Teach Beginning ESL/EFL and Survive!

Clear, Practical Lesson Plans for Teaching Adult Beginners

Ellen Lockwood

Many thanks to Martha Garcia-Jimenez and Susan Locke for their professional feedback and to Tom Donovan for his voluntary and valuable input. Also many thanks to Joanne Gordin, Pat O'Neill, Randy Akerson, Alex Leviloff, Phil Brown, and George Lockwood for giving me the benefit of their experience as artists and writers.

www.CreateSpace.com/5731316

ISBN-13: 978-1517290177
ISBN-10: 1517290171

First edition: September 2015
10 9 8 7 6 5 4 3 2

Introduction

What Is In This Book?

This book is not a textbook for students. It is a set of detailed lesson plans using simple, classic techniques for teachers of beginning level ESL classes, either adult or secondary. It is a manual and a reference to enable you, the teacher, to teach a basic ESL class or supplement your required textbook as quickly as possible.

You have to teach a class three times to become good at it. The first time you're just trying to survive. The second time you've analyzed your mistakes and you're fixing them. The third time, you finally feel as if you know what you're doing. The goal of this book is to make your first time a success.

The biggest mistake of inexperienced teachers of beginning ESL students is aiming their materials too high. These lesson plans will help you level them appropriately.

Using this book, new teachers of beginning ESL students can follow a logically organized sequence, providing a framework for courses which do not already have one. There are 80 lesson plans. The manual provides a lesson plan for a 2-hour class, although you may not be able to finish all of the activities in that time. Even if you use only some of the pages in additional textbooks suggested for writing practice in class and at home, there is more than enough material for one school semester of work for students who started with no English at all.

The first page of each lesson plan is for preparation. It has a vocabulary list matched to the grammar taught that day and useful for homework. There is an agenda which can be projected or copied on a board or used to help you write required lesson plans. There is also a list of materials needed for that day, such as pictures, flashcards, and maps.

If your required textbook lacks speaking and listening exercises, this book provides oral routines and examples which show you how to use students, classroom objects, and everyday materials to create your own practices. If your text doesn't help you to explain grammar, here you have easy ways to explain grammar concepts.

For written grammar practice, the plans refer to specific pages in proven textbooks to reinforce the lesson of the day, with written exercises simple enough to use for homework. The recommended texts also provide pictures, ideas, dialogs, and additional listening exercises. The manual section entitled "Texts" tells you which texts are best suited for each type of student and where to find them.

The manual offers suggestions on grading, leveling, and promotion. There are ideas for quizzes and suggestions on how to prepare the class for mandated unit tests. Four extra days with activities appropriate for a substitute teacher are provided.

Why Did You Write This Book?

I wrote this book in response to situations that I have experienced personally. I taught English as a Second Language to secondary students and adults for 30 years. For much of that time, I was working with absolute beginners, meaning students knowing very little or no English and speaking different languages, although many spoke Spanish. Some people can't understand how students can learn from a teacher who does not share their language. Other people assume that any English speaker can teach ESL because ESL must be so simple.

Even English teachers of English-speaking students need a new approach when taking a beginning ESL class. Students who would be considered remedial in a regular English situation speak fluently and have a large passive vocabulary. In an ESL class, vocabulary must be built up from nothing. Listening practice is essential, and commonly taught composition skills are only appropriate for ESL students in about their third year. Poetry and humor are fraught with difficulties, and reading material that a teacher considers low-level turns out to be much more difficult than it first appears.

Several times I have volunteered to help new teachers. One taught semicolons, even though many beginning students don't use periods for about six months. One wanted to write her own more creative materials because the books I showed her had such simple sentences that she, the teacher, was bored. Like their students, these teachers were beginners.

Unfortunately, I couldn't help them much, because with beginners, every word spoken in class has to be carefully controlled. It's hard to understand what to do without actually doing it, preferably for long enough to see how your system produces results. I realized that I couldn't help these teachers without providing them with extremely detailed lesson plans. That's why I wrote this book. It is an attempt to reduce the time-consuming and labor-intensive preparation of the first year for beginning teachers, who have to create a class while changing their whole approach to communication.

Who Needs This Book?

You have volunteered in a church program to teach English to new immigrants. You realize that you don't know where to begin. Should you have them read and write, or just speak? Will they be embarrassed if you correct them? What should you do first? You just don't know.

You have just received a master's degree in Teaching English as a Second or Foreign Language. You start working in a private language program with young adults from different countries. The school insists that you use their company's textbooks. The materials are okay, but scanty. Your supervisor tells you to get more out of the materials. You need ideas, the sooner the better.

You are hired to teach in a large metropolitan area adult school. You look at the provided curriculum and realize that it's just an outline. You will have to prepare every class from scratch. Only the test has been written for you.

You are a secondary school teacher and your district has just adopted a state-approved textbook for ESL students. You look at the beginning level text and realize that it has allotted 70 pages for your 90-day semester. Other supplied materials have lots of tiny little dialogs and practices with only five questions. The kids finish them in ten minutes, leaving you with an hour to fill. You cry in the training meetings, but the trainer just tells you to repeat the same material over and over. The older, very experienced ESL teachers are also protesting, but at least they're not in tears.

You are a high school or middle school teacher with low seniority. You would like to keep your job in an era of layoffs, and your principal wants you to teach a beginning ESL class. You say okay. The first day of school, your class has five students who speak no English at all. By the end of the semester, 15 more students have trickled in at the rate of one or two per week. Most of them are struggling. You have no idea of how to help them catch up or whether to pass them at the end of the semester.

Your school needs an ESL teacher, and your district requires ESL teachers to have an English credential. Your school does not hire a language teacher, who knows how to teach language skills. They hire you, though your only training is in teaching literature. When you realize that your beginning ESL students can't read the simplest paragraph in English, you panic.

You are a new English teacher, and you are also a native Spanish speaker. A school district hires you to teach English, and they also want you to teach ESL because of your language skills. You think you will be able to reach the kids by teaching them in Spanish. You walk into class on Day One and realize that eight of your students are Asian.

You are on your way to teach in an unfamiliar situation. You may be asked to teach complete beginners. You may even be asked to train other teachers to teach beginners. You don't yet have a stash of "most valuable support texts." You may not have 24-7 Web access, and you haven't yet discovered that valuable bookstore in the center of your foreign city. You are worried.

In short, you need experience. But first, you need to survive.

Who Doesn't Need This Book?

Teachers in Bilingual Programs Bilingual programs teach primary school children in both English and their home language. Some techniques in this book could be used in such programs, but in general, this book is not appropriate for children attending U.S. elementary schools.

Teachers of Standard English Learners Standard English Learners are students who do not speak what is considered standard English. They may speak a regional dialect or be from neighborhoods where Black English is used. These students may have a class to practice using standard English in certain situations. English is not their second language. They will be offended and bored to tears in an ESL class. This book would be valuable for their teacher only to explain the structure of very basic standard English grammar.

Teachers of "Sheltered English" "Sheltered English" is an attempt to help former ESL learners and others who lack higher-level English skills to understand academic classes by reducing the difficulty of the language used in textbooks and in the classroom.

Beginning ESL students are wasting their time in sheltered English classes, because there is no way the teacher can "shelter" the material enough for them. They need an ESL class geared to beginners to build their English skills starting at the basics. Most schools offer only 2-3 years of ESL. After that, the student can go into a sheltered English class.

On the other hand, some children, if they speak another language at home and have failed an ESL placement test, may be placed in an ESL class, possibly a beginning class, even after attending a U.S. school for several years. These children should not be in ESL classes because they speak English fluently, though not perfectly. They should go to a "sheltered English" class where their English skills can be improved.

Index

Before Using the Lesson Plans

How Should You Use this Manual?

If you do not have a textbook chosen by your program, you should go to the "Text" section at the back of this manual and decide what text to buy to provide reading and writing practice for your class. Decide how many of the other recommended texts you can buy. All of them are valuable in their own way.

Look at the "Essential Equipment" section, and start assembling a collection of materials. Start collecting pictures from newspapers and magazines to use with vocabulary lists and practices. Look under the "Stuff" section of the lesson plans to see what stationery supplies you will need for flashcards and activities.

You should skim through the different sections of this book and then start using the lesson plans. If they seem too easy and the explanations too simple, try them for a while before making a final judgment. In a beginning class, you will see very soon if the students understand you. If the students are too advanced for the first few lessons, skip the first units or skim the material as a review and then move ahead faster.

Goals

The goals of a beginning ESL course are for the students to listen, speak, read, and write English at a basic level. Your objectives are to introduce the material, practice and review the material, and connect newer material to older material. You will be required to evaluate student progress and occasionally provide a little fun while still using English. Other objectives of the class will depend on your mandated curriculum.

This manual is not intended to be a scripted program, although a "script" is provided for grammar explanations. Use the oral routines and examples like a scripted program until you feel secure. Feel free to loosen up as you get more experience. You should always change the examples to refer to your own students and classroom. I haven't given you every single sentence to say.

However, if you try to think of examples or explanations at the moment you are teaching, you may find that the examples which spring to mind are actually exceptions to a rule or involve vocabulary which is too difficult for your class. You should be very careful not to make your own examples more difficult than the ones given here. Be careful not to add too much new material too soon, or to make examples more challenging as you try to make them more interesting. The idea is that the students should get lots of practice at one level, which helps them to understand the sentences more naturally.

I do suggest that you follow the general sequence of topics in the manual, which is the order found in most textbooks for beginning ESL students. I also suggest that you use all the exercises in listening practice that you can find, because students really need it.

You may have to change the lesson sequence, cut some sections due to time constraints, and adjust the balance of listening, speaking, reading, and writing practice depending on the needs of your class. This manual was intended to make it easy for teachers to use as they see fit and easy for students to understand.

How the Lesson Plans Are Organized

Classes are organized the same way almost every day. This minimizes confusion for the students and leaves the teacher with less to explain.

There is no Table of Contents. The Index gives you only the page number where a topic is first explained. You can assume that there will be more practice on that topic in following pages. The agenda is the table of contents for each lesson. In the "Lesson Plan" section, I explain how to use each technique or activity the first time you do it. That's why the lesson plans at the beginning of the manual are much longer than those at the end.

The difficulty of the activities varies to provide for students who know more. For example, you introduce basic vocabulary, but make the students do a dictation the following day. The vocabulary introduction is easy. Writing each word after hearing it only three quick times is difficult. Writing each word perfectly is even harder.

What's the Approach?

There are different approaches to teaching beginners, of which the Natural Approach, Total Physical Response, and Notional-Functional are the best known.

You will use the Natural Approach by giving lots of spoken input appropriate to the level of the class. The amount of correcting you do depends on your opinion of the Natural Approach, which advises to avoid specific correction as much as possible.

You will use the Total Physical Response approach when you ask the class to respond to words, questions, and commands with pointing and actions.

Some people believe in teaching language for specific situations, using dialogs and dramas. This Notional-Functional approach could easily be increased in these lessons by adding your own original dialogs and others from the recommended textbooks.

Each approach is valuable in its own way, and in using this manual, you will use them all. By using different approaches, you can address the differing learning styles of your students and avoid doing the same thing every day.

Using all three approaches, this book organizes the lessons based on grammar difficulty, as most books for beginning language students do. A class organized like this gives you, the teacher, a way to organize your own thoughts. It provides a basis for explaining harder lessons and gives the students general rules to follow. Grammar was overemphasized in the past, but that is no reason to ignore its value today.

Practicing the Lesson Directly

Students should experience their new language in a natural situation with as little explanation as possible. That's why you avoid using their first language as much as you can. That's why you show pictures, point, or ask the class about things they see right in the classroom.

You must find ways to explain as quickly and simply as possible. For example, to teach the concepts of singular and plural, at the beginning, you say "one" and "two, three, four" while showing them a pencil in one hand and several pencils in the other. Then you say "one" and "more than one" while holding up the pencils. Later, you say "one (singular)" and "more than one (plural)" together. After a while you can say "singular" and "plural" and they will know the meaning of the words. You check their knowledge by asking, "And what is plural?" They should instantly answer that it is more than one.

You do need to teach some grammatical terms like "present," "past," "future," and "continuous," but students will understand and remember better if you associate these grammatical ideas with specific words and gestures. When you use the word "present," you add "every day" and later "or regularly." When using the term "present continuous," you point to the floor and say, "right now." With "future," you point ahead of you and with "past," you point behind you. You can teach and review the terms on a time line, with specific times shown as X and a continuous action shown as a squiggly continuous line. Then you can elicit a present continuous verb from them by making a continuous wavy line with your fingers. You want to avoid too much analysis.

Although you will need some grammar terminology, you should use grammar words only to make it faster and easier for students to understand the content of the course, which is how to use English like a native speaker. Terminology words are very hard to remember and add a layer of interference between the content and the form of the sentence. You should not test students on their knowledge of grammar terms. Most teachers have not been taught traditional grammar terms themselves, so it is best to stick with words in common use, like "past" and "continuous."

When introducing new grammar, you should review previous grammar and then use the differences between the old rule and the new rule to help the students understand the new material. You shouldn't jump around too much between grammar topics, but try to provide a logical sequence. Rather than expecting immediate mastery of each topic by every student, you repeat and recycle concepts.

When introducing new material, practice should involve only the new concept and not address every other grammar item which may appear in a reading or dialog. If you assign a worksheet to practice new grammar or new vocabulary, the number of new vocabulary words in the worksheet should be limited, or illustrated so they are instantly understandable. You stretch the students' knowledge a little at a time, so nobody gets stressed out.

All of the recommended textbooks are extremely simple and clear. They may strike you as boring, but beginning students never complain that they are bored. Fear and lack of confidence are bigger problems for them.

Teacher Talk

"Teacher Talk" is an ESL term which refers to the limited range of speaking which a teacher of beginning ESL students must use. Beginner topics are universal and easy to point to. That means numbers, time, money, clothing, common food and drinks, and objects within the classroom, putting everything possible into a context which the students can easily understand. You point to objects and say, "I have, There is a, Look at, It's a." Act out the meaning of "I'm writing, I'm running."

You use photos and draw pictures to avoid talking too much. You talk about things in the plainest way. For example, commands are simpler than description. Description is simpler than telling a story. The class doesn't have to understand every part of the sentence at first. They just have to get the general idea. You avoid abstract topics until you can explain them using language the class already knows.

Repetition, Repetition, Repetition

ESL teachers become notorious among their friends for saying everything four times, because people rarely remember things that they have heard only once. Children learn language by hearing words in the same context again and again until they understand their meaning. In a beginning class, you are just trying to speed up this process. That's why you recycle vocabulary so often over the course of the lesson, the week, and the class.

Day 1

Vocabulary

zero - 0
one - 1
two - 2
three - 3
four - 4
five - 5
six - 6
seven - 7
eight - 8
nine - 9
ten - 10

Agenda

1. Greeting routine - first few days
2. Attendance routine - first few days
3. Date routine - first few days
4. Agenda routine - daily
5. Information card - fill out, collect

PRETEST HERE IF NECESSARY

6. Numbers 0-10 vocabulary - introduce on board, oral practice
      HOMEWORK - copy list 20X for quiz
      Explain quiz procedure for tomorrow
7. Personal information dialog (attached) - introduce, read as class 2-3X,   copy 1X
      Oral practice as group, then pairs
      HOMEWORK - copy dialog 2X more
Explain procedure for handing in 2 separate homeworks

AND/OR

8. Personal information dialog or forms - written practice - optional
9. Homework - repeat homework instructions quickly at very end of class

IF TIME

10. Information card conversation in pairs or small groups - limit to name, country of origin, phone number, favorite activity

Stuff

1. Wall calendar, the bigger, the better
2. Set of large flashcards of vocabulary, numbers on one side, words on the other
3. 3x5 or 5x7 cards so students can write personal information for you
4. A pad of gigantic "Post-it" paper to cover up vocabulary list
5. Several groups of small objects, like pencils, pens, markers, books, reachable on desk
6. Paper copies or projectable file of personal information dialog (attached)

Lesson Plan

1. Opening Routine - First day You need to establish a regular pattern of behavior without much explanation. Some teachers of teenagers and even adults give written rules, but you cannot explain rules well without using the students' native language, so your behavior sets the pattern. Avoid being late or starting class late. If students come in late, don't interrupt class activities to interact with them. If a student comes late every evening, deal with it after class.

At the exact time class begins, or after the bell rings, say to the students,

"Hello, class, this is ESL One, and I'm your teacher, Mrs. Lockwood." On the board, have your full name and title, the day of the week, and the date written in formal style, **September 9, 2015.** Point to your name and say, "I am your teacher, Mrs. Ellen Lockwood. You can call me Mrs. Lockwood."

"This is ESL 1." If you like you can have a little graph with levels and little arrows pointing up from a lower level to the next one higher.

```
ESL 4 _____
ESL 3 _____
ESL 2 _____
ESL 1 _____
```

"Is everyone (wave your hand toward the whole class) here in ESL 1?" Point to the ESL 1 level. Hold up a registration card as an example and go around to check each student's registration document. It's possible to have high school students who speak perfect English sitting in your Beginning ESL class or to have confused students who are in the wrong room.

2. Attendance Routine - First few days Pull out your attendance list ostentatiously and take attendance every day at the very beginning of the class. While you're practicing the words "who" and "where," you're also checking that everybody belongs there. You're also showing them that you expect everybody to listen and answer verbally in class.

Go down your list and call everybody's name. "Rodriguez, Martha. Where is Martha?" Or, "Where is Mrs. Rodriguez?" Stare around the room, making it clear that you are looking for someone. Don't go on until Martha Rodriguez has answered. When she answers, say, "Hello, Mrs. Rodriguez," or "Martha Rodriguez is here."

"Cho, Linda. Who is Mrs. Cho?" When she answers, you say, "Ah, you are Mrs. Cho. Hello, Mrs. Cho."

"Hernandez, Olivia. Where is Mrs. Hernandez? . . . She isn't here? She is absent. Mrs. Hernandez is absent. She isn't here." Write "present = here" and "absent = isn't here" on board. Indicate the negative by waving your index finger sideways and shaking your head sideways. Show a positive response by nodding, smiling, waving hello, or showing thumbs up, if that's okay in the culture of your students. For "here," point to the floor.

"Where is she?" Make an "I don't know" face and shrug. "She's not here."

"Ramirez, Juan. Mr. Ramirez. Is he here? Okay, he isn't here. He's absent. He isn't here. He isn't present."

Tell the class that they can say "I'm here" or "Present." Show them how to raise their hand, repeating "I'm here" several times.

About halfway down the list, start using only Mr. and Mrs. to see if they understand the difference. Don't explain Miss and Mrs. at this time. Just say Mrs. for older or married women and Miss if they are younger.

Repeat this in every class until the class list stabilizes and the students can respond "present," "here," "absent," or "not here."

Optional - Seating chart If you work in a K-12 setting, you can repeat this procedure while placing students on a seating chart.

3. Date Routine Do this on the first few days of class and occasionally afterwards. Write out the day of the week and the date on the board completely, September 9, 2015. Many students are from countries where the day is written first, then the month, then the year. You want them to get used to the American system of month first, then day. Also, in Spanish and other languages, the month and day of the week are not capitalized. Writing the date in formal style in every class will accustom them to spelling and capitalizing the month, and using the right form for business letters. Including the day of the week will give them lots of practice in spelling the names of the days, which can be confusing.

Point to the day and say, "This is Monday." Point to the class and then to your ear to indicate that they should repeat it after you several times.

"What day is it?" "It's Monday." You ask the question and then answer it. Have them repeat each after you several times.

Point to the month and say, "It's September." The students repeat it.

Point to the date and say, "It's September 9th." Have them repeat it. Don't get into explaining about the "th" at this point. They won't even hear the "th."

Point to the year and say, "It's two thousand fifteen. It's twenty-fifteen." They repeat each.

Then read the whole phrase. "It's Monday, COMMA, September 9, COMMA, twenty-fifteen." Point to the commas and stress the word "comma." Repeat this several times. Indicate punctuation marks with gestures and a loud voice, because if you don't, most students won't notice them. You will limit punctuation to the most basic at this level, but you should stress basic punctuation and dictate punctuation marks when you do dictations.

Point to the day. "What day is this?" "Monday." Underline the M and make it twice as big. Say, "Capital M."

Point to the month. "What month is this?" "September." Underline the S and make it twice as big. Say, "Capital S."

Point to the date. "What's the date?" "It's September 9th. It's the 9th." Have them repeat.

Point to the year. "What year is this?" "It's 2015." If students can't answer these questions, have them repeat the answers after you.

Note that you're not explaining the vocabulary or the question form at this time. You'll explain those things later. For now, you're just using English words in a context the students can understand. If anyone seems confused, go to the large classroom calendar and point to the day, week, month, and date.

4. Agenda Routine Every day of the course, have the agenda on the board. Pointing to the agenda, quickly summarize out loud what you will do in the class. You can make a yapping gesture or point to your mouth for spoken practice, and make a writing gesture for a written assignment.

Having students copy the agenda is not a valuable use of time.

Write down what you think you can finish each day with a little extra IF TIME. You should always have something extra to do in case you finish early. You don't want students to think that if they finish the work quickly, they will be rewarded by doing nothing.

5. Information Card - Written practice Write on the board or project the following words and have the students copy the words on a 3x5 or 5x7 note card and then fill in their information. K-12 students may have this information on their program card or their student ID card. If they don't want to put down their real information, tell them that they can make up a phone number or email address. Write on the board "1-000-000-0000" and point to it, or write "aabbcc@examplemail.com" and point to it. The main idea is for them to practice address formats and numbers and learn words like "telephone number" and "email." It also provides information in a convenient form for you and helps you know the class better.

Just this small amount of writing will show you which students have low writing skills and poor handwriting. Clear writing and cursive writing (instead of printing) indicate a higher level of education in the home country.

Name

Address - house number, street, city, state, zip code Have students put their information in this order, with city, state and zip code on a second line. Many students don't understand that the address on an envelope has a customary order and format. If they don't understand, ask to see their driver's license or registration material and point to the address section. Don't insist on perfection if this is hard for them.

Family phone number Encourage students to write this clearly.

Family email address Only ask for phone and email if it is acceptable to your school, the students, and you. Having the students' personal phone number and email could be problematic.

Where did you study English before? How many years? This will give you lots of information as to how much English the students have been exposed to. Even if they placed into your low-level class, they may have had quite a bit of English before, which will affect their achievement in your class. Students who don't speak much may have had extensive written practice in English, often the case with students from Asia. Sometimes students have gone to elementary school in the U.S. and then returned to their home country, losing their English temporarily. It will help you to be aware of this.

For adults, you may want to add a "Languages you speak" category. Experience with other languages will help them in your class.

Favorite sport or activity Give examples they will understand easily, like "football" or "dancing."

Don't expect perfect understanding or performance on the information card activity. Let them work until most students are finished, helping as many as you can. Collect the cards to use later.

NOTE ON PRETEST WHICH CAN GO HERE: Based on your experience in your school, especially in a public school K-12 situation, you may not be sure that the students are leveled accurately. You can give them a multiple-choice pretest here. If you give a multiple-choice grammar test as a part of your final exam, you can use that as a pretest. You can write your own or find this type of test at the end of many textbooks. You can limit the length to one-half or one-third of a final test, because if the students are True Beginners, they won't finish it and may not understand any of it. You want to ensure that you have a True Beginners class, with students who know almost no English.

Don't include a composition or phonics questions on a pretest, because very few incoming students have been trained in these.

6. Numbers 0-10 Vocabulary - Introduce Have the words for the homework vocabulary written or projected on the board. For numbers, include the figures. If students insist on translating for weaker students, allow them to do it, but ask them to keep their voices down. Try to discourage this habit. Do not allow a teaching assistant to translate all of the vocabulary for anyone, even a special education student, during the introductory phase of the vocabulary. The teaching assistant should explain in the native language only if the student has tried and cannot understand any other way. You do not want your students to become dependent on a translator.

Pointing to each number, read the entire list quickly once. If students start to read with you, gesture "No" with your index finger moving sideways or motion "Halt" while shaking your head, "No." Point to them and then to your ear. Read the whole list once or twice. Then say, "Now, you (point to them) AFTER me." Say each word with your hand up for "stop" and then point to the group to say it until they understand to do it after you, not with you. If they don't pronounce the number correctly, have them repeat it 1 or 2 times after you. Don't expect them all to pronounce every word perfectly. If they continue to pronounce something very incorrectly, just move on to the next number. If you want them to say it together with you a few times, point to the words on the board and repeat each one while motioning to the whole class to "come on" with the other hand.

Numbers 0-10 - Pronounce After the whole class has practiced the list several times, you can point to individual students and have each read or repeat one difficult number. Believe it or not, this will amuse them. Pump up the entertainment value of your class by pronouncing things in an exaggerated way, making faces and dramatic gestures. Sounds in foreign languages are difficult to distinguish, so the more exaggerated you make the sound at first, the easier it is for the students to hear. Later you can tone it down so they hear the word closer to what they will hear in real life.

People have "boxes" in their brains which separate the sounds of their native language, one sound per box. They are going to try to fit the sounds of English into their accustomed brain boxes. Your job is to gradually provide them with extra boxes to fit in the sounds of English. Some students will stun you with the accuracy of their hearing and ability to imitate. Others are less sensitive to phonetic differences and may never lose their accents. That's why you don't strive for perfection in pronunciation.

However, if a student is very difficult to understand, you should repeat words for them a few extra times and continue to focus on their speaking. If you politely ignore a student's terrible pronunciation, the student will assume that he is understandable and that everything is okay. You are their English teacher. You need to convey in a loving way that the person needs to work on their pronunciation and that you are there to help them.

After doing the numbers in order, point to the numbers out of order without pronouncing them and have the class as a group read them as quickly as they can. Do each number several times.

Numbers 0-10 - Oral practice Hold up different groups of fingers and say, "How many?" The students answer with the correct number. Write simple math problems on the board and have them give you the answers. Use the words "plus, and, minus, take away, times." Don't get into division. Don't go above 10.

Point to your eyes, ears, and nose, and hold up groups of objects which you grab from your desk, like pens, paper clips, and books. Your goal is only to practice "How many?" with the vocabulary numbers. Don't teach them vocabulary for the objects now. You can say, "How many pens?" or "How many fingers?" but don't ask them to use the word to reply, only to supply the number. Try to practice all of the numbers at least twice except zero, which gets too complicated.

Getting out your flashcards, show the class that the words are on one side and the figures on the other. Read the word sides in order once. Show them the number sides in order and see if they can give the correct words without looking at the list on the board. Some will cheat, but that's okay. Cover up the vocabulary list on the board with a giant Post-it sheet if you want. Then mix up the numbers and have them say the names without looking. If they make mistakes, turn the cards around and show them the words on the back.

Numbers 0-10 - Written practice - Homework Tape 2 pieces of notebook paper on the board. On one, show the class how to copy each word with its number on a list. Then on the other piece, show them how to copy zero - 0, zero - 0, etc. until they get the idea. Write 20X on the board. Listen to them groan and complain. Write a big 1 in a circle on the top of the page, and show them that they will get one point in your book for this homework paper.

Write the words "quiz," "exam," and "test" on the board and look scared. Tell them they will have a quiz in the next class, a little examination. On the board, write the numbers from 1 to 11 in a vertical list with circles around them. Tell the class, "I say the word 'three,' " and you write "three-3" next to the number 1 on the board. Then tell them, "I say the word 'six' and you will write 'six-6.' " Put "six-6" next to the number 2 on the board.

Show them how you will collect a paper from each of them, and pointing to each word with its numeral on the board, say, "One point for this, correct, one point for this, if correct." Write another short list of numbers 1 to 3. Write "tree - 3" on the board next to the number one. Draw a big X over it and say, "Incorrect!! Zero points!" and write a zero there. Write it correctly. Next to the circled number two, write "five - 7." Draw a big X over it, say, "Incorrect!" and write a zero there. Fix the number. Next to the circled number 3, write the word "five" alone. "Incorrect!" Write the figure 5 next to the word.

Go over to the vocabulary list and count the numbers on it. Write the number 11 above the list and put a circle around it. "You will get 11 points if you have all of the numbers and words right." Show your hands scrambling the numbers around and say, "Not 1, 2, 3! No! I will say 5, 2, 8, 1, like that!" so they understand that they cannot just copy their list and turn it in. (Yes, someone will try that.)

7. Personal Information Dialog - Introduce Project or write the dialog (attached) on the board and have the class repeat each line after you several times. Try to get them to do it with natural intonation and stress. They copy it 1 time.

Show them how to write the dialog with colons by pointing to the names and circling the colons on one side of the board and then show them that the sentences to speak are lined up on the other. Read the names with the dialog and shake your head "no." Read a few lines in a male voice and a female voice. Point to a boy and say, "You are Alberto." Point to a girl and say, "You are Maria." Don't let them put quotation marks around the dialog.

This is not important for adult education students. However, K-12 students will eventually be tested on their knowledge of drama, and they will need to know that the names are characters and a drama script is written with colons. Also, you want them to start paying attention to different types of punctuation. The colon will not be on the final exam. Just point it out whenever it's used in a dialog.

Personal Information Dialog - Oral practice Practice the dialog. You can do it boys vs. girls a couple of times. Then you can have individual pairs stand up or come up front and do it as a dramatic dialog. Then divide the class into pairs and have them practice it several times reading the copies. You can count the class off using 1 and 2 to create the pairs, or you can put them in groups of 4 or 6 and ask them to practice it in different combinations. Don't let this take too long. If each student does it twice, it's enough.

Personal Information Dialog - Homework Tell class to copy the dialog 2 more times as homework. Explain that you want the dialog on a separate paper from the numbers homework by drawing on the board two little papers, one with numbers and the other with the dialog lines. Or you can take your sample paper from before in one hand, and your dialog paper in the other and say that you want two different papers. Each homework paper is worth 1 point.

"First, you give me this one." Indicate the numbers paper. "Then you give me this one." Hold up the dialog sheet. You want them to turn in separate types of homework separately because it's easier to grade and roster at 1 point each. It's very hard to process homework quickly if some students are turning in two assignments on a page.

AND/OR

Personal Information Dialog - Written practice - Optional Most texts and activity books have fill-in blanks and dialogs about personal information. If you use a written practice from your mandated text or other recommended text in addition to or instead of the dialog above, make sure that you go over the sentences or questions orally first, and then check the answers orally again after students have completed the writing exercises. **Practical English, p. 2; Side by Side, pp. 1-6; New American Streamline Departures, pp. 1A-2A; Access (literacy level, with dialogs and listening scripts in the back of the book), pp. 35, 37-39, 55, and 91-92; Lifeskills, pp. 10, 13; Skill Sharpeners, pp. 1-2; GrammarWork, p. 3.**

8. Homework - First day - Review procedure Allow students a few minutes to prepare for the end of class. Point to each part of the agenda that says "HOMEWORK." Ask, "What is your homework for tomorrow?" They can tell you, or you can read the assignments together. Show them the sample papers again and repeat that you want the different assignments on paper 1 and paper 2. Say, "AND quiz!" Point to the word "quiz" on the agenda. Ask, "What else do we have tomorrow?" and point to the word "quiz" on the agenda. "A test! A little examination!"

IF TIME

9. Information Card - Pair practice Leaving the students in their groups, pass the information cards back. Have them practice the dialog with the information on the cards, and ask each other questions about the information on the cards. Write the question forms below on the board. Don't insist on correct grammar or pronunciation in the questions or answers. Just encourage them to get any information from the other student. You and your teaching assistant should help them here. Encourage them to use only English. Write on the board.

What's your _____? My _____ is _____.
                 name
                 address
                 phone number
                 favorite sport

Personal Information Dialog

ALBERTO: Hi!

MARIA: Hi! You're in my class! What is your name?

ALBERTO: My name is Alberto.

MARIA: Where do you live, Alberto?

ALBERTO: I live in Santa Monica.

MARIA: Oh, what street?

ALBERTO: I live on Pico Boulevard.

MARIA: I live in Santa Monica too. Where are you from?

ALBERTO: I'm from El Salvador. Where are you from?

MARIA: I'm from Mexico.

ALBERTO: What is your phone number?

MARIA: 310-649-2703. Call me sometime. Or text me.

ALBERTO: Okay! See you later.

MARIA: Bye-bye now. See you later.

Day 2

Vocabulary

ten - 10
eleven - 11
twelve - 12
thirteen - 13
fourteen - 14
fifteen - 15
sixteen - 16
seventeen - 17
eighteen - 18
nineteen - 19

Agenda

1. Opening routine - repeat greeting and roll routine for first few classes (See Day 1.)
2. Date routine - teach paper heading, review formal date
3. Agenda routine - (See Day 1.)
4. Numbers 0-10 - collect homework
   Review numbers for quiz - flashcards with numbers and words
   Do quiz
Numbers 10-19 - Introduce vocabulary, repeat 2-3 times
   Oral practice stressing "teen"
   Math with flashcards, symbols and math words, 0-19
   Talk about ages if students are teenagers
   Number practice activities
   Review vocabulary with flashcards
   HOMEWORK 20X, quiz tomorrow
5. Personal information dialog - repeat practice dialog with copies
   Pair practice with real information, volunteer pairs in front of class
6. Information card - conversation (See Day 1.)
   Information card - speech (See Day 1.)
7. Personal information - written practice - 1-2 pages
8. TPR orders - begin TPR with classroom objects (TPR routine attached)

Stuff

1. Large calendar for date routine
2. Flashcards with numerals 0-10 and words on the back
3. Flashcards with numerals 10-19 and words on the back
4. Flashcards with math terms and symbols - and, plus, minus, take away, times
5. Large elementary school chart with numbers 1-100
6. Copies of personal information dialog (See Day 1.)

Lesson Plan

1. Opening Routine For the first few days of the class, continue the greeting and roll routine, but don't practice it as long. Use it with new students. (See Day 1.)

2. Date Routine Repeat the date routine from Day 1, using the calendar, repeating the date as it is written out, and stressing date format. Require students to write the date in traditional format. It's easier to practice the spelling and writing of the months and dates daily. Draw or project a homework paper on the board with an example of the heading you want to see on class papers. Tell the class if you want their first or last names first. Some students don't realize that you want their full name. Having a format for their homework and quiz papers conveys the idea that attention to format and detail is expected in a school setting.

3. Agenda Routine Quickly point to and read the basic activities from the agenda list. Then say, "Okay, that's the agenda for today. What are we going to do first?" Point to the words "collect homework," "review for quiz," and "quiz." Say, "Please pass up your homework and get out a piece of paper for the quiz." Some students think that "pass up your homework" means to walk to the front and give you their homework individually. Show them how to give their work to the student in front of them.

4. Numbers 0-10 - Review for quiz Quickly repeat a few of the number practices. (See Day 1.) Then show the flashcards in order twice with words and twice with figures. Make sure that everybody has a single piece of paper out and that nobody has books or bags on their desks. Ask them to put headings on their papers, and circulate around the room to make sure that everyone has a name and the complete date on the paper. Again write the numbers 1-11 on the board in a list, circling each number. Say, "Number one," and then dictate a number, like "ten" and show them that they must write "ten - 10" next to the circled number 1. Write it on the board as a freebie. Make sure everyone understands that they are to write the numbers in mixed order on the list together with the numeral. They are not supposed to write the number next to the same number on the list.

You always want students to write dictation words next to numbers so you know which word they're trying to write. If their words are correct, but not in the order that you dictated them, they're either copying or very confused. Look out for answers written on desks. Collect homework before the quiz so they can't copy from it. If you give them any extra time to cram for the quiz, some students will count on cramming during that time and won't study at home.

Vocabulary - Dictation quiz Dictate the vocabulary list in mixed order, repeating the numbers slowly and clearly no more than three times. Walk around the room making sure that everyone is writing the numerals as well as the words. At the end, slowly read all of the numbers only one more time, allowing people to include the ones they missed. Resist all calls to repeat them more than once. If you notice anyone copying, take the paper immediately.

Collect the quiz very quickly. With teenagers, watch out for kids copying from papers being passed in from behind. Do not allow them to turn quiz papers in late. Hide the papers in your bag or a folder because students may copy the answers and then run up and thrust their papers into a stack on your desk.

At least for the first week of this quiz routine, you should return the papers the next day, graded with one point for each correct answer, word and numeral. Some students will not study at all for the first quiz. If you return papers quickly, results will gradually improve because students don't like to see low numbers on their papers when others are doing better. Certain students will realize that you are serious and will decide to do homework and study. The quizzes will also help you notice writing problems and hearing difficulties.

If you are teaching adult education where academic skills are not as necessary, you should still do dictations and vocabulary, but you can use them more as an activity. Have the students correct their own papers or exchange papers to grade. You could make the quizzes more of a competition or game.

For more on tests and copying, see the "Rationale" section at the back of this manual.

Numbers 10-19 - Introduce Read and repeat numbers on the list as before. (See Day 1.)

Numbers 10-19 - Oral practice - Teenagers Go down the list again, saying the "teen" part of the numbers very loudly. Don't let students accent the first syllable.

If students are in high school, go around the class and ask each one, "How old are you?" They answer, "I'm _____." Write their answers on the board. If they don't understand at first, pick a student, write his date of birth on the board, and calculate his age.

Then pick out a few students, and ask, "Are you fourteen or sixteen?" "Are you twelve or fifteen?" etc. Don't let them say, "I have fifteen." Allow them to answer with the number only.

With the numbers they know so far, perform some tasks. Using the number chart, have them count by twos from 2 to 20. They can count the number of boys in the room versus the number of girls. They can write all the odd numbers or all the even numbers. They can do basic math problems. Finish by reviewing with the flashcards. (See Day 1.)

5. Personal Information Dialog - More oral practice - Optional Students get out their homework or handouts from previous day. Repeat the dialog together several times. You can have them stand face to face in two lines and practice the dialog, with one line moving to speak to a new person after they finish with the first.

After the students sit down, have several couples come to the front and try to do the address dialog with their real information. Collect the dialog homework.

6. Information Card - Oral practice - Pairs - Optional Return the information cards from yesterday. Write or project these sample information sentences on board.

My name is _____(Juan)_____ .
I live in _____(Los Angeles)_____ .
I live on _____(Alvarado Street) _____ .
I'm from _____(Guatemala)_____ .
I like _____(football)_____ .

Make sure everybody understands the idea by offering possible answers. Put students into pairs counting them off by number 1 and number 2, or ask them to practice with the person sitting next to them.

Information Card - Speech - Optional - Volunteers If the information card conversations have gone well, ask for volunteers to stand up at their seats and give one or two pieces of information from their card. If they are reluctant, choose several students and ask each of them the questions. Let them use their information cards to help.

If students are not talking at all, put your own personal information on the board and talk about it. Then take cards from several volunteers and write their information into the blanks on the board. Collect the information cards after this activity. Often the information is more current and more useful to you than official records.

7. Personal Information - Written practice Do an additional 1-2 pages from **references, Day 1. Also Lifeskills, p. 13.**

NOTE: The textbooks and pages are given for written practice supplemental to your text or for use if you have no text. You can use as many of them as you need, but don't do all of the pages at once. You can do 1 or 2 pages per class, do1 or 2 additional pages later as review, and use an additional page to review before a test.

Students should not spend the entire class writing, but oral practice should be broken up by writing practice, since it is very stressful for beginners to have to focus on listening for 1-2 hours at a time. Secondary school students usually need a lot of written practice. As long as you preview and review a written practice orally, you can assign it for homework and go over it the next day.

First, read the dialog in the text at least once. Review the vocabulary. If students don't understand a word, explain it with pictures, gestures, or examples. They practice the dialogs orally first. They can copy the dialog at least once in class or at home.

If the written practice involves filling in blanks, students should copy the whole question with punctuation and write the answer in a complete sentence. Most students can fill in blanks perfectly, but when they write complete sentences, they make mistakes. You can correct papers much more easily if you are reading complete sentences, and it is not as easy for students to copy.

Students should spend some time in every class writing so you can see their work. Walk around the room and point out mistakes in capitals, periods, and question marks. If they are not leaving margins on their papers, fold their papers back on the pink margin lines to show them how to conform to the margins. Draw pencil lines halfway through the spaces to show them how high the small letters should be. Insist that they use lined paper.

Pay attention to the students' written form. Their letters may be all the same size, words may float off the lines, or the student may write in all capitals. There are worksheets to practice printing in education supply stores and some of the recommended textbooks. Students should do cursive writing or printing practice at home for extra credit. You will not have time to teach beginners traditional cursive writing, and it's not likely that their printing will improve much in the time you have them, but you should communicate the idea that readable writing is desirable.

When the majority of students are finished, go over the whole exercise again, having them read the question and give their answers. If they seem to be doing well, they can finish an exercise for homework and you can check it orally the next day. Check all written work orally, because students don't pay attention to written corrections on their written work. They also need the speaking practice.

Take note of who never finishes and which students seem to depend on copying. Don't allow slower students to finish while you are checking the work. Tell them to check what they have and they can finish for homework or after school. It's more important for them to hear the sentences orally than to finish writing all of them.

If the worksheet involves an ID card exercise, have them pull out their ID cards and talk about them first. Most secondary schools and community colleges provide IDs. This might cause privacy concerns. Use your judgment. **Lifeskills, p. 10; Skill Sharpeners, p. 2.**

Numbers - Page numbers Use the textbook as a way to practice numbers. Write the page number and text title on the agenda. At the beginning of the course, when you tell the students to open their books at a certain page, hold up your text, point to the page number, and repeat it several times. As the class goes on, just say the page number and see who can find it without help. You don't try to trick the students while teaching, but you do test their comprehension level. It helps you decide who to promote.

8. TPR - Introduce TPR stands for a language teaching method called "Total Physical Response." The theory is that when physical action is involved in learning, the student will learn better and understand more directly.

In TPR, the teacher gives a sequence of orders to the class. The students respond with a physical action. When you first give the order, you do the action yourself as an example. If the order is "Stand up," you stand up or motion to the class to stand up. If the next order is, "Sit down," you sit down or motion to them to sit down. You repeat the orders until most of the students are following correctly without your prompting. The teacher can see immediately who understands the order. Students learn these actions very quickly. Even if

15

they don't understand at first, they can imitate the other students. When most students appear to understand the order, you stop modeling it. Practice a few more times by asking a volunteer do the action alone or having small groups do it. Then go on to new actions and combinations of actions.

When using TPR, you don't write down the vocabulary or teach it first. You can review a TPR exercise as a beginning warm-up, or at the end of class with only a few minutes left.

Although the technique is great for beginners to learn vocabulary, once you start thinking this way, you can use the TPR technique to teach more advanced grammar. Adults may be less enthusiastic than teenagers about using TPR, but they will usually do it at least for a while because they realize that it makes learning really easy. Giving them some tricky or funny orders can be exploited for laughs.

The attached sentences are examples of TPR order sequences.

TPR Orders

1. Stand up.
2. Sit down.

3. Point to the teacher.
      the door
      the window
      the board

4. Stand up and walk to the door.
5. Stop.
6. Walk to the window.

7. Stop! Don't walk to the window. Walk to the door.
8. Stop! Don't walk to the door. Walk to the board.

9. Write your name on the board.
10. Erase your name. Walk to your desk and sit down.

11. Look at the teacher.
      the board
      the class
      a student
      a boy and a girl
12. Look at the clock. Stop! Don't look at the clock.

13. Point to a book.
      2 books
      3 books and a pencil

14. Pick up a pencil.
      a pen
      a pen and a pencil

15. Pick up a pencil. Put down the pencil.
      Pick up a book. Put down the book.
      Pick up a book. Show me the book. Put down the book.

16. Show me a pencil.
      Stop! Don't show me a pencil. Show me a pen.
      Stop! Don't show me a pen. Show me a book.

Day 3

Vocabulary

10 - ten
20 - twenty
30 - thirty
40 - forty
50 - fifty
60 - sixty
70 - seventy
80 - eighty
90 - ninety
100 - one hundred
a hundred
200 - two hundred
1,000 - a thousand
one thousand
2,000 - two thousand

Agenda

1. Opening routine - greeting, roll, date, agenda
2. Numbers 10-19 - review 10-19 with flashcards, number chart
    For teenagers, review ages and math problems. (See Day 2.)
    Collect numbers homework only
    Do quiz 10-19, collect
3. Numbers 10-100 - introduce, repeat 2-3X
    With large number chart, teach to count by tens, read by tens forward and backward
    Spelling problems
    Plural of hundred and thousand, oral practice
    Pronunciation - fourteen vs. forty - pronunciation stressing "teen" and "ty"
    Practice with #1#2 technique
    Oral practice with ages of teacher and students (for older students)
    Numbers - written practice
    HOMEWORK 20X, quiz tomorrow
4. Classroom words - oral practice with TPR - classroom objects and locations
5. A, an, the - TPR oral practice - classroom objects, singular only
    the - TPR practice - optional
    a, an - written practice
6. To be - long forms and short forms - introduce and practice with pointing
    Oral practice with names of students and your name
Short forms of am, is, and are - introduce and explain
    Pronunciation
    Sentence stress

Stuff

1. Flashcards with numerals 10-19 and words on the back
2. Flashcards with today's vocabulary in figures with words on the reverse side
3. Large elementary school number chart with numbers from 1-100
4. On a table or desk in the front of the room - a pen, pencil, book, notebook, etc. plus an orange, an apple, and an eraser. Use only one of each item.

Lesson Plan

1. Opening Routine Follow previous routines. (See Day 1 and Day 2.)

2. Numbers 10-19 - Quiz Students read number flashcards in order, then in mixed order. Do a little oral practice with ages and math problems. (See Day 2.) Collect homework and give the quiz. (See Day 2.)

3. Numbers 10-100 - Oral practice Read the large number chart from 10 - 100 by tens. Be sure to stress the first syllable of the words. Then have students repeat each number after you several times. Use the large number chart to count by tens forward and backward.

Point out the odd spellings of "forty" (no U) and "fifty." Write "fourty" and put a big X over the U. Write "fivety" and put big X over the VE. Change it to F and then write the word out, "fifty." Underline GHT in "eighty" and give students a rule. "It's always GHT, not GTH, TGH, or anything else." Write and then X out GTH and TGH. (Don't mention "strength" and "length." Leave exceptions for later.) Draw a big arrow pointing to the E in "ninety."

Plural Numbers Review the basic plural rule with examples: 1 boy, 2 boys. 1 pencil, 4 pencils. Pronounce the S with a lot of stress and hissing. Point to the list and show them that there is no S on hundred or thousand. Write "200" and "two hundreds" on board, then cross out the S with a big X. Then write "2,000" and the words "two thousands" on the board. Ask, "Correct or incorrect?" Someone will yell, "Incorrect!" and you then cross out the S on "thousands." Write on the board 4,000 and 5,000. Have them repeat 4,000, stressing the lack of S, and 5,000, NOT "five thousands!"

Comma on thousands Point out that 1,000 has a comma, not a period. Write "1.000" on the board, point to the period, stare at it dramatically, and write a big giant comma over the period. Don't explain any other number formats at this time.

Numbers - Pronunciation - "teen" vs. "ty" Write several pairs of numbers on the board.

> fourteen - forty
> sixteen - sixty
> seventeen - seventy

By saying the stressed syllables very loudly, show how the accent on "fourteen" is on the second syllable, but the accent on "forty" is on the first syllable. Have students repeat the pairs several times. Write large dark accent marks over the stressed syllables on the board.

#1#2 Listening Practice Use the #1#2 technique to help students hear the difference between "thirteen" vs. "thirty," "fourteen" vs. "forty," etc. Read the pair "fourteen - forty" from the board several times, pointing to the words. Ask, "Can you hear the difference?" as you point to your ear. Write #1 next to "fourteen" and #2 next to "forty." Say "fourteen" and hold up one finger. Say "forty" and hold up two fingers. Say, "When I say 'fourteen,' you hold up one finger." Repeat "fourteen" once or twice. They should hold up one finger each time. Then say "forty" once or twice, watching each time to see if they are holding up two fingers. Then say the two words at random. After mixing up the words several times, repeat the same word 3 or 4 times to see if students actually hear the difference or if they are simply guessing. Repeat with two more pairs. Students like this game, but don't do it very long, since some students will not be able to hear the difference.

If your students are teenagers, ask them, "How old are you?" If they say "fifteen," you say, "Fifteen or fifty?" If they don't understand, write the two numbers on the board. Use your approximate age and ask, "Am I sixty or sixteen?" Then ask them, "Are you fourteen or forty?" "Are you seventeen or seventy?" This should get a laugh, since teenagers are so insulted by being asked if they are forty.

If your students are adults, ask volunteers how old they are. Write the age on the board and then write it as follows: 52 = 50 + 2. 43 = 40 + 3. Write out the numbers "fifty-two" and "forty-three," pointing out the hyphens.

Don't practice for too long. Numbers are difficult to learn because they are so similar, so you need to practice them regularly, but briefly.

Numbers - Written practice - Access, pp. 69-70; Lifeskills, p. 11; Skill Sharpeners, p. 8.

4. Classroom Words - TPR Introduce classroom objects and fixtures with TPR routines. (See Day 2 for a sample routine.) You can introduce any object or location in the classroom that they can point to, walk to, or pick up. Practice each new word a few times. It's okay to add two objects or two commands. You are introducing and previewing vocabulary which they will get on dictation quizzes later. Don't use clothing or people. Save those for later.

Classroom Words - Written practice If you have a worksheet or text with classroom vocabulary, do it now. **Side by Side, pp. 7-9; Lifeskills, p. 17; Skill Sharpeners, p. 11.**

5. A, an, the - Introduce with TPR Have on a table in the front of the room a pen, a pencil, a book, and a notebook, plus an orange, an apple, and an eraser. Use one of each item. Do the routine several times, ordering the class and individual students with natural pronunciation.

Point to a pen.
Point to an orange.
Point to a pencil.
Point to an apple.

Point to a book.
Point to an eraser.
Point to a table.

Write each sentence on the board and repeat it several times. Make sure they hear the accent on the last word in the sentence and the lack of accent on "a" and "an." Show them that they are only going to hear a change in the rhythm; they won't hear "a" and "an" as full words. Say "pen" followed by "a pen." Stress the N in "an orange," "an eraser," and "an apple."

On the board, write "a apple," "a orange," "a eraser." Pronounce each phrase for the students. Shake your head sadly, frown and point to your ears, indicating that it doesn't sound good. Write "a apple, an apple" together and pronounce them both. Put a big X over "a apple." Repeat with the other two words.

Write A, E, I, O, U vertically on the board. Then add the words apple, eraser, iPhone or ice cream, orange, umbrella (with little pictures). Underline the first letter of each word. Write "an" before each word, and draw an arrow from the N in "an" to the first letter of each word to show that it is the first letter of the word that requires the use of "an" before it.

Practice "the" - TPR - Optional Practice the difference between "a" and "the."

> Look at a pen. Point to the pen.
> Point to a book. Pick up the book. Show me the book. Put down the book.
> Point to a book. Pick up the book. Stop! Don't pick up the book! Pick up a pen.

Give students the rule. Use "a" for the first time you refer to an object, and after that use "the." Another rule is that if both people in a conversation know what object they are talking about, use "the." Give the example orally and then on the board.

Do you have a pencil?   Yes.
Please give me the pencil.

I have a coffee cup. The cup is on the desk.

Give only two or three examples. Don't try to explain too much. Practice the above examples briefly, or optionally. The class will get more practice in later TPR routines. Expect the students to know the difference between "a" and "an," and correct them on that, but don't test them on how to use "the." It's too difficult for beginners.

A, an - Written practice Choose between "a" and "an." **Practical English, p. 11 (bottom); New American Streamline Departures, p. 3A.**

Do the written exercises out loud first. (See Day 2.) If the practice is a dialog, act it out. "What is it?" Act out the "I dunno!" gesture. "It's a pencil!" Stress "it's" several times because this is a very difficult sound for most students to hear. When they write, make sure they put apostrophes on "it's." Point to the example in the book.

6. To be - Long forms - Introduce Write forms on the board.

I am	we are
you are	you are
he is she it	they are

Show students the meaning by pointing to yourself, to one of them, to a boy, to a girl, to the desk, to all of you at once in a circling motion, to several of them at the same time, and to two people who sit close together while you stand off to one side.

Make sentences while pointing.

> I am your teacher. I am Mrs. Lockwood.
> You are students. You are in class.
> She is Maria. She is from Guatemala.
> He is Juan. He is a boy.
> It is a desk. It is a TV. It is my book.
> We are in school now.
> We are in Los Angeles. We are in California.
> They are girls. They are boys.
> They are windows. They are computers.
> You are Juan. You are Jose.
> You (indicating all of the students) are in my class.

Subject Pronouns - Oral practice "I," "we," and "you" tend to become confusing, so draw a circle around "he," "she," "it," and "they," and practice only those now. Put different students standing in different parts of the room. You want 1 boy, several boys, 1 girl or woman, 2 or 3 girls or women, 1 chair by itself, and 2 chairs together. Show the class where to point at first. As you say, "he," "she," "it," and "they," the students point to the appropriate place. Make sure all are pointing in the right direction.

The idea is for them to practice the differences between "he," "she," and "it," and to realize that several boys, several girls, and 2 chairs are all called "they." This will be more difficult for them than you expect. Many students have trouble distinguishing H from SH, and students from some languages will expect to hear different words for a group of males versus a group of females. They may drop the personal pronouns "he" and "she" and just use "is" or "are" alone, especially when writing.

To be - Short forms - Introduce Go back to your list on the board in activity #6 above. In the space below the long forms on the your list, write the short forms. Make the apostrophes very obvious. Have students repeat both forms together 2 or 3 times. Continue with the other forms. "I am, I'm. You are, you're," etc.

For each verb, point to the long form and say it. Put your hands together in front of you and then move them out as if you were showing a big object. Then point to the short form and say it. Move your hands back together, or move your thumb and forefinger closer together to indicate a small size.

Go back to "I am." Underline each word of the long form and count out loud, "1 word, 2 words." Write "2 words" on the board. Underline the whole short form and count, "1 word." Write "1 word" on the board. Do this for all the forms.

Then go back and draw a little arrow pointing toward the space between "I" and "am," "we" and "are," etc. Write the word "space" above each arrow. Draw a little empty square in between the words. Show them that the short form does not have any space between the words except for the area filled by the apostrophe. You do this because many students will write short forms with the apostrophe hanging in a huge empty space and the **'re** and **'s** parts of the short form standing alone like a separate word.

Go back to the board and write each long form as 2 separate words. Put a big X over the A in "I am." Show the class that you are erasing the A and replacing it with an apostrophe. Then push the I and the M together with your hands and rewrite it as "I'm." Do the same with "he is" and with "you are" and with "we are" and with "they are." Students have to understand that the apostrophe stands for a missing letter, so they can't just insert apostrophes at random. There must be a letter missing.

To be - Short forms - Pronunciation Show students correct pronunciation by repeating the short and long forms together. "I am, I'm. I am, I'm." Press your lips together to show them how to pronounce the M. Some may try to say, "I'n." Don't allow them to say "his" for "he's," "were" instead of "we're" or "iss" instead of "it's." When going over written exercises, always correct pronunciation, because these forms are so essential.

To be - Short forms - Pronunciation - Stress Write these sentences on the board.

I'm a **TEACH**er. Normal, no stress on I'm. It's information.

I **AM** a teacher!!! Yes!!! Stress on long form shows you are insisting it's true.

I am a **TEACHER**!!! **YOU** are a **STUDENT**! You're stressing the different ideas. Also show them that the word "a" is not stressed, but they should hear it in the rhythm of the sentence. Many students don't hear the "a" beat, and will leave it out.

From now until the end of level one, you should say long forms of "to be" and short forms together until students understand the short forms easily when used alone. Right now, on Day 3, teach affirmative only, no negative.

Day 4

Vocabulary

door
window
board
chair
desk
table
pen
pencil
pencil sharpener
eraser
marker
book

Agenda

1. Opening routine - greeting, roll, agenda
2. Numbers 10-100 - repeat numbers by ten with number chart
    Count by tens forward and backward
    Practice multiplying and dividing by ten (add zero, subtract zero)
    Review with flashcards in order, then in mixed order
    Correct or Incorrect? - spelling review
    Collect homework
3. Date routine - review
    Writing date in full
    Say the year - twenty-fourteen and two thousand fourteen
    How to head papers
4. Numbers 10-100 - quiz, check date format while dictating quiz, collect
5. Hyphenated numbers - optional - written practice
6. To be - plural - oral practice - TPR
    Written practice - 1 or 2 pages
7. Classroom words #1- introduce or review today's vocabulary - TPR - singular only
    Review spelling on board
    Pronunciation and repeating
    HOMEWORK 20X, quiz tomorrow
8. Plurals with S - introduce regular plurals with small objects, include vocabulary words
    Written practice - 1 page

IF TIME

9. Have with numbers and plurals - optional - oral practice
10. This/that - introduce this vs. that (singular only) briefly
    Written practice

Stuff

1. Flashcards with numerals 10-100 by tens and words on the back
2. Large number chart showing all numbers 1-100
3. Flashcards of today's vocabulary
4. List of vocabulary so far, with each day's words written under the complete date
5. Small groups of small classroom objects such as pens, pencils, markers, erasers, books

Lesson Plan

1. Opening Routine Do the opening routine with greeting, date, roll call, and agenda as in the first few days of class, but in much shorter time. Roll call can be silent. You can also add announcements and review your rules for heading papers or other concerns which don't fit in anywhere else in the agenda.

2. Numbers 10-100 - Oral review Review numbers orally as before. (See Day 3.) For practice, you can talk about multiplying and dividing by ten. This allows you to use the vocabulary in context.

Numbers 10-100 - Correct or Incorrect? Quickly do a spelling review for the difficult numbers forty, fifty, eighty, and ninety. Write these number words on the board, two of them correctly and two incorrectly. Point to each number and ask, "Correct or Incorrect?" If the students tell you the number is written incorrectly, ask them to spell it correctly or fix the error on the board. If necessary, you rewrite the number correctly. Don't forget to erase these numbers before the quiz.

3. Date Routine - Written practice Before doing the daily quiz, review the date format and ways to say the year. During the test, walk around to make sure students have written the date correctly in their quiz paper headings. You should review the date format periodically.

4. Numbers 10-100 - Quiz (See Day 2 for quiz procedure.) When dictating this quiz, include 200 and 2,000. When checking the papers, make sure they have not put S on the ends of "hundred" and "thousand."

5. Hyphenated Numbers - Written practice - Optional, adults only If you want to teach hyphenated words ("twenty-seven," "ninety-two"), you could give the class one practice page on numbers. For adults, hold up your checkbook and ask them using gestures if they use one. If they are still using checkbooks, you can do a practice with check formats. **Skill Sharpeners, p. 8 OR Lifeskills, p. 11; GrammarWork, p. 29.**

Using number examples, show that the hyphen puts together 2 complete words to make one different word. For secondary school students, the value of writing hyphenated numbers is to show them that some words must be spelled with a hyphen. This is enough time to spend on hyphenation at this level. Discourage students from hyphenating words at the right margin of their papers. Many secondary students who try to use hyphens carry over only a single letter to the next line.

Also, explain on the board with arrows and boxes that there are no extra spaces in a hyphenated word. (See Day 3.) Write two hyphenated numbers with hyphens floating in a large space between the words. Draw a box in each of the extra spaces around the hyphen. Put an X over each box and show by bringing your hands closer together in front of you that you are making the word shorter. Write the hyphenated word again correctly (without spaces) under the wrong version. Correct this error when the class writes hyphenated numbers.

6. To be - Long and short forms - Written practice Preview and check written practice orally as explained on Day 2. **Practical English, pp. 3-5.**

Make sure that students write apostrophes in short forms correctly, since apostrophes and contracted verbs are tested constantly at every level of regular English classes. Insist that they write the apostrophe with a curl, since straight apostrophes tend to degenerate into blobs, become commas by floating down to the lines on the paper, or completely disappear.

Students become careless, so encourage them from the beginning to write clearly and to think that punctuation is important. Each punctuation mark means something, and somebody (you) actually looks at what they write. Walk around the class while they're doing writing practices and point to each error. Explain, show with a gesture, or write in yourself the missing punctuation or capital letter. By the end of the course, some students will be able to correct a mistake if you simply point to it.

7. Classroom Words #1 - Introduce and review Review today's vocabulary of classroom words with TPR routines from Day 2 and Day 3. For pronunciation practice, have them repeat, name the objects in the room, and read flashcards. (See Day 1.) Quickly point out possible spelling problems - W on "window," CH on "chair" vs. SH on "sharpener," two words on "pencil sharpener," C on "pencil" vs. S on "eraser." (See Day 2, Day 3, and #5 above for techniques to point out problems with spaces and spelling.)

Master Vocabulary List - Optional Before students copy their list for homework and the quiz, pass out a sheet in which each day's number vocabulary has been typed under headings of each day's date written out in complete form. Or write on the board.

> **September 9, 2015**
> zero
> one
> two
> **September 10, 2015**
> ten
> eleven
> twelve

Show students that you want them to write today's date in their notebooks, and list today's vocabulary underneath it. Tomorrow's vocabulary list will go underneath tomorrow's date in the same list. They will use this big word list to study for exams. You could collect the list each Friday and give one point for having all of the days complete. This ensures that absentees will get the vocabulary from someone else and helps the students to have an organized study system. It also saves them paper.

8. Plurals with S - Introduce with TPR Use today's vocabulary words, which all have regular S plurals. Add a few other words which have regular plurals, like student, teacher, boy, and girl. Hold up or point to one or two objects at a time. Example:

Hold up a book. Say, "A book."

Hold up two books. Say, "Two books." Stress the S.

Continue with "a marker - two markers," " a pencil - three pencils," etc.

Point to a window and say, "A window."

Point to two windows. "Two windows"

Holding up or pointing to different objects, see if the students can say the words in singular and plural. Hold up one finger and point to an object for singular. Hold up two fingers and point to two objects for plural. Give them the answers if necessary. Make sure that you hear the S on plural words. Correct them by repeating the plural word, stressing the final S, and asking them to repeat it.

Many students are not sensitive to final S as we are in English. They may not hear it, or the S may be present in their language but minimized or even ignored. They may confuse it with SH. Also, S in English may be pronounced in several other ways, such as "SS" or "Z." That's why you correct for a missing S from the beginning of the class. You can't assume that the student will pick it up later.

Plurals with S - Oral practice - Choose correct item - TPR Using small groups of items on your desk (pen, pencil, eraser, marker, book), you pick up one item in one hand and two items in the other hand and use the following routines.

> Point to 1 pencil. Point to 2 pencils.
> Point to 1 eraser. Point to 2 erasers.

If students can do this easily, you can use other sentences for the plural forms. You are not asking them to make the sentences, only to choose between one item and several items.

> Point to a pencil.
> Point to 3 pencils.
> Point to the pencil. (Show the pencil very obviously.)
> Point to pencils.
> Point to 1 pencil.
> Point to some pencils. (Slightly stress the S.)

Mix these examples up until students are getting them right. You want them to hear the S on the end of the plural. Then go on to pens, erasers, etc.

Plurals with S - Written practice Do 1 page. **New American Streamline Departures, p. 3B**.

9. To be - Singular and plural - Oral practice Write the following two sample questions on the board. Hold up classroom objects one at a time or several at a time. Ask the questions. Students answer in a complete sentence.

What is it?   It's a _____.
What are they?   They're _____.

Make sure students do not say, "They're a _____."

IF TIME

10. "Have" with numbers and plurals - Oral practice - Optional Review quickly. Give 2-3 examples and get about 5 answers for each sentence type. In the first, they answer with a number.

(Hold up 2 pens.)   How many pens?   Two pens.
(Point to three desks.) How many desks?   Three desks.

Write these models on the board. They change the object from one to two.

I have a marker.   I have 2 markers.
I have 1 marker.   I have 2 markers.
We have a door.   We have two doors.
You have a book.   You have two books.

Don't teach "has" at this time. Point to the objects you are asking about. Ask,

How many markers do I have?   Three markers.
How many doors do we have?   We have two doors.
How many books do you have?   I have 4 books.
How many shoes do you have?   I have 2 shoes.

Tell the students to answer with "yes" or "no."

I have 2 pens.   YES
I have 100 TVs.   NO
I have 1 shoe.
I have 2 cars.
I have 25 houses.
I have 2 girlfriends.

11. This/that - Introduce - TPR (See Day 2.) Set up 2 groups of small classroom objects so that one group is next to you and the other is on a table or desk a little way across the room. Give the class some orders.

> Point to this pencil. (Point to the pencil on your desk.)
> Point to that pencil. (Indicate the pencil on the table across the room.)
> Point to this pen. (Hold up a pen or point to a pen close to you.)
> Point to that pen. (Indicate the pen on the distant table.)
> If you have two sets of windows, walk to one window and say, "Point to this window."
> Point across the room to a distant window. Say, "Point to that window."
> Call on a student. Say, "Walk to this window." Then say, "Walk to that window."
> Point to one girl near you and say, "This girl is Maria."
> Point to a girl across the room. Say, "That girl is _____."
> Pointing to boys close to and far from you, say,   "This guy is _____."
>   "That guy is _____."

This/that - Written practice To practice "this" and "that," texts often indicate a faraway object with pictures of a pointer stick, a pointing finger, or an arrow. Go over the exercises with students answering orally before they write. Make sure they pronounce "th" correctly. **Practical English, pp. 6-7; Writing Practical English, p. 9; GrammarWork, p. 34.**

Day 5

Vocabulary

notebook
ruler
stapler
paper clip
rubber band
TV
computer
scissors
paper
liquid paper
chalk
tape

NOT FOR QUIZ
singular
plural
count
noncount

Agenda

1. Opening routine - greeting, roll, date, agenda
2. Classroom words #1 - oral review with TPR, flashcards
        Collect homework, quiz
Classroom words #2 - introduce, oral practice
        TPR - practice singular, plural, and noncount words
        HOMEWORK 20X, quiz tomorrow
3. a/an - written practice
4. this/that - introduce or review quickly - oral practice (See Day 4.)
        Start, finish, or correct written page (See Day 4.)
        Written practice - 1 more page
5. these/those - introduce, oral practice
        Written practice
6. this/these pronunciation - #1#2 game (See Day 3.)
        Which is correct? - oral practice
        More oral practice - difficult examples
IF TIME
7. Alphabet - with alphabet chart - pronunciation
8. Vowels vs. consonants - memory saying, say vowel or consonant
9. Short reading, then copy in class or do answers as HOMEWORK
LAST 1/2 HOUR - BINGO

Stuff

1. Flashcards - divided into homework vocabulary and today's vocabulary
2. Three examples of each item in vocabulary list (not computer or TV), a package of paper
3. Elementary school chart of letters and capitals printed (not in cursive writing)
4. Tape of alphabet song, if available
5. Short reading from text, grammar book, or copies
6. Bingo game and candy or prizes

Lesson Plan

1. Opening Routine Greeting, roll, review, agenda

2. Classroom Words #1 - Oral review Use TPR to review words for the quiz in singular and plural. (See Day 4.) Students point to the objects placed separately or in pairs and groups in the room.

Point to a _____.
Point to 2 _____.

Review once more with flashcards, collect the homework, and give the quiz.

Classroom Words #2 - Introduce and oral practice This vocabulary list has singular, plural, and noncount words. Practice them with the TPR routines below. Don't stress the rule too much at this time. Hold up each object or stand next to it while you give the commands.

I have a ruler. Point to the ruler.
I have a notebook. Point to the notebook.
I have a paper clip. Point to the paper clip.
I have a rubber band. Point to the rubber band.
I have a stapler. Point to the stapler.
I have a computer. Point to the computer.
I have a TV. Point to the TV.

Distribute the notebook, ruler, stapler, paper clip, and rubber band to individual students. Ask those students to answer in a complete sentence.

What do you have?
I have a ruler.
I have a _____.

Make sure they use "a" and the correct stress. If you need to, repeat "I have A ruler. I have A notebook," to make sure they use the "a." Then, holding up or pointing to the same objects in mixed order, have the students say, "A ruler. A notebook," etc. Use the objects about 3 times each.

Go on to "scissors." Because it is plural, they can't answer with "a" or "an." Put on the board.

I have scissors.
I have (some) scissors.

Hold up a pair of scissors and read each sentence, emphasizing the S at the end. Say, "Scissors" has an S because you have two." Point to the two blades of the scissors as you count "one, two." Point to a pair of pants and count the legs. Say, "One, two, pantS," stressing the S. Show them a pair of glasses and count the lenses. Say, "One, two, glassES," stressing the final S. Give the following TPR orders.

Point to scissors.
Point to pants.
Point to some scissors.
Point to some glasses.
Point to glasses.
Point to some pants.

Go on to the words which do not take "a." Use TPR orders.

Point to the paper.
Point to the liquid paper.
Point to the chalk.
Point to the tape.

Write the question on the board, and point to the paper.

What is it?
It's _____.

Point to the paper. They should say, "It's paper." If they answer, "It's a paper," shake your head no and say, "It's paper." Write on the board, "It's a paper." and then put a big X over the "a." Ask the student to repeat "It's paper." Repeat for the other 3 words.

Hold up a piece of paper and say, "I have paper." Then hold up several pieces of paper and say, "I have paper." Then hold up a pack of paper and say, " I have paper." Do the same with several bottles of liquid paper, several sticks or boxes of chalk, and several rolls of tape.

Don't explain the rule of count/noncount words any further in this lesson. Simply correct students who say, "I have a paper." or "It's a chalk." This grammar will be repeated often during the course, because students have problems with it for a long time.

Vocabulary with two words On the vocabulary list, point to each word, such as "notebook" and "paper clip," and say, "One word" or "Two words." On the terms with two words, point to each word separately and draw small boxes in the spaces between the words. (See Day 2.)

Review the vocabulary for homework by going through the flashcards twice.

3. A/an - Written practice Do one more page of practice with "a" and "an." See **references, Day 3.**

4. This/that - Introduce, complete, or review Do oral and written practice from Day 4.

This/that - Written practice Do one additional page. See **references, Day 4. Also, New American Streamline Departures, p. 4A.**

5. These/those - Introduce - Oral practice - TPR Using small objects, quickly review "this" and "that." (See Day 4.) Have a table in the front of the room set up with 2 collections of single objects which are clearly visible to the class. Stand closer to one of the groups and repeat the TPR routine. For example, "This is a pencil. That is a pen."

Then use objects from classroom words #1 and #2 to practice "these" and "those" in the same way. Add objects to the 2 groups, so that instead of 1 pen, you have 2 pens. Instead of 1 pencil, you have 3 pencils in a group. Repeat the TPR routine with the plural objects. For example, "These are pencils. Those are pens."

Hold up the objects near you and point to the items farther away to make it very clear which ones you're talking about. You can use two fingers, or point separately to each object out of 2 or 3 in a group to show that you are referring to more than one thing. Continue practicing with more of the classroom objects on the vocabulary list.

These/those - Written practice Use an exercise which practices only "these" and "those" or one which also includes "this" and "that." **New American Streamline Departures, p. 3B; Practical English pp. 8, 13; Writing Practical English, p. 10; GrammarWork, p. 35.**

6. This/these - Pronunciation with #1#2 Students will have a lot of problems distinguishing and pronouncing "this" and "these." Write "#1 this" and "#2 these" on the board and pronounce the words together several times. Ask the students to repeat them together. Use the #1#2 game to practice the difference between "this" and "these." (See Day 3 and Sub work 1.)

This/these - Pronunciation - Which is correct? Hold up 1 or 2 objects and ask the question.

    (1 pencil) Which is correct? This pencil or these pencils?   This pencil
    (3 erasers) Which is correct? This eraser or these erasers?   These erasers
    (1 ruler) This ruler or these rulers?
    (2 books) This book or these books?

Continue with other vocabulary words until most of the answers are right. If the students are doing very well, you can get tricky. Repeat the choices very clearly and loudly.

(2 pencils) These pencil or these pencils?   These pencils
(1 pencil) This pencil or these pencil?   This pencil
(3 books) This books or these books?
(3 books) These book or these books?
(1 pair of scissors) This scissors or these scissors?   These scissors

IF TIME

7. Alphabet Point to the alphabet chart. Students repeat each letter after the teacher and then repeat the most difficult letters several times. Doing the alphabet song with a tape or the teacher singing is an option. Students can sing along if they want to, but don't force them to sing. Say the song again in phrases showing how the rhythm helps memory. (See Sub Work 1 at the end of the manual for a longer lesson on consonants.) **For a listening practice, Access, p. 54. For pair interviews, Access, p. 55.**

8. Vowels vs. Consonants Write the vowels on the board. Students repeat them 2-3 times. Students copy the phrase "A E I O U and sometimes Y" in their vocabulary list. (Y is a vowel, as in "gym" and "psychology," and a consonant, as in "yes" and "yellow." Turn the alphabet chart over and erase the vowels from the board. Repeat 5 or 6 letters and students say "vowel" or "consonant" for each.

9. Short Reading Read and copy a short reading or dialog from a text. Write answers for homework. (See Day 6 about how to use a short reading.)

LAST 1/2 HOUR - BINGO

Rewards - Bingo At the end of the week, everybody needs a break, and Bingo is a great listening exercise. Students should play Bingo no longer than 1/2 hour at the end of a class, usually on Friday or the day before a holiday. After they have played Bingo for a month or two, instead of "BINGO" as a title, substitute other words with difficult letters, like QUIET, WACKY, PALMS, FRESH, JUMPY, QUICK, and ZEROS.

Pass out the cards yourself so students will not waste time looking for their lucky card. Try not to have duplicate sets of cards, because friends will look for duplicates and copy from each other. Tell students that only the first to yell "Bingo!" gets the prize. You can show them that the "B" column only has numbers 1-15, the "I" column numbers 16-30, etc. The teaching assistant or other students may help new students, but only by pointing to the number, not by translating it.

The teacher cheats. . . At the end of each Bingo game, the caller returns all of the numbers to one big pile. However, I kept the used numbers off to one side and pulled numbers for the next game from the unused numbers. That way we practiced more different numbers in each game. Also, with completely different numbers in each game, the better students are less likely to win twice. Only one adult student ever caught me doing this, and when I explained to her that the real goal of the game was to practice all the numbers, she was okay with it. The younger students never figured it out.

Day 6

Vocabulary

shelf
closet
bulletin board
(2 words)
file cabinet
(2 words)
clock
teacher's desk
student's desk
table
chair
box
bag

NOT FOR QUIZ
in
on
under
pick up
put down
put in
take out

Agenda

1. Opening routine
2. Classroom words #2 - review with TPR routines, this/that/these/those
      Collect homework, quiz
Classroom words #3 - introduce vocabulary, repeat 2-3X
      Oral practice using in, pick up, and other "not for quiz" vocabulary
      HOMEWORK 20X for quiz
3. Reading selection - introduce, finish or review from Day 5
      Practice reading paragraph - several pairs of students read to class
      Copy reading and questions, write answers in complete sentence
4. Irregular plurals - introduce - rules and examples on board (list attached)
      Written practice - 1 page
5. To be - review affirmative long and short forms
      Introduce negative long and short forms
      Negative and short forms (oral routine attached)
      Written practice

Stuff

1. Flashcards for vocabulary - today's quiz and today's homework
2. Classroom objects - small items including a box and a bag
3. Flashcards with "to be" - affirmative on one side, negative on the other

Lesson Plan

1. Opening Routine - Greeting, roll, date routine, agenda Continue to practice grammar and numbers with the roll, date and agenda. For example, you can comment incorrectly when taking the roll. "Oh, Mrs. X isn't here." See if anybody corrects you. Point to the date and read the month or the day incorrectly. See if anybody corrects you. Students love to tell the teacher that he or she is wrong. It shows you if they understand and if they are paying attention.

If students don't understand a page number, write it on the board for them. Never translate it.

2. Classroom Words #2 - Review or introduce Briefly, use TPR and flashcards to review. Collect homework and give the quiz.

Classroom Words #3 - Introduce and practice (See Day 1.) Point out the vocabulary items with 2 words by drawing little boxes in the spaces between them. (See Day 2.)

Classroom Words #3 - Oral practice Students point to each vocabulary word and say, "That is a _____." Use each word on the list several times.

Location Words in the vocabulary Using only the location words in the vocabulary list, point to each object in a location and say,

> The shelf is in the cabinet.
> The books are on the shelf.
> The clock is on the wall.
> The bulletin board is on the wall.
> The paper is on the bulletin board.
> The bag is on the teacher's desk.
> The bag is on Maria's desk.
> The box is on the shelf.
> The box is in the closet.
> The box is under Juan's desk.
> Now the box is under the teacher's desk.
> The box is under the student's desk.

Don't teach the rules of possessive with **'s** right now. You're just introducing it in context. In the same way, you are practicing "in" vs. "on" in context, but don't explain it yet. Many students do not hear the difference, so correct it if someone uses it incorrectly.

Classroom Words #3 - TPR Practice a routine with the box, bag, closet, and desks.

> Pick up the pencil.
> Put the pencil in the bag.
> Take the pencil out of the bag.
> Put the pencil on the teacher's desk.
> Pick up the pen.
> Put the pen in the box.
> Pick up the box.
> Put the box on a student's desk.
> Point to the bag.
> Pick up a book.
> Put the book in the bag.
> Pick up the bag.
> Put the bag on Juan's desk.
> Take out the book.

You can use "this/that/these/those" with today's vocabulary words for review.

> Pick up this pencil. Put it in that bag.
> Pick up that bag and put it on this desk.
> Pick up this box and put it under that chair.
> Pick up that box and put it on the shelf in the closet.
> Point to that bag. Pick it up and put it on the file cabinet.
> Pick up that chair and put it on the teacher's desk. (What!!!!)

Don't do TPR exercises too long, just until most students understand the instructions and you've used the words enough to help the students remember them for the quiz the next day. You are allowing them to learn the vocabulary directly.

3. Reading Selection - Introduce It's very important when reading a new selection to have mostly words which the students know or a picture which is easily understandable, so that everyone understands the situation and so that you can point to the answers in the picture.

Read the paragraph or dialog first with students following along in the book. Point to the picture as you read. Then go over the reading sentence by sentence and ask questions. For example, the sentence says, "Juan is going to the supermarket."

Point to the boy in the picture and ask, "Who is Juan?" Students say, "a boy" or "a man."

Make a walking motion with your fingers. "What is Juan doing?" "He's walking," or "He's going."

Point to Juan and then move your finger to the supermarket door. "Where is Juan going?" "Store" or "Market."

"Who is going to the supermarket?" If nobody answers, point to Juan. "Juan."

"Is Juan going to the supermarket?" Point to Juan and then to the supermarket. Someone should say, "Yes." You repeat, "Yes, he is. Juan is going to the supermarket."

Don't require a complete answer or a grammatically correct sentence. The idea is for the class to understand the questions and give basic answers. If nobody can answer a question, give them the answer and go on to the next sentence.

Reading selections should be from the required class text or from textbooks written for Beginning ESL students. Newspaper articles and even cartoon books are too difficult for students at this level, no matter how simple they may appear to an English speaker. This includes most materials written for elementary school English speakers, although some might be useful. Even commercial reading storybooks which are labeled Level One for ESL speakers are usually not appropriate for the first semester of ESL. The exception is the **True Stories** series, which are low enough and which provide reading support. (See "Texts.")

When you use a reading selection, you should add numbers either before each sentence or in the margin next to each line of the reading. You can photocopy the reading so students can mark it up, or have them write the numbers lightly in the book in pencil. That makes it easy for everybody to follow where you are in the book. Especially in the first weeks of the course, point to the word or sentence you're talking about.

If the selection has written questions, ask each question orally and have students answer them out loud before they write answers. When they have finished copying the questions and writing the answers, have the students read each question out loud. Help them to give their answers in complete sentences. Start with the stronger students, so the others get the idea. The reading should be written so that a good answer can be copied directly from the story.

Reading Selection - Written practice Before answering written questions about a paragraph, students should copy the paragraph. That allows them to see the answers before they read the questions. Also, copying is an easy way for students to internalize rules of formatting and punctuation. They should copy the paragraph in correct paragraph format with an indent and margins, capitals, periods, commas, and question marks. Some books for beginners don't have indents. You can ask your students to put them in, but many won't. With beginning ESL students, limit the reading to one paragraph.

If the text does not provide specific questions in a logical sequence, you can write them yourself and attach them to the reading. The questions for a reading selection should begin at the beginning and follow an obvious sequence to the end. Show students how to search for the answer starting at the top of the paragraph and to look for the same words that they see in the question. At the beginning level, the questions should be very specific and use the exact words from the paragraph. You are not testing their knowledge. You are training them to search a paragraph for specific information. If you want to elicit student emotions or opinions about the reading, you can do so in an oral discussion where you can help them answer.

Some students will answer by simply copying complete sentences directly out of the paragraph. For example, the reading says, "Ted is a good student in Mrs. Lockwood's class," and the question is, "Is Ted a good student?"

The answer should be, "Yes, he is." OR "Yes, Ted is a good student." OR "Yes, he is good." They don't need to copy the entire sentence. It's okay at the very beginning of the course, because at that point, the students don't know many ways to answer a question in English. However, if they continue to copy the whole sentence in their answers, it's possible that they don't understand the questions.

At the beginning of the course, have students do all of the reading work in class. When the students get the idea of how you want them to answer, they can write answers for homework and you can correct them orally in class the next day. Never give them any homework without previewing it orally first. This shows them how to answer, and gives them the general idea of the reading.

When you collect their work, glance over it to see if they get the main idea and to note what each individual's problems are. At this level, the students shouldn't give lots of wrong answers because the paragraphs are so simple. If it seems that a student doesn't understand the questions or the paragraph at all, he may be copying somebody else's answers, in which case the answers may go with the wrong question, or there may be lots of odd spellings from copying another student's handwriting. Sometimes students simply copy the paragraph and questions with no answers at all. Sometimes they wait to fill in the answers when you go over the work in class.

Reading Selection - Oral review of answers Always go over answers orally just to give students a little more speaking practice and allow them to associate the written word with the spoken version. Have a student read both the question and the answer, or have two students question and answer in front of the class. Give credit for work which is mostly completed.

If you want to give the class extra review, you can do some of the dictation practices below. Going over the same material again is good, but you should do it a different way each time. That way it seems new to the students, while the material is becoming more automatic for them.

Reading Selection - Dictation - Extra practice - Optional After you have finished a reading selection, you can assign a short paragraph for dictation. For homework or in class, the students can copy the paragraph several times or repeat it to themselves. Dictate several sentences from one paragraph in correct order. They search for each correct sentence in the paragraph and copy it on their paper. To make the dictation harder, mix up the order of the sentences.

To make the task even more difficult, you can simply dictate chosen sentences without allowing students to look at the reading, or you can dictate a whole short paragraph. Then they correct their work by looking at the reading.

Reading Selection - Sentences to paragraph - Extra practice - Optional Some texts have beginning readings shown as numbered sentences in a list instead of as a paragraph. In this case, after reviewing the sentences orally, you can have students copy the sentences into correct paragraph format, without numbers.

Reading Selection - Main idea, details, conclusion - Preview - Optional If the paragraph you are reading has a clear main idea in the first sentence or a clear conclusion in the last sentence, you can start teaching these ideas. Write these words on the board.

main idea = general idea, big idea, most important idea, paragraph begins

details = facts, information, small ideas, middle of paragraph

conclusion = end, finish, emotion or opinion, paragraph ends

Don't do this in the first few weeks of class. Save it for the end of the course. Don't test them on these concepts at the beginning level. Simply introduce the concepts and vocabulary. You can ask them questions you know they can't answer, as long as you give them the basic idea and show them how to get the answer. To give them the word "idea," point to your head. It's not too difficult to introduce these concepts when your paragraph and details are very simple.

4. Irregular Plurals Rules - Introduce Write the irregular plurals chart (attached) on the board and go over the rules. Practice pronouncing "man - men" and "woman - women" using the #1#2 technique. (See Day 3.) Practice the pronunciation of S and the pronunciation of words with ES with an extra syllable. Students should copy the chart in their notebooks for reference.

Irregular Plurals - Practice Write the list of words from the plurals chart on the board. The students copy the singular words and write the plurals according to the rules. Correct the work by having students write their answers on the board. Repeat the correct forms again.

Irregular Plurals - Written practice When reviewing answers for this work, write the irregular plurals on the board. **GrammarWork, pp. 30-33 (easy vocabulary); Lifeskills, p. 40 or Skill Sharpeners, p. 74 (both higher level vocabulary).**

5. To be - Short forms - Introduction See Day 3 for an introduction to short forms. If not already done, do a written practice. **Practical English, pp. 3-8.**

It's easier to do oral practices with "he," "it," and "they" than to use "I," "you," and "we." First and second person are more confusing, because you can question the students, but they can't question you. However, there are many texts and workbooks with written dialogs and practices for all three persons. It's best to explain each form of "to be" (long form, short form, negative, question, and short answer) separately and then do a written practice on each, stretching the material over several weeks. For all forms, **Practical English, pp. 3-13, 17-21; Writing Practical English, pp. 13-19; New American Streamline Departures, pp. 1A-1B, 2A-2B; GrammarWork, pp. 1-2.**

To Be - Affirmative - Review long and short forms - Oral practice Write on the board.

I am here. We are here.
I'm here. We're here.

You are here. (Point to 1 person.)
You're here.

You are here. (Indicate class.)
You're here.

He is here.
He's here.

She is here.
She's here.

They are here.
They're here.

It is here.
It's here.

Putting your palms together in front of you, pull them apart slowly while saying "long form" very slowly. Then bring them back together quickly, saying "short form" very quickly. Go to the board and draw circles around the verbs and the 're and 's. Draw a little arrow to show that the "are" becomes 're and the "is" becomes 's.

Ask the following questions to individuals or the class as a whole. When they answer in long form, say, "OR" and indicate with your hands that you would also like to hear the short form. If they use the short form, say, "OR" and indicate by stretching your hands out that you would also like to hear the long form.

"Juan, where are you?" He answers, "I am here." Then get him to also say, "I'm here."

"Maria, are you here?" She should answer, "I'm here," and "I am here."

"Class (indicating everyone), where are we tonight?" "We are here," and "We're here."

Point to one person. "Juan, where am I?" He answers, "You are here," and "You're here."

Get a student to come to the front with you. Ask the class, "Where are we tonight?" They should answer, "You are here," and "You're here." Help them to answer if necessary.

Pick up your purse or your briefcase, and put it on the table. "Where's my bag?" They should answer, "It is on the table," and "It's on the table."

41

Get two pencils and put them on the table. Pretend to look for something and say, "I need a pencil. Where are my pencils?" Students say, "They are on the table," and "They're on the table."

If the students don't answer the way you would like, give them the answer and wait for them to repeat it after you. Then practice that form a little bit more. Have students copy the chart into their notebooks. Walk around to check that apostrophes are written accurately.

To be - Written practice Do another written practice with "to be" and positive short forms. See **references above.**

To be - Negative - Long and short forms - Oral practice Use the following pattern.

> He is here.
> He's here.
> He is not here.
> He isn't here. (Leave "He's not here" for later.)

Give examples of negative sentences with people in the class.

Where's Juan?   He's here.
Where's Jose?   He isn't here.

Continue with other examples.

Where's President Obama?   He isn't here.
Where is Shakira (or other female star)?   She isn't here.

Write on board,

> I am here.
> I am not here.
> I'm not here.
>
> You are here.
> You are not here.
> You aren't here.
>
> He is here.
> He is not here.
> He isn't here.
> She isn't here.

It is here.
It is not here.
It isn't here.

We are here.
We are not here.
We aren't here.

You (plural) are here.
You are not here.
You aren't here.

They are here.
They are not here.
They aren't there.

Have the students repeat each sentence one time after you and then copy the forms into their vocabulary notes.

Go over all over these forms again with students repeating each sentence after you. Listen for pronunciation errors. Stress the M in "I'm" because a lot of students will want to say "I'n" or will not hear the M. Stress the "aren't" by growling like a dog on the R and stressing the T. Make a barking sound for "aren't."

Go back to "I am" and show them that there is no form for amn't (in American English). Write "I amn't" under "I'm not" and then cross it out. Show that "amn't" is too difficult to pronounce by saying it several times, emphasizing the difficulty in getting it out. Then say "I'm not" and show a thumbs up or smile. Repeat "I amn't" and show thumbs down or frown and shake your finger sideways to indicate "no."

Have them repeat the negative forms several more times. Review with flashcards with "to be," affirmative on one side and negative on the other.

To be - Negative - Written practice Do 1- 2 pages using negative long and short forms. See **references above.**

To be - Short answers, affirmative and negative - Compare If you want, you can do questions first, then do short answers. (See Questions, #4 on Day 7.) If you do short answers first, don't explain the question form yet. You ask the questions and then model the long and short answers, using gestures to reinforce the meaning. Use the attached routine. Don't finish the whole routine if students appear too bored. You can also leave part of it for another day. Before you do the routine attached, write these sample sentences on the board.

Is Juan here?
Yes, he is. OR Yes, he's here.
No, he isn't. OR No, he isn't here.

To be - Short answers - Correct a typical problem - Optional In the attached oral routine, read the questions and their affirmative short answers only. Use these examples to show that with an affirmative short answer, you cannot use a short form. If you use a positive short form like "he's," something must come after it.

For example, you can say, "He's a student." You can say, "He's here." But you cannot say, "Is he a student? Yes, he's."

Write the question and wrong answer on the board. Extend the answer to make it "Yes, he's a student." Then write "OR" and under it write "Yes, he is."

If students make this error in oral responses, at first just model the correct answer. If only one student is making the error consistently, give a few more examples to that person individually. Don't try to correct the problem with the entire class unless several students are making the mistake. If a student asks why you can't use a short form in a short answer, just shrug your shoulders elaborately and say, "That's English." Don't get too involved in explaining a point that doesn't concern the whole class.

To be - Short answers, affirmative and negative - Compare - Written practice Do 1-2 pages from the above references. Don't make students answer with both long and short answers in writing. It's too boring and not typical of conversational English.

To be - Short answers, affirmative and negative - Compare - More oral practice Use the information in textbook sentences to ask the class questions. Ask them to answer both "yes" and "no" with short answers. **From the above references, Practical English, pp. 17-19 and p. 21; Writing Practical English, pp. 5-6.**

Irregular Plurals Rules

in general	with s, x, ch, sh, ss	with y	irregular
add s	add es	change y to ies	memorize
girls	bus-buses	baby-babies	man-men
students	box-boxes	city-cities	woman-women
friends	watch-watches		child-children
	bush-bushes		
	glasses-glasses		

(except with vowels)
boy - boys
tray - trays

Change these words to plural.

teacher

kiss

fox

mailman

lady

match

secretary

ashtray

toy

Show the meaning of the words above with gestures, pictures, or by acting out smoking a cigarette with a match and an ashtray.

You will have to continually correct students on these rules throughout the course, especially to pronounce the extra syllable with "es," and not to change the "y" after a vowel to "ies." Write "BOIES" on board, and count the vowels, 1, 2, 3. Shake your head "No." Say, "We don't want 3 vowels together." Don't teach exceptions or give other examples at this time. Focus on the rule and pronunciation.

To Be - Short Answers - Oral Routine

Try to get short answers and longer answers. Provide the longer answers yourself if necessary. Stress pronunciation of "isn't" and "aren't."

(Point to a student.)
    Are you present?   Yes, I am. AND Yes, I'm present.
    Are you absent today?   No, I'm not. AND No, I'm not absent.

(Point to yourself.)
    Am I here today?   Yes, you are. AND Yes, you're here.
    Am I absent today?   No, you aren't. AND No, you aren't absent.

(Indicate the whole class.)
    Are we in Room 100 right now?   Yes, we are. AND Yes, we're in Room 100.
    Are we at home right now?   No, we aren't. AND No, we aren't at home.

(Point to a desk.)
    Is this a desk?   Yes, it is. AND Yes, it's a desk.

(Hold up a pencil.)
    Is this a desk?   No, it isn't. AND No, it isn't a desk.

(Hold up 2 pens.)
    Are they pens?   Yes, they are. AND Yes, they're pens.

(Hold up 2 pencils.)
    Are they pens?   No, they aren't. AND No, they aren't pens.

(Point to a man in the class.)
    Is he from Mexico?   Yes, he is. AND Yes, he's from Mexico.
    Is he from Guatemala?   No, he isn't. AND No, he isn't from Guatemala.

(Point to a woman.)
    Is she from Thailand?   Yes, she is. AND Yes, she's from Thailand.
    Is she from India?   No, she isn't. AND No, she isn't from India.

Vocabulary

FOR QUIZ
door
window
floor
flag
wastebasket
trash can
light
ceiling
wall
screen
projector

NOT FOR QUIZ
stand up
sit down
point to
touch
walk to
run to
stop

Agenda

1. Opening routine
2. Classroom words #3 - review with TPR, flashcards. Collect homework, quiz
Classroom words #4 - introduce - TPR
       Repeat list 2-3X, review with flashcards
       HOMEWORK copy 20X, quiz
3. Irregular plurals - review rules with flashcards and on board
       HOMEWORK - copy both forms 10X, unannounced quiz tomorrow
4. To be - questions - introduce question form
       Oral practice
       Introduce short answer, affirmative and negative (or review from Day 6)
       More oral practice
       Written practice 1-2 pages
5. Colors - Introduce with color square flashcards
       Oral practice - point to clothing, jewelry, and classroom objects and say colors
       Test knowledge - teacher points and students answer with the color of object.
IF TIME
       Oral practice - "My favorite color is _____." or "I like _____."

Stuff

1. Flashcards of vocabulary for quiz and for homework
2. Flashcards with one object only (no words) on front and two objects on back
3. Flashcards with words from irregular and regular plurals list
4. Flashcards with squares of common colors plus gold and silver. See vocabulary list, Day 8. Make sure the colors are distinct so you don't have arguments over whether a shirt is orange, red, or reddish-orange. Use only colors from the vocabulary.
5. Flashcards with names of colors

Lesson Plan

1. Opening Routine

2. Classroom Words #3 - Review Use TPR, flashcards, and pictures to review. (See Day 1 and Day 2.) Collect homework and give the quiz.

Classroom Words #4 - Introduce Use TPR, pictures, and flashcards to introduce and practice the new vocabulary. HOMEWORK is to copy the words 15X for a quiz tomorrow.

3. Irregular Plurals - Review rules Use flashcards with only pictures, one object on the front and two of the objects on the back. Students see one object and give the name. When they see two objects, they give the plural form. Make sure they pronounce S and add the extra syllable to words with ES. Make sure they pronounce irregular plurals as correctly as possible and don't add an S to them, like "mens" or "childrens." Review the rule chart one more time.

Irregular Plurals - More written practice See **references, Day 6**. For pronunciation only, **Practical English, p. 54**; **Writing Practical English, p. 32.**

You will give them a surprise plurals quiz with the words on the list attached to Day 8. Write the list and have students make the plurals. HOMEWORK is to copy both forms together 20X. You can add words they already know. On a surprise quiz tomorrow, the class will hear the singular and write the singular and plural together.

4. To be - Question form - Introduce Complete work with negative and short answers from Day 6 if necessary.

When teaching questions, do not include negative questions. Their meaning is too subtle for this level. Also, don't try to explain questions which are sentences in regular order but with question intonation. It will just confuse the students. If someone continually answers this way, give a few examples. Then ask the student to use the reverse order for the question.
Insist that students include question marks and change the capital letter when converting the sentence to a question. Also require them to put the comma after "yes" and "no."

Forming questions - Introduce the rule Write on the board.

He is here.

is He here

Draw crossed arrows showing that "is" moves to be the first word in the sentence and "He" moves to being the second. Underline "i" and change it to a capital. Say, "First word in sentence, capital letter!" Take the capital off "He" and replace with a small H. Ask, "What do you need here?" pointing to the end of the sentence. The answer is, "Question mark." Dramatically draw a large dark question mark at the end of the sentence.

Is he here?

Write on board.

He is here. (INFORMATION) (SENTENCE)
Is he here? (QUESTION)

Draw the arrows again between "is" and "Is," "He" and "he." Hold two fingers up in the victory sign with palms toward the students. (Make sure beforehand that this gesture is not offensive to your students.) Then flip your hand around so that your fingers are now facing toward you, indicating that the two words are now in a reverse position. Flip your hand back and forth several times, saying, "Sentence, question, information, question."

You can also hold up your two index fingers and or cross your arms so that your fingers or arms form an X. You should make these gestures every time you review the material and every time you introduce the question form of a verb. To correct a student who answers with a sentence that should be a question, make the question gesture.

Subject and verb - Introduce the idea Write on the board.

He is here.   Write SUBJECT over "He" and VERB over "is."

Is he here?   Write VERB over "Is" and SUBJECT over "he."

Point to "He is" and say, "Subject, verb." Flip the two fingers and say, "Verb, subject." Repeat "Verb, subject" as you point to "Is" and "he."

Say, "Information, subject, verb," and point to "He is here." Then say, "Question, verb, subject." Point to "Is he here?"

To be - Questions and short answers - Oral practice Go to the short answer oral practice routine attached to Day 6. Help the students change the questions to sentences by flipping the subject and verb.

"Are you here today?" becomes "You are here today." Dramatically take the question mark off the sample sentence. Circle the capital on "You," and the period at the end of the sentence. Continue.

Am I here today?	I am here today.
Are we in Room 100?	We are in Room 100.
Are we at home right now?	We are at home right now.
Is this a desk?	This is a desk.
Are they pens?	They are pens.
Is he from Guatemala?	He is from Guatemala.
Is she from Thailand?	She is from Thailand.

After the students change all of the questions to sentences orally, they go back and change each answer to a short answer with "yes" and "no" as they did in Day 6.

Distinguish questions from information On the board, write the words "Sentence (Information)" and "Question." As you read each of the following sentences, students say "Sentence" or "Question."

Am you here today?	Question
He is absent today.	Sentence (You add "AND information.")
Are we in Room 100 right now?	Question
Are we at home?	Question
This is a desk.	Sentence (and information)
They are pens.	Sentence (and information)
He is from Mexico.	Sentence (or information)
Is she from Guatemala?	Question

To Be - Questions and short answers - Written practice Do 1- 2 pages with negatives, questions, and short answers. **Practical English, pp. 20-21, 27-29; Writing Practical English, p.7; GrammarWork, pp. 20-21 and 23-25.**

4. Colors - Introduce Using flashcards with squares of color only, introduce the colors on the vocabulary list on Day 8. Have the students repeat the colors after you several times. Then choose 4-5 simple items of clothing, like pants, tee shirt, or shoes, which have colors on the list and ask students what color they are. Do very common colors first, like black, white, red, and blue. Go on to the more difficult colors, including gold and silver if someone is wearing jewelry. Don't ask about colors you can't see or garments with unclear colors.

IF TIME

Each student says, "My favorite color is _____." or "I like _____." Write the models and the color list on the board. Don't let them choose unusual colors. They have to choose from the list. Show each answer with the color square flashcards. Prompt them with the color square flashcards if necessary. Finally, students review with flashcards of the color words.

Day 8

Vocabulary

red
white
blue
green
yellow
orange
black
gray
brown
tan
pink
purple
gold
silver

Agenda

1. Opening routine
2. Classroom words #4 - review, collect homework, quiz
3. Unusual plurals quiz (attached), self-correct
4. Colors - introduce or review and practice with color square flashcards and color word flashcards
   Oral practice with TPR routine (attached)
   HOMEWORK 20X, quiz tomorrow = dictation, color words only
   Quiz for day after tomorrow = you only show color cards, they write words
5. Locations - review, written practice
6. Numbers + simple clock time - review time questions
7. Adjectives + opposites - oral review
   Written practice - 1 page
8. If time, practice numbers with money, amounts, questions about cost of products

Stuff

1. List of words with unusual plurals for quiz (attached) on board or poster
2. Set of "rods," colored pencils, or crayons in basic colors and 4-6 large cups in basic colors
3. Flashcards with squares of colors mounted on cardboard, including gold and silver
4. Flashcards with words naming the colors on today's vocabulary list
5. Clock face with moveable hands
6. Cash, Monopoly money, or text with pictures of money - dollar (buck), quarter, dime, nickel, penny (cent), 5-dollar bill, 10-dollar bill, 20-dollar bill

Lesson Plan

1. Opening Routine

2. Classroom Words #4 - Review
Go over the vocabulary with pointing and flashcards. Collect homework and give the vocabulary quiz. Don't collect papers yet.

3. Irregular Plurals - Pop quiz
Ask students to turn over their color words quiz. Tell them that they will have a "pop quiz" on plurals. Use the attached list. Say that two of the words are regular plurals and the rest are irregular. Write the words, "Regular" and "Irregular" on the board. Ask the class, "What is a regular plural?" Answer, "Put S on the word." Write the words on board. Students copy the list and for the quiz, they write the plurals next to the words. Because a "pop quiz" is unannounced, allow students to correct their own papers by putting a big X on mistakes. Ask students for the answers and write them on the board. Collect the papers. If they do well, give credit.

Review these rules later in the course each time that students learn words with irregular plurals. At that time, first ask them if they can repeat the rule. Then review it.

4. Colors - Introduce
Show flashcards of colors only (without words on the board) to see how many of them students know. Write the colors on the board and repeat them a few times. Practice pronunciation. Their quiz tomorrow will be a dictation of the color words only.

Colors - Oral practice - TPR Practice the colors using a set of colored "rods," which are educational materials made of shorter or longer bars of various colors, or use colored pencils or crayons. You need about 6 big plastic cups in the basic colors from your list. The attached TPR colors routine has examples of orders to give the students. For each order, repeat similar orders with different colors of crayons and cups until students appear to understand most of the colors. When you read each order for the first time, demonstrate by putting the crayons into the cups and taking them out. Then you give directions to different individual students. If a student makes a mistake, allow the class to correct him. If nobody corrects him, correct him by doing the action correctly. When students begin to answer correctly, then let the class order you to put in or take out some crayons. Do the actions correctly at first and then test the students by doing some wrong. See how quickly they notice the mistakes. Don't spend too much time on this routine, although the students will enjoy it.

Colors - Oral practice with clothes Practice colors by pointing to students' clothing. Only do the easiest clothes - shirt, tee shirt, pants, shoes, jeans, backpack, and purse. Then, as a quick review, point to a flashcard or a piece of clothing and have them write the color on used paper. (Make a note of the flashcards or clothing that you used.) Check by pointing again to the same clothing or card to see how many they got right. Inform them that their quiz tomorrow is writing the dictated color words only, but that the following day they will have to write the words when they see only the color cards.

5. Locations - Basic - Written review Do **Practical English, pp. 9, 30; Writing Practical English, p. 8.**

6. Numbers Review - Clock time Using your classroom clock and a cardboard clock which allows you to change the times, ask simple questions.

What time is it now?	It's 8 o'clock. (Point to the classroom clock.)
Now what time is it?	It's 8 twenty-five. (Ask about 5 different times while moving the hands on the cardboard clock.)
What time does this class start?	7:30
What time does this class finish?	9 o'clock

Don't do more complicated times, such as "half past," "a quarter past," or "twenty-five after." Teach "a.m" and "p.m." by writing on the board "a.m. = morning, p.m. = afternoon." Ask, "Is this a.m. or p.m.? Do you eat breakfast in a.m. or p.m.? Do you go home in a.m. or p.m.?"

From now on, review by occasionally asking students to check the time for you. "What time is it? How many minutes do we have left? What time should we go on break? How about five minutes for break? What time are you going to come back?"

Clock Time - Written review Do an exercise writing the time with "It's" and figures. "It's" is one of the most difficult words for students to hear, remember, and use. Stress it whenever you use it - IT'S!!! Make sure they hear and use the T. Don't let them say "Is 9 o'clock." The following sources have written exercises with clock faces. **Practical English, p. 26; Writing Practical English, p. 21; GrammarWork, pp. 26-27; New American Streamline Departures, p. 26; Access, pp. 80-82 (listening, drawing), 79, 83 (dialog), 115-119; Lifeskills, pp. 31-32; Skill Sharpeners, pp. 9, 10.**

If you are teaching hyphenation, have students repeat some of the same sentences with the numbers written as words. Remind them of the hyphen, as in "twenty-five."

7. Adjectives - Opposites - Introduce It's good to teach basic adjectives with their opposites, because you can practice "to be" in negative and affirmative forms at the same time. "He is tall. He isn't short. She is rich. She isn't poor." Many texts introduce adjectives this way. **New American Streamline Departures** and **Side by Side** provide the best introduction, with pictures to make the idea of opposites very clear. Go over the exercises orally at first. Use gestures as well as the pictures. Show "tall" and "short" with your hand. Show an empty wallet for "poor," write many dollar signs for "expensive" or "rich." Make horrible faces for "ugly." Pretend to smile into a mirror for "beautiful." Then write the exercise in class. This is not a good homework assignment. **Practical English, pp. 22-23; Writing Practical English, pp. 14-16, 38-39; New American Streamline Departures, p. 5A; Side by Side, pp. 35-39, 157, 165; GrammarWork, pp. 6-7; Skill Sharpeners, p. 37.**

As a review, quickly call out words and ask the class to yell out the opposites. If you don't have a text to introduce opposites, see the routine at the end of Day 9. Day 9 has some suggestions for your picture collection. You should have a "qualities" folder in your picture collection, to prompt students to describe people and things with their adjectives and opposites words. This also allows you to review the qualities without constantly referring to the same pages in your text.

IF TIME

Money - Introduce Using coins and bills, ask the class very easy questions.

How much is this? (showing each coin)
How many pennies in this nickel?
How many quarters in this dollar? (Show the quarter and the dollar bill.)

How much is gas now? "It's _____ a gallon."
How much is a pair of sneakers? (Draw them on board.)
What is the cost of a house in (your town)?
How much does a pen cost?
How much is an iPhone?

Write the amount on the board for each answer. Use dollar and cent signs and also show the amount as a decimal number with just a dollar sign.

These are great exercises when you have only a few minutes left before the end of class. Everybody loves to talk about the prices of real estate, gas, and clothes from the discount store.

Numbers Review - Money - Oral and written practice Find or write an exercise where students read price tags or choose between three amounts when they hear a price from you. **Access, pp. 93-100.** Or simply talk about money. **Lifeskills, pp. 20, 21; Skill Sharpeners, pp. 20, 21.**

If you don't have worksheets or exercises, you can make your own by photocopying combinations of coins onto worksheets and asking the class to add and report the totals.

Plurals Quiz (words written on the board)

1. girl

2. apple

3. glass

4. box

5. man

6. child

7. pot

8. orange

9. class

10. woman

11. secretary

12. baby

13. boy

Colors - TPR - Sample Routine

1. Put a yellow crayon in the orange cup.

2. Put a red crayon in the orange cup.

3. Take the yellow crayon out of the orange cup.

4. Put 2 brown crayons in the yellow cup.

5. Put 3 red crayons in the blue cup.

6. Put 5 white crayons in the white cup. Stop! Don't put 5 crayons in. Put 4 crayons in.

7. Put 1 red crayon and 1 purple crayon in the green cup.

8. Put the green cup in the orange cup.

9. Put the green cup and the orange cup in the blue cup. Now put the green cup and the orange cup on the blue cup.

10. Put 2 brown crayons in the yellow cup. Take 1 brown crayon out of the yellow cup. Put it in the green cup.

11. Put 3 red crayons in the blue cup. Take 2 red crayons out of the blue cup. Put 1 in the green cup and 1 in the orange cup.

Repeat each of these commands until the students answering know what to do, or until the class is correcting the student following the commands. Don't spend too much time on each command, but don't change the tasks too much. Restrict the commands to the basic concepts of colors, numbers, and very easy locations.

Day 9

Vocabulary

No new words today. The quiz will be to write the color words when only squares of color are shown.

Agenda

1. Opening routine
2. Colors - review colors with TPR and color square flashcards

   Practice questions and negatives

   Review spelling with color word flashcards

   Collect homework, quiz on spelling of color words

   Explain quiz for tomorrow - they will see only color square flashcard, then write the color

   Review colors with clothing pictures

   Optional color review - a worksheet using crayons (younger students) OR

   Written practice (older students)

   HOMEWORK - study colors and spelling for quiz
3. Money - review - oral practice - very simple money exercise

   Written practice

   Order food from menu as a class, then in pairs, total the bills and report
4. Tips and taxes - calculate - optional
5. Opposites - introduce, continue, or finish written work (See Day 8.)

   Practice questions and negatives when checking written opposites work

   Oral practice - opposites and short answers (routine attached)

Stuff

1. Color square flashcards
2. Color words flashcards
3. Pictures showing clothes with colors on the vocabulary list
4. Worksheet where students can color pictures - optional
5. Very simple menu from a text, workbook, fast food restaurant or teacher-made
6. Monopoly money, if available
7. Text pages with pictures of opposites
8. Pictures which illustrate adjectives like tall, short, rich, poor, cheap, expensive, dirty, clean
9. Flashcards of adjectives with their opposites on the back

57

Lesson Plan

1. Opening Routine

2. Colors - Oral review - TPR Show 2 color square flashcards at a time. Tell students to point to the color you name. They point to the left or the right.

Quickly review TPR activities from Days 7 and 8.

Practice colors with questions and short answers. Show the color square flashcards.

       Is this red?   No, it isn't. It's blue.

Review color spellings with the color word flashcards. Give the quiz and collect homework. Explain that in the quiz tomorrow, you will show only the color flashcards, and the class will have to write the color word with correct spelling. (You can choose whether to give credit for misspelled words on tomorrow's quiz.)

Colors - Oral practice with clothes words In the next few days, students will have clothing words as vocabulary. You can preview these words and practice colors at the same time. Use your color word flashcards and pictures of clothes with colors from the vocabulary list. Don't use any clothes with checks, patterns, or in-between colors. Point to the item of clothing in a picture and start the sentence. Students complete the sentence. If they don't remember the color name, show the color word flashcard and say the sentence.

These shoes are _____.
This sweater is _____.
This sweatshirt is _____.
These glasses are _____.
These pants are _____.
This bag is _____.
This shirt is _____.
These socks are _____.
This bracelet is _____.
These sweatpants are _____.
These boots are _____.
This jacket is _____ and _____.

Colors - Review - Optional for younger students Use crayons and a worksheet where the class can color in a rainbow, fruit, animals, etc., available in elementary materials at an educational supply store. OR you can create a worksheet with object outlines and give students written or dictated sentences about which colors to fill in. When you introduce and go over the sheet, review "this," "that," "these," "those," and plurals. This is only suitable for younger secondary students.

Colors - Review - Oral and written practice Older students can review colors with **New American Streamline Departures, p. 8.**

3. Money - Oral practice Ask students to read the following numbers.

46   forty-six

$4.06   four dollars and six cents (After students read this answer, make the period very large and dark to emphasize that the period indicates cents. Read the number several more times.)

406   four hundred and six; four hundred six

4,006   four thousand and six; four thousand six (After they read this answer, make the comma much larger and darker to emphasize that in English, a comma indicates thousands.)

$40.06   forty dollars and six cents

Money - Written practice Review numbers and money quickly with a worksheet or teacher-made exercise. See **references, Day 8. Also, Practical English, p. 45; Writing Practical English, pp. 29-30, 88.** Correct students if they say "a 5 dollars bill" or write the dollar sign after the number.

Money - Review - Menu As a class and then in pairs or small groups, order food from a simple menu with a limited amount of money. One person should be the waitress and write the order. Students should total their personal orders. Then one person should add the individual orders to get a group bill. **Lifeskills, p. 63; Skill Sharpeners, p. 46.**

4. Tips and Taxes - Optional When the groups are finished, as a whole class, calculate a tip of 20% (or amount normal for your area) on a few of their orders and add it to their bills. Add a sales tax if there is one in your state. If the class doesn't understand the concept of a tip, act it out this dialog with one student acting as the server.

A: Here's your check.

B: Thank you very much. Is that $22?

A: Yes. Your bill is $20 and sales tax is 10%.

B: Okay. Here's the $22 and $4 for you. Thanks a lot.

A: Oh, thank you very much.

5. Opposites - Oral and written practice - Continue Do 2 more written pages from texts illustrating adjectives and opposites. After checking the written work, you can hold up the illustrations and say, "Point to the tall boy." "Point to the bad student." "Point to the thin cat." Mix up the order of the pictures. They raise their textbooks and point to the correct picture. See **references, Day 8**.

Opposites - Oral practice Use pictures which illustrate different qualities. Put model sentences on board. Students say the quality in a complete sentence. "He's tall. He's short." Then go through the flashcards again and they give you the opposite. "He's tall. He isn't short. He's poor. He isn't rich."

Some possible pictures for collection

Basketball player or giraffe for tall or thin
Jockey for short or light or small
Sumo wrestler for fat
American football player for heavy or big
Homeless person for poor
Fashion model for thin or beautiful
Man or woman with an expensive watch or jewelry for rich
Dracula or a witch for ugly
Luxury car for expensive
Necktie from the Seventies for wide
Necktie from the Sixties for narrow

For more oral practice, use the attached routine, which also practices short answers.

Opposites and Short Answers Routine

Hold up a short pencil.	Is this long?	No, it isn't. It's short.
Hold up a long pencil.	Is this short?	No, it isn't. It's long.
Point to a tall student.	Is he short?	No, he isn't. He's tall.
Point to a short student.	Is she tall?	No, she isn't. She's short.

Point to yourself. (The question should be the opposite of what you actually are.)

	Am I tall?	No, you aren't. You're short.
	Am I young?	No, you aren't. You're old.
Point to a young student.	Is he old?	No, he isn't. He's young.

Point to an old object, like a TV, purse, or book.

Is this new?	No, it isn't. It's old.

Hold up a new, unsharpened pencil or a brand-new book.

Is this old?	No, it isn't. It's new.

Hold up the pencil.	Is this expensive?	No, it isn't. It's cheap.
Point to a computer.	Is that cheap?	No, it isn't. It's expensive.

Point to a student.	Are you rich?	No, I'm not. I'm poor.
Point to yourself.	Am I rich?	Yes, you are.

No, I'm not. I'm so-so.
(Wave your hand back and forth for "so-so.")

Continue to ask questions about objects which are not in the room.

Is gas cheap?	No, it isn't. It's expensive.
Is an iPhone cheap?	No, it isn't. It's expensive.
Are we cold today?	No, we aren't. We're warm.
Are we happy today?	Yes, we are. OR
	No, we aren't. We're mad.

You can use this routine with pictures in your text or with your opposites flashcards.

Continue with simple questions about people they recognize - Optional For example,

Is Shakira ugly?	No, she isn't. She's beautiful.
Is a vampire beautiful?	No, it isn't. It's ugly.

Day 10

Vocabulary

OPPOSITES
big - little
large - small
tall - short
long - short
old - new
old - young
thick - thin
fat - thin
wide - narrow
cheap - expensive
poor - rich
full - empty
heavy - light
beautiful - ugly
strong - weak

Agenda

1. Opening routine
2. Colors - review - color squares and color words flashcards
   Quiz - show color squares, they write color
3. Opposites - written practice, continue (See Day 8 and Day 9.)
   Review with flashcards
   HOMEWORK - words with opposites 20X. Homework due in 1 day, quiz in 2 days
4. Clothes - introduce - very basic clothes vocabulary using students' clothes
   Ask questions and talk about students' clothing
   Oral practice - order of color and object
   Written exercise - match clothing names and pictures
5. Pronunciation - long vowels but not Y (5 minutes)

LAST 1/2 HOUR - BINGO

Stuff

1. Flashcards with squares of color
2. Flashcards with color words
3. Big sheet of Post-it paper to cover up qualities listed on board.
4. Flashcards with adjectives (qualities) on front and opposites on the back
5. Bingo game and candy rewards

Lesson Plan

1. Opening Routine

2. Colors - Quiz on color squares Quickly review for quiz with color word flashcards, then color square flashcards. Students write numbers 1-14 on paper. For each number, teacher shows color flashcard and students write colors. Give the class time enough to write the answers, but don't hold up the color too long. That just gives students time to whisper the answer. At the end, go back and show each color again quickly for students who missed one or two. Answers must be readable, but teacher decides whether or not to count spelling. Do not give credit if answers are in the wrong order.

3. Opposites - Test review - Introduce Show vocabulary list of adjectives and their opposites. Students copy list from the board and repeat the qualities with their opposites. Correct pronunciation.

Explain that on the quiz tomorrow, you will dictate a word, and they will write the word and its opposite. With a big sheet of sticky Post-it paper, cover the right side of the list. Ask students to go down the list, reading the quality, then giving its opposite. Then put the blank Post-it paper over the left side of the list. Again, students read the word and give the opposite. If needed, practice a little more with opposites flashcards.

Opposites - Written practice - Continue See **references, Day 8 and Day 9.**

3. Clothes - Introduce Introduce basic clothes vocabulary by pointing to clothes that students in the class are wearing. Clothes words will be vocabulary words soon, so they don't copy the following list for homework. Don't write them on the board until the end of the oral practices if at all. Limit the first few oral practices to the following.

> pants
> jeans
> shorts
> tee shirt
> shirt
> shoes
> sneakers (or tennis shoes or the most common term in your area)
> socks
> sweater
> sweatshirt
> sweatpants
> jacket
> backpack
> bag

Clothes - Oral practice - TPR Use these examples to ask about clothes in the class.

> Point to the white shoes.
> Point to my green jacket.
> Point to a black shirt.
> Point to a black and pink backpack.

Clothes - Oral practice - Complete the sentence Teacher points to clothing and students complete the sentence.

> Her jacket is _____.
> His shoes are _____.
> Her backpack is _____.
> His pants are _____.

Clothes - Oral practice - Use "has" to talk about clothes Put sample sentences on board.

> Maria has white shoes.
> Juan has a green jacket and a black shirt.
> She has _____.
> He has _____.
> She has a _____ and a _____.

Color Order - Correct or Incorrect? Quickly review rules for adjective order and number. Adjectives do not add S for plural. Adjective comes before the thing. Write the correct or incorrect sentences on the board. Then point to each sentence and ask, "Correct or Incorrect?"

Juan has shoes blacks.	Incorrect!
Maria has shoes black.	Incorrect!
Maria has blacks shoes.	Incorrect!
Maria has black shoes.	Correct!
Backpack pink	Incorrect!
Pink backpack	Correct!
Pink backpacks	Correct!
Purple shoes	Correct!

Clothes - Oral practice Match clothing names with pictures, label the clothes on a model, or name the colors of clothes. **Side by Side, pp. 67-71 and 77; New American Streamline Departures, p. 24 (using pictures and "has"); Lifeskills, p. 19; Skill Sharpeners, pp. 18, 19.**

5. Pronunciation - Long vowels - Introduce List the 5 vowels plus Y on the board.

Repeat several times, "A E I O U and sometimes Y." Cover the list and ask, "What are the vowels?" See if students can repeat the saying confidently as a class.

Write the words LONG VOWELS over the list. Then show them that you are erasing Y from the list. Say, "We're not doing Y right now."

Say, "These are the long vowels," and move your hands out to each side slowly, showing that they are long sounds. Repeat each slowly, showing that you can make the sound very long. "See, it's long! AEEEEEEEEEE, EEEEEEEK, AIEEEEEEE, OOOOOOOOOH, YOUUUUUUU!"

Next to each vowel, write several words with the sound.

     A - okay, day, date
     E - he, she, we, eek! (scared)
     I - I, hi!, iPhone, ice cream
     O - oh!, okay, go
     U - you, ooh!, too

LAST 1/2 HOUR - BINGO (See Day 5.) Before starting, have class spell out BINGO. Point to the I and say, "Long I. Ayieeeeee." Point to the O and say, "Long O. Oooooooooh!"

Day 11

Vocabulary

NO QUIZ - will practice regularly in class
a quarter after
a quarter past
to
before
half past
noon
midnight
a.m./p.m.

NO QUIZ - write and draw in notebook
in
on
over
under
in front of (3 words)
in back of (3 words)
behind
next to (2 words)
at
by

Agenda

1. Opening routine
2. Opposites - review with both sides of flashcards - pronounce and spell
   Collect homework of pairs copied 20X
   HOMEWORK - study for quiz on the opposite of the word you hear
   Practice with flashcards - say opposites of word you see. If students know most
   answers, do opposites bee below in the last 15 minutes
   Oral practice - word order - "tall boy" or "boy tall"
3. Money - 2-3 short practices
4. Time vocabulary - oral practice - clock face, questions
   Written practice - 1 page
5. Location words - oral practice - locations in room with TPR (routine attached)
   Copy graphic of location words and illustrations
   Written practice - 1 page
   Pronunciation of in/on with #1#2
   Written practice - 1 page

LAST 15 MINUTES - optional - opposites bee with rewards

Stuff

1. Flashcards - adjectives with opposites on back
2. Clock with moveable hands
3. Large colored cups with colored pencils, crayons, or "rods" of different colors and lengths
4. Candy or other rewards for opposites bee
5. Teacher-made graphic of location words - list the words from today's vocabulary on board and show their meaning with drawings or shapes. On photocopies or copied from board.

Lesson Plan

1. Opening Routine

2. Opposites - Review Practice spelling only of opposites with flashcards. Collect homework. Review for the quiz tomorrow in which the teacher shows flashcards and students write the opposite.

Adjective Word Order - Oral practice Using all the vocabulary words from tomorrow's quiz, students answer by repeating the correct phrase.

> boy tall or tall boy?
> beautiful girl or girl beautiful?
> handsome man or man handsome?
> dog ugly or ugly dog?
> pizza large or large pizza?
> small Coke or Coke small?

Be careful not to always put the correct choice last. For review, do the opposites bee below.

3. Money - Review Do 2 or 3 short practices. See **references, Day 9.**

4. Time - Introduce Practice more difficult time vocabulary using a large cardboard clock face with moveable hands. Ask, "What time is it now?" and students answer with vocabulary words from today, "a quarter past," " quarter to," etc. Repeat each term from the vocabulary list several times each. You will not test them on these.

Time - Oral Practice Ask, "What do we do at _____ o'clock?" Ask about times common to all students, for example, the start of class, the end of class, twelve midnight, six a.m., etc. They can answer with just a phrase, like "sleep" or "go home." Then ask individuals, "When do you _____?" (eat lunch, get the bus for school, watch your favorite TV show)

Time - Written practice Do 1 page. **Practical English, pp. 46-47; Writing Practical English, p. 44; New American Streamline Departures, p. 26 (time zones); Access, pp. 117, 118 (listening); Skill Sharpeners, pp. 27-28, 84, and 85 (time zones).**

If you don't have many resources for practicing time, you can pass out worksheets with blank clock faces and have students draw the times you dictate on the clocks.

5. Location Words - Review Practice the vocabulary location words using cups and pencils, students, and classroom locations. (See attached routine.) Don't use "at" or "by" much.

Location Words - at and by - TPR - Optional Use a separate TPR routine to practice "by" and then "at."

> Juan, stand up.
> Walk to the door. Stop! Stand by the door.
> Now walk to the file cabinet. Stand by the file cabinet.
> Don't stand by the file cabinet. Stand by the window.
> Maria, stand up. Walk to the door and stand by the door.

Now repeat the routine with "at."

Location Words - Illustrate Have students copy the location vocabulary words from the board. By each word, the teacher draws a little illustration showing the meaning. You can use colored squares, circles and squares, stick figures, letters, etc. For example, a circle is behind a square, a stick man is next to a stick lady, the A is by the B, but it is not by the C. Allow students to do this if they can. If nobody volunteers, have students copy your illustrations. An alternative is to pass out copies of the vocabulary list with the meanings illustrated.

Location Words - Written practice 1 page. **Practical English, pp. 40-41; Writing Practical English, p. 31; Lifeskills, p. 37; Skill Sharpeners, pp. 29, 30.**

Pronunciation of in/on - Oral practice Using the #1#2 technique, quickly practice the difference between "in" and "on." (See Day 3.)

Pronunciation of in/on - Written practice Do **GrammarWork, p. 43.**

LAST 15 MINUTES

Opposites Bee Game Students stand in two lines to compete as teams or in one long line to compete as individuals. You can divide students into teams by gender, by age, by giving each student a number of 1 or 2, by drawing a line in your roll book, or in any other way that will result in a good competition and be different every time.

Read out the word. They must say the opposite word. If it's wrong, they have to sit down. A reward system is always flexible. If the students are doing very well, you can give a candy bar only to the last person standing in each game. If few are doing well, you can give a candy bar to the last student standing on each team, or the last boy and the last girl standing, or the last two or three people standing, or the last ones standing when the end of class bell rings. You can set a timer and pay off anyone still standing when the timer sounds. You can bribe very strong winners to sit out the next round by giving them a reward for not doing the game.

Location Words Routine Using Colored Cups and Pencils

Repeat each order with different cups and pencils until the students understand the order. Then move on to the next one. It will not take them long to catch on. Stress the separate words, like "in front of," "in back of," and "next to." Stress the two T's in "next to."

1. The blue cup is in the red cup.

2. (Turn the red cup over and place the blue cup on it.) Now the blue cup is on the red cup.

3. The blue pencil is in the blue cup. Now the blue pencil is in the red cup.

4. Where is the blue pencil now? It's in the red cup.

5. (Take the blue pencil and balance it on top of the red cup.) The blue pencil is on the red cup.

6. The blue cup is next to the red cup.

7. (Being sure to face the students directly. Put the blue cup between them and the red cup.) The blue cup is in front of the red cup.

8. (Move the blue cup so the red cup is now in front.) The blue cup is in back of the red cup. The blue cup is behind the red cup.

9. (Again place the blue cup on top of the overturned red cup, touching the red cup.) The blue cup is on the red cup. (Lift the blue cup in the air.) Now the blue cup is over the red cup. The red cup is under the blue cup.

10. (Put the red cup inside the blue cup and turn them upside down and put them on the table.) Where's the red cup? It's under the blue cup.

11. (Pick up both cups and hold them over the table.) The red cup and the blue cup are over the table.

12. (Hold them under the table.) Now the cups are under the table.

13. Steve is (behind) Maria. Maria is (in front of) Steve. Nancy is next to Maria. Maria is next to Nancy. (Use your hands to point to spots in back of you, in front of you, and directly next to you as you give these orders.)

14. Steve, walk to the door. Stop! Where is he now? He's next to the door. OR He's at the door. OR He's by the door.

Day 12

Vocabulary

pants
jeans
tee shirt
shirt
skirt
blouse
shoes
sneakers
socks
suit
jacket
tie

Agenda

1. Opening routine
2. Opposites - review with flashcards
      Oral practice - respond with opposite word only
      Collect homework, quiz - give word and they write opposite only
3. Time - oral practice - class times, appointments
      Written practice - 1 page
4. Clothes #1- introduce clothes vocabulary with pictures
      Talk about clothing of students
      Written practice
      Review with flashcards
      HOMEWORK is 20X, quiz

Stuff

1. Flashcards with words and opposites on other side
2. Large moveable clock face
3. Pictures and flashcards of all clothing words
4. Pictures and flashcards of clothing words on tomorrow's quiz in a separate group

Lesson Plan

1. Opening Routine

2. Opposites - Review Use flashcards to review. First, students read all the flashcards. Then they give opposites of the word they see. Collect homework. Do the quiz, where students write the dictated word and its opposite.

3. Time - Appointments - Oral practice Using a text illustration or calendar, agenda book, or class schedule, introduce the idea of appointment times. Ask students to name one appointment they have. Orally fill in these blanks written on board.

I go to the doctor on _____ at _____ .

The ESL One class is at _____ on _____ and _____ .

Time - Appointments - Written and listening practice For example, **GrammarWork, pp. 39-40; Access, pp. 83, 86, 115, 118-119; Lifeskills, pp. 35-36.**

4. Clothes - Introduce Introduce all clothes vocabulary with pictures. If students don't know the name of the item, tell them. Go through all clothes pictures several times.

Separate out the pictures for today's clothes vocabulary #1. Students read and repeat them several times. Most of the clothes on the list should be familiar to them. Draw pictures on board to show the difference between shirt and skirt. Draw pictures to illustrate the difference between a man's style shirt and a woman's blouse or top. HOMEWORK is to copy the words 20X for the quiz.

Clothes - Oral practice - Review The teacher points to and talks about the clothing on the list worn by people in the class.

    Maria has white shoes.
    I have a green jacket and a black skirt.
    Juan has a black jacket and black shoes.

Clothes - TPR practice - Review Review the vocabulary list using clothing in the class with students pointing. See how much they have remembered.

    Point to white shoes.
    Point to black shoes.
    Point to a green jacket.
    Point to a black jacket.
    Point to a skirt.
    Point to a tie.

Clothes - Question review - Oral practice Teacher points to the item of clothing and asks question. Students answer following the model on the board.

What is it?	It's a _____ .
What are they?	They're _____ .
What is it?	It's a black shirt.
What is it?	It's a black tee shirt.
What is it?	It's a blue shirt.

What are they?	They're shoes blacks.
Shoes blacks?	No, black shoes.
What are they?	They're jeans blue.
Jeans blue?	No, they're blue jeans.
What are they?	They're black and white shoes.
Or?	Black and white sneakers.

If you don't use the word "sneakers" in your area, you can substitute "tennis shoes," "gym shoes," "sports shoes," or whatever term is common where you are.

Be sure to correct students who reverse the order of the color and object or add an S to the color word. Spanish speakers will have trouble with this.

Clothes - Written practice Use **Lifeskills, p. 19; Skill Sharpeners, pp. 18, 19; GrammarWork, pp. 36-38; Side by Side, pp. 67-78, and video; New American Streamline Departures, pp. 8, 24.**

Pronunciation - skirt vs. shirt Use the #1#2 technique to practice the difference. (See Day 3.) Review with flashcards only the clothes on the quiz tomorrow.

Day 13

Vocabulary

dress
pantyhose
shorts
belt
sweatpants
sweatshirt
bathing suit
cap
hat
gloves
sweater
scarf

NOT ON QUIZ - POSSESSIVES

I - my
you - your
he - his
she - her
it - its
we - our (compare to are, hour)
they - their

Agenda

1. Opening routine
2. Clothes #1 - review clothes #1 - pictures, flashcards
   Collect homework, quiz
Clothes #2 - introduce - examples from class, pictures
   Flashcards of tomorrow's quiz words
   HOMEWORK is copy 20X, quiz
Clothes - written practice - 1-2 pages
3. Possessives - introduce on board, repeat several times
4. Clothes and possessives - reading and writing practice
5. Family clothes poster - optional
6. Their, They're and There - difference between three words which sound the same
7. Pronunciation practice with #1#2 - you vs. your, they vs. their

Stuff

1. Pictures of all clothes, with those on today's vocabulary in a separate pile
2. Flashcards of clothing words for quizzes, separated into today's quiz and tomorrow's quiz
3. A knitted sweater and a sweatshirt
4. White paper or small poster paper and colored pencils or crayons for pictures of family

Lesson Plan

1. Opening Routine

2. Clothes #1 - Quiz   Review the clothes #1 list with pictures and flashcards. Collect homework and give the quiz.

Clothes #2 - Introduce   Use pictures and examples in class. (See Day 12.) Show the difference between a knitted sweater and a sweatshirt. Practice with flashcards for tomorrow's quiz. HOMEWORK is to copy the list 20X for the quiz.

Clothes - Written practice - Continue   Do 2 pages. See **references, Day 12 and below.**

3. Possessives - Introduce   Use this oral routine.

(Point to your purse.) I have a bag. It's my bag.
(Point to a student's bag. Speak directly to the student.) You have a bag. It's your bag.
(Point to a woman with a phone on the desk.) She has a phone. It's her phone.
(Point to man with a book on the desk.) He has an English book. It's his book.
(Point around the classroom.) We have a big classroom. It's our classroom.
(Indicate all of the students.) You have a teacher. I'm your teacher.
(Move two students over to a corner of the room.) I'm their teacher too.
(Hold up your purse again.) My bag has a color. Its color is black.

NOTE: You can give examples of "its" as a possessive, but most texts for beginners don't use it or practice it. It's too complicated for the beginning level. Don't include it on tests.

Possessives - Introduce Write the list on board and point out problems.

I - my	not "mee"
you - your	Remember "r" - "youR book," not "you book"
he - his	Careful! his mother, his sister - matches the owner of the thing
she - her	Careful! her father, her brother - matches the owner
it - its (no apostrophe)	"Point to the computer. Point to its keyboard."
	"Point to the file cabinet. Point to its top drawer. Point to its bottom drawer."
we - our	Careful! It sounds like "are" OR "hour."
they - their	Remember "r" - "theiR car," not "they car"

4. Clothes and possessives - Reading and writing practice Read about people and their possessions. **New American Streamline Departures, p. 8; Side by Side, pp. 73-74. Also Practical English, pp. 89-90; Writing Practical English, p. 63.**

5. Clothes - Project - Begin a poster - Optional Draw pictures of family members in their usual clothing. Label each picture with the person's name. When finished, each student tells the class what one family member is wearing. Write examples on the board.

This is my mom. She has a blue dress. Her dress is blue. She has black shoes. Her shoes are black.

This is my dad. He has black jeans. His jeans are black. He has white shoes. His shoes are white.

6. Their, They're and There - Introduce Write "there" and "they're" under "their." Call the class's attention to the three words. Repeat the words to show how they sound exactly the same. Write the sample sentences and rules on the board and have students copy them in their vocabulary lists.

Their shoes are white. (Point to two people with white shoes.)
COMES BEFORE A THING
BELONGS TO TWO OR MORE PEOPLE, LIKE A FAMILY, A COUPLE, OR A CLASS

My shoes are over there. (Point to the other side of the room.)
TELLS WHERE

They're my shoes. (Point to your own shoes.)
They are my shoes.
THEY'RE = THEY + ARE
COMES FIRST IN THE SENTENCE
HAS THE VERB IN THE SENTENCE

Give a few more examples of each, but don't do a lot of practice on this now.

7. Possessives - Pronunciation practice - you/your, they/their Practice with the #1#2 technique.

Day 14

Vocabulary

watch
wallet
purse
glasses
sunglasses
umbrella
uniform
suit
pajamas
robe
bathrobe
necklace
bracelet
ring
jewelry

NOT ON QUIZ - POSSESSIVES
I - my
you - your
he - his
she - her
it - its
we - our (compare to "are," "hour")
they - their

Agenda

1. Opening routine
2. Clothes #2 - review with flashcards, pictures, gestures, TPR. Collect homework, quiz
Clothes #3 - introduce with gestures, TPR, pictures, flashcards
      HOMEWORK - copy 20X, quiz
         Oral practice with clothes and possessives - questions, TPR, and gestures
3. Clothes - written practice - 2 more pages
4. Clothes - reading or dialog
5. Clothes - project - optional - finish family clothes poster (See Day 13.)
6. Possessives rule - optional - 's
7. Pronunciation - compare short vowels to long vowels with memory words

Stuff

1. Pictures and flashcards for clothes words, separated for today's quiz and homework
2. Paper and colored pencils for posters of family members in typical clothes

Lesson Plan

1. Opening Routine

2. Clothes #2 - Review Use pictures, gestures, and TPR, with flashcards at the end to review. Collect homework and do the quiz.

Clothes #3 - Introduce Use gestures, TPR, pictures, and flashcards. Using pictures, show the difference between a business suit and a uniform. HOMEWORK is to copy the words 20X for the quiz.

Oral Practice with Clothes Talk about clothes from the vocabulary list. Write the models on the board. Ask students to point to or hold up the possession.

> Who has a wallet?
> Who has glasses?

Repeat the practice with possessions that are not in the room (sunglasses, an umbrella, a uniform, a suit, pajamas). Show pictures of the objects to help them.

Oral Practice with Possessives Use TPR and gestures. Use the jewelry and accessories which you see in class to practice today's vocabulary as in these examples.

> Point to my watch. Point to his watch. Look at your own watch.
> Point to our clock, the clock in this room.
> What is our room number?
> (Indicating the whole class.) Who is your teacher? Point to your teacher.
> Who has a ring? Maria has a ring. Point to her ring.
> Who else has a ring? Juan has a ring. Point to his ring.
> Here's my purse, and here's my wallet. (Show your own purse and wallet, and hold
> them up far away from each other.) Point to my wallet. Point to my purse.
> Who has a wallet? Juan has one. Juan, show us your wallet. Point to his wallet.
> Who has a purse? Maria has one. Point to her purse.
> Who usually has a purse? Yes, girls and women.
> Who usually has a wallet? Men and women.

3. Clothes - Written practice Do 2 pages. See **references, Day 12 and Day 13.**

4. Clothes - Dialog or reading on shopping or clothes See **references, Day 13. Jazz Chant "Shoes and Socks"; Side by Side, pp. 69, 75; Access, pp. 98-100. Also Lifeskills, pp. 26, 45, 22-23; Skill Sharpeners, p. 36; New American Streamline Departures, p. 24 (more difficult).**

5. Clothes - Project - Optional Finish or create a poster of family members. See Day 13.

6. Possessives - Rule - Optional You can give them this rule, but don't practice it. It's too difficult at this level. However, correct anybody who uses "it's" for the possessive. Use an apostrophe with a person's name, but never on a possessive word.

> Maria's desk, Juan's desk, the teacher's desk - OKAY
> her's desk, it's color - NOT OKAY

7. Pronunciation - Short vowels - Introduce Put on the board two lists under LONG and SHORT, with their memory words.

> LONG
> A = okay
> E = me
> I = I
> O = okay
> U = you
>
> SHORT
> A = hat (Draw a picture.)
> E = bed (Draw a picture.)
> I = hit (Show the action.)
> O = hot (Fan your face.)
> U = hut (a small house, like a cabin) (Draw a picture.)

Repeat the lists of memory words several times quickly. Then repeat long A and short A words together several more times. Stretch out your arms to show that "okay" has a long A. Bring your arms back in close while you pronounce "hat" quickly. (See Day 3.) Repeat for the other vowels. Erase the memory words and see if anybody can say the vowels correctly without them.

Don't use pronunciation symbols, because nobody can remember them.

Look at today's vocabulary and find the words or word parts that are short (glasses, sun, umbrella, bath, neck, ring). Repeat them a few times. Then read the flashcards for homework one more time.

Day 15

Vocabulary

house
home
room
kitchen
bedroom (1 word)
bathroom (1 word)
living room (2 words)
family room (2 words)
dining room (2 words)
baby's room
garage

Agenda

1. Opening routine
2. Clothes #3 - review with pictures, flashcards
       Collect homework, do quiz
       Written practice - optional
3. Rooms #1 - introduce with text and pictures
       Oral practice - identify rooms
       Oral practice - rooms and activities
       Oral review - "What room is this?" with pictures
       Written practice
       Oral practice with rooms in text
       Pronunciation - bathroom v. bedroom with #1#2
       Quick review - flashcards
       HOMEWORK - Copy 20X, quiz tomorrow
4. Location words - review
5. There is/there are - introduce with pencils and cups
6. LAST 1/2 HOUR - BINGO

Stuff

1. Pictures and flashcards of clothing vocabulary
2. Large pictures of rooms
3. Flashcards with names of rooms
4. Colored pencils and large colored cups
5. Bingo game and reward candy or cookies

Lesson Plan

1. Opening Routine

2. Clothes #3 - Review Use pictures and flashcards to review. Collect homework and do the quiz.

Clothes - Written practice - Optional See **references, Day 12, Day 13, and Day 14.**

3. Rooms in a House - Introduce Showing pictures of rooms in a house, have the students repeat the names of the rooms. Then talk about the pictures and their houses.

What is this room?	It's a bedroom.
	It's a kitchen.
Where are they?	They're in the bedroom.
	In the kitchen.

How many bedrooms/bathrooms do you have in your house?
Do you have a garage/dining room/garden?
Do people in California have attics? What about basements?

You can talk about all the parts of a house with pictures. If everyone where you live has an attic and a basement, include them in the vocabulary list. Only test on words which students use in their daily lives or which are in their textbook.

Pronunciation of bedroom vs. bathroom Practice with the #1#2 technique. (See Day 3.)

Rooms in a House - Written practice The best references are **Side by Side, pp. 10-12 and video; GrammarWork, pp. 44-49; New American Streamline Departures, p. 6.**

Also **Lifeskills, pp. 46-47, 48, 53; Skill Sharpeners, pp. 56-57.**

Rooms in a House - Review When checking written work on rooms, you can introduce verbs which you will practice later. For example, the exercise has pictures of people doing activities in rooms, and you are answering the question, "Where are Juan and Maria?"

They're in the kitchen.

Then you can ask, "What are they doing?"

They're cooking.
They're eating breakfast.

And you continue, "What do you do in the kitchen?"

You wash plates.
You open the refrigerator.

If the students make errors in the answers, model the answers correctly, but don't teach or correct these verb forms unless they are included in the written exercise.

Rooms in a House - Oral practice Using the pictures of rooms and names of students in the class, ask questions.

Where's Juan?   He's in the _____.
Where am I?   You're in the _____.

Rooms in a House - Oral practice only - Optional Continue with oral practice only, **Side by Side, pp. 17-21; Skill Sharpeners, p. 60; Lifeskills, p. 48.**

4. Location Words - Review Use TPR, cups and pencils to review location words quickly. "Put the blue pencil in the red cup," etc. (See Day 11.)

5. There is/there are - Introduce - TPR Use cups and pencils as before to introduce "there is" and "there are" in a TPR routine.

Put the blue pencil in the red cup. There's a blue pencil in the red cup.
Put the blue pencil in the green cup. There's a blue pencil in the green cup.
Put a red pencil in the blue cup. There's a red pencil in the blue cup.
Put 2 black pencils in the green cup. There are 2 black pencils in the green cup.
Put 3 pencils in the red cup. There are 3 pencils in the red cup.
Put 2 pencils in the green cup. There are 2 pencils in the green cup.

Practice the sentences a few times. Don't practice in, on, etc. You are just focusing on "there is" and "there are." Then write on the board, lining up "there is" and "is there" as shown.

A.   Put a blue pencil in the red cup.

            There's a blue pencil in the red cup.
            Is there a blue pencil in the red cup?
        Yes, there is.
            Is there a black pencil in the red cup?
        No, there isn't.

B.   Put 2 black pencils in the green cup.

            There are 2 black pencils in the green cup.
            Are there 2 black pencils in the green cup?
        Yes, there are.
            Are there 2 red pencils in the green cup?
        No, there aren't.
            Are there 4 black pencils in the green cup?
        No, there aren't.
            There are 2.

Use arrows between "there" and the verbs to illustrate how the subject and verb reverse for the question and go back to regular order for the answer. (See Day 7 about how to explain this with arrows.) In this case, "there" acts as the subject and reverses as a subject just like "he" or "she" would.

There is/there are - Oral practice Write model sentences on the board and do the routine.

> There is _____ pencil in the _____ cup.
> There are _____ pencils in the _____ cup.

Hold up the cups with the indicated number of pencils. Ask and answer following the model.

How many pencils are in the red cup?	There is 1 pencil in the red cup.
How many pencils are in this blue cup?	There are 2 pencils in the blue cup.
How many pencils are in the green cup?	There is 1 pencil in the green cup.
How many pencils are in the blue cup now?	Now there are 5 pencils in the blue cup.

Write the next model on the board.

> Yes, there is.
> No, there isn't.
>
> Yes, there are.
> No, there aren't.

Hold up a cup with 1 pencil.

> Is there a pencil in this cup? Yes, there is.

Hold up a cup with 3 pencils.

> Are there any pencils in this cup? Yes, there are.

Hold up a cup with a blue pencil and a red pencil.

Is there a red pencil in this cup?	Yes, there is.
Is there a blue pencil in this cup?	Yes, there is.
Is there a green pencil in the cup?	No, there isn't.
Is there a black pencil in the cup?	No, there isn't.
How many pencils are there in this cup?	There are 2.

If the class is having trouble, practice each sentence several more times with different colors.

Add two more pencils to the cup.

| Are there 4 pencils in the cup now? | Yes, there are. |
| Are there 5 pencils in the cup now? | No, there aren't. |

Hold up a cup with 3 pencils.

| Are there 3 pencils in this cup? | Yes, there are. |

Don't do any written practice on this today. You will continue the oral practice tomorrow.

Rooms in a House - Review vocabulary Quickly review vocabulary flashcards for quiz tomorrow.

6. LAST 1/2 HOUR - BINGO (See Day 5.)

Day 16

Vocabulary

stove
sink
refrigerator
table
washer
dryer
shower
carpet
picture
sofa
plant
desk
television
window

Agenda

1. Opening routine
2. Rooms #1 - review all room pictures from yesterday's vocabulary
      With today's furniture vocabulary, show picture, ask "Which room?"
      Review with room flashcards, collect homework, give quiz
3. Furniture #1 - introduce with pictures
      Complete sentences using model
      HOMEWORK - copy 20X, quiz
4. There is/there are - question form
      Written practice or dialog
5. Pronunciation - continue list of short vowels, compare to long vowels
      Short vowels - examples with known words
      Consonant-Vowel-Consonant rule
      Two consonants = one consonant rule

Stuff

1. Pictures and flashcards of rooms
2. Pictures and flashcards of furniture, with today's homework vocabulary in one group
3. Pictures and flashcards of routine activities done in specific rooms - cooking, taking a shower, etc.

Lesson Plan

1. Opening Routine

2. Rooms #1 - Review
Review room words #1 with pictures. Show pictures for today's furniture vocabulary. Ask, "Which room?" Don't ask them to give the furniture word, just the room word. Review for the quiz with room flashcards, collect homework, and give the quiz.

3. Furniture #1 - Introduce
Show pictures of the new vocabulary again. Ask class to name each item of furniture. They will know some of them. After naming the pictures several times, go over spelling with the list on the board.

Using the model, complete some sentences. Mix up the order of the vocabulary words.

    The stove is in the _____.
    The carpet is in the _____.
    The television is in the _____ and the _____.
    The shower is in the _____.
    The sink is in the _____ and the _____.
    The washer and dryer are in the _____.
    The refrigerator is in the _____.
    The table is in the _____ and the _____.
    The sofa is in the _____.

HOMEWORK is to copy the vocabulary 20X for a quiz.

4. There is/there are - Question form
Write the following models on the board. Use arrows between "he," "there," and "is" to show the reverse order in the questions. Write the words SUBJECT over "he" and "there" and VERB over "is" to show that "there" is the subject, and it changes places with "is" or "are" just as a regular subject like "he" does.

    He is _____.
    Is he_____?

    There is _____.
    Is there _____?

Fill in the blanks to complete the sample sentences with suggestions from the class. Point out the question mark. Write INFORMATION and QUESTION on the board next to each sample sentence. Ask the whole class to repeat each example after the teacher. Stress the normal intonation and then the question intonation.

Add a short answer to each question and write INFORMATION next to it. Show that in the short answer, the question intonation and reverse order change back to normal intonation and order. (See Day 3, Day 6, and Day 7 for how to explain short forms and question forms.)

He is here.	INFORMATION, REGULAR ORDER
Is he here?	QUESTION, REVERSED ORDER
Yes, he is.	INFORMATION, REGULAR ORDER AGAIN

Go on to a plural example.

There are red pencils on the table.
Are there red pencils on the table?
Yes, there are.
No, there aren't.
There are black pencils.

Explain that for a plural subject talking about 2 things or 2 people, you must use "are" but the rule stays the same. They repeat the plural example several times with regular and question intonation. Don't make them say "there're."

Don't expect students to get this question form correct right away. It's difficult to practice "there is" and "there are" and to constantly correct students on singular and plural, but it's worth the trouble, since these forms are so commonly used in conversation.

There is/there are - Written practice Do 1 more page of written exercises or a dialog about renting or buying an apartment or house, including rooms and furniture. **Side by Side, pp. 59-60, 61-62; New American Streamline Departures, p. 6 (good); Practical English, pp. 109-110; Writing Practical English, pp. 67-68, 79; GrammarWork, pp. 44-49 (good).**

4. Pronunciation - Short vowels - Continue Quickly review short vowels. Put on the board the lists LONG and SHORT with memory words from Day 15.

LONG
A = okay
E = me
I = I
O = okay
U = you

SHORT
A = hat
E = bed
I = hit
O = hot
U = hut

Repeat the work from yesterday, but very quickly. For each vowel, repeat the long and short forms together several times with long and short arm actions. Draw out the long vowels with your voice. Erase the memory words and ask the class to say the vowels correctly without them.

Dictate the memory words in mixed order and ask students to respond with "long" or "short." If they are making a lot of mistakes, do the dictation again, but exaggerate the length of the long vowels and say the short vowels very quickly.

Short A vs. Short E - Pronunciation Practice "tan" and "ten" with #1#2. (See Day 3.)

Consonant-Vowel-Consonant = Short Rule - Introduce Write the short memory word list on the board. Write CVC = CONSONANT, VOWEL, CONSONANT on the board. Underline the first letters in the words "consonant" and "vowel." Point out the pattern Consonant -Vowel- Consonant in the short memory words. The rule is CVC = short vowel.

Write on the board known words which follow the rule. Under this heading, write bag, cat, fat, ten, bed, red, pen, six, sit, big, box, top, rug, cup. Have students repeat the list several times and then read the words as you point to them in mixed order.

Two Consonants = One Consonant Rule Write the following known words on the board. Tell the students to watch as you underline the two consonants at the beginning or end of each word. After doing a few examples, you can ask students to underline the two consonants.

flag, black, half past, trash, desk, shelf, rich, thick, thin, sink, stop, clock, socks

Write CC = C on the board.

Explain that the rule is CVC = short vowel. But, if you have 2 consonants, it's a combination, or "combo" like a hot dog plus a bun or a hamburger plus cheese, and the 2 consonants = 1 consonant.

Put on board: CVC = short vowel

But C = CC

So   CCVCC = short vowel (Change each C in CVC to CC.)

Read the list with 2 consonants several times.

This is only an activity. Don't expect perfection. Practicing pronunciation will help student accents, and it will help them read better when they come across strange words.

Repeat the rule many times later in the course. When students are reading out loud and hesitate in pronunciation, remind them of the rule. Write CVC on the board, saying, "Consonant, vowel, consonant equals short vowel," and see if they can give you the short vowel and then the correct pronunciation.

Day 17

Vocabulary

chair
couch
rug
coffee table (2 words)
end table (2 words)
lamp

fireplace
chimney (Draw on the board a fireplace and a chimney. Draw the fire in the fireplace and show smoke curling up the chimney. Spanish speakers will confuse these two words.)

bed
curtain
dresser (or bureau, or other locally used word)
bathtub
mirror
shelf
dishwasher

Agenda

1. Opening routine
2. Furniture #1 - review - actions, pictures, flashcards
        Collect homework, quiz
Furniture #2 - introduce - pictures, acting
        Place item in correct room
        Pronunciation review - short vowels in vocabulary list
        HOMEWORK - copy 20X for quiz
        Written practice - 1 page - rooms and furniture - there is/are
3. Present continuous verbs - introduce with written and oral practice

Stuff

1. Pictures and flashcards of today's furniture vocabulary
2. Pictures of rooms in the house
3. Pictures of common activities at home
4. Large Post-it paper to cover vocabulary list

Lesson Plan

1. Opening Routine

2. Furniture #1 - Review with TPR, pictures, and flashcards. Collect homework and do the quiz.

Furniture #2 - Introduce Use pictures and acting to introduce the words. Orally place each item in its correct room. "The couch is in the living room." Quickly review for homework with flashcards. HOMEWORK is to copy the words 20X for the quiz.

Cover the words on the board. Write four list titles on the board: living room, bedroom, kitchen, and bathroom. Mix up the order of the flashcards and show them to the class one by one. Ask them to suggest rooms for each item. Some words will be in more than one room. Write their answers under the rooms.

Then students complete these sentences, either on the board or in their notebooks.

There are chairs in the _____ and the _____.
There are rugs in the _____, the _____, and the _____.
There's a couch in the _____ and maybe the _____.
There are lamps in the _____ and the _____.
There are curtains in the _____, _____, _____ and _____.
There's a mirror in the _____ and the _____.
There's a dishwasher in the _____.
There's a dresser in the _____.
There's a bathtub in the _____.

Pronunciation - Short vowels - Review Find the short vowels in today's vocabulary list. Answers are: rug, end, lamp, chimney, bed, dresser, bath and tub, mirror, shelf, dish but not washer. Say, "Washer doesn't follow the rule."

Furniture - Written practice - There is/ are - Continue Include rooms. See **references, Day 16.**

3. Present Continuous Verbs - Introduce A good introduction of action verbs in rooms of the house is in **Side by Side, pp. 17-21, 22-23.** Or do one or two pages where present continuous action verbs are used with pictures making very clear what activities are happening. **Practical English, pp. 68-78; Writing Practical English, pp. 47-52; New American Streamline Departures, p. 21; Skill Sharpeners, pp. 45, 58, 75.**

Present Continuous Verbs - Oral practice After writing exercises, ask questions about pictures in the texts and other available pictures of common home activities like playing video games, watching TV, sleeping, doing homework, and playing with the dog.

What's he doing?   He's _____.

Day 18

Vocabulary

porch
patio
deck
balcony
yard
garden
basement
attic
den
home office
TV room

Agenda

1. Opening routine
2. Furniture #2 - review with pictures, flashcards, collect homework, do quiz
3. Rooms #2 - introduce words about house and yard
      Draw a house with porch, attic, etc.
      Oral practice - talk about your house
4. Present continuous - everyday activities with today's vocabulary
5. Present continuous - introduce and practice - TPR
      Explain rule
      Written practice - 1-2 pages
6. Pronunciation - short I with CVC and VC rules (list attached)

Stuff

1. Pictures and flashcards of yesterday's furniture words
2. Pictures and flashcards with today's vocabulary
3. Pictures of activities in the house and yard
4. A cup of coffee and a bottle of water
5. Copies or projectable file of short I pronunciation list

Lesson Plan

1. Opening Routine

2. Furniture #2 - Review Use pictures and flashcards to review furniture vocabulary. Collect homework. Do a quiz.

3. Rooms #2 - Introduce Explain new vocabulary with pictures. Show or draw a house which shows the location of the porch, the attic, etc. Repeat the vocabulary list several times.

Rooms #2 - Oral practice Talk about your house.

Do you have a house or is it an apartment?
Is the apartment in a big building or a small building?
Do you have a balcony? Is it large or small? What room has the balcony?
Do you have a porch? Do houses in California have a porch?
Do you have a patio or a deck? Where is the patio? Where is the deck?
Do you have a den or a home office?
Do you have a computer? Where is the computer?
Where do you watch TV? How many TVs do you have in your house?
Are there stairs in your house or apartment building? Are they inside or outside?

Rooms # 2 and Activities - Oral practice Using your pictures of activities in the house and yard, ask students what they do in each place on today's vocabulary list. Don't insist on correct grammar or complete sentences. One-word answers are okay.

Review for the quiz with flashcards of tomorrow's words. HOMEWORK is to copy the words 20X for the quiz.

NOTE: "Porch," "patio," "deck," "attic" and "basement" or "cellar" are regional. Use location words to explain them if students do not have them at home. "Porch" is in front of or around the house, and people sit there in hot weather to drink beer and watch their neighbors. "Patio" is a flat stone or cement area in the front, back, or side of the house. "Deck" is a wooden floor which is several feet up and attached to the house in back. You can get large pictures from home decoration magazines and catalogs like IKEA.

Houses in hot areas like California may not have full attics or basements. Students in apartments may not have them either. However, you can use these words to practice "over" and "under."

Leave words out of the quiz if they are not common in your area.

4. Present Continuous - Oral practice Use pictures of typical activities in the places listed in today's vocabulary, such as the yard and the TV room. Prompt students to give you the name of the activity for each picture. Then model sentences in the present continuous form for the class as you show them the pictures.

They're playing video games.
She's drinking water.
They're eating dinner.

If available, use the **Side by Side video.**

91

5. Present Continuous - Introduce - TPR Discuss actions with present continuous verbs.

Hold up a cup of coffee. "I have a cup of coffee."
Drink from the cup. "I'm drinking the coffee right now."
Point to the floor, "Right here!"
Point to the clock, "Right now!"
Put the coffee cup far away from you on the desk. "Am I drinking the coffee right
    now? No, I'm not."
Grab the coffee and take another drink. "Am I drinking the coffee now? Yes, I am."

Repeat the sequence with a bottle of water.

Present Continuous - Practice with TPR Help students to answer your questions.

Ask a male student to stand up.
Ask, "Is he standing right now?"   "Yes, he is."

Tell him to sit down.
Say, "Is he standing up right now?"   "No, he isn't."
"What is he doing?"   "He's sitting down."

Tell a student to walk to the door. As the student walks, say to the class, "She is walking right now."

Tell the student to stop.
"Is she walking now?"   "No, she isn't."
"What is she doing?"   "She's standing."

Tell the student to walk back to her desk.
"Is she walking right now?"   "Yes, she is."

Tell her to sit down.
"What is she doing right now?"   "She's sitting."
"Is she walking right now?"   "No, she isn't."

Present Continuous - Explain written form Write on board and review a chart of "to be." Then add a verb + "ing." Leave the sentences in pieces with the plus sign. Talk about actions which are happening right now.

I am + drink + ing water (right now)
You are + drink + ing coffee (right now)
She is + stand + ing (right now)
He is + sleep + ing (right now)
We are + study + ing English (right now)
You are + look + ing at the teacher (right now)
They are + walk + ing (right now)

In each sentence, underline the subject, the verb "to be" and the "ing" on the verb. Say, "Put these 3 pieces on the verb." Count 1, 2, 3 as you point to the subject, the "to be," and the "ing." Point again while saying, "Number 1, the subject. Number 2, 'to be.' Then the verb. Then number 3, 'ing.' "

Use your hands to make a flowing motion in front of you. Say, "The verb is continuous. It continues for a long time."

Tell a student to walk to the door. While he is walking, you say, "He's walking, he's walking, he's walking, he's walking," while making the "continuous" motion with your hand.

Go back to the sentences on the chart. Point to some of the sentences and ask,

What is she doing right now?   She's standing.

Write this answer with all the parts together next to the one on the chart. Use the short form and leave out "right now." Ask,

What is he doing right now?   He's sleeping.
What are we doing right now?   We're studying English.
What are they doing right now?   They're walking.

Continue to ask and write the answers for all of the sentences in the chart.

Point out the short "to be" forms on the verbs.

Then tell the students that "She's standing" means "She's standing right now," and "What is she doing?" means "What is she doing right now?" Go through the questions and draw a line through "right now" in each sentence. Then erase it in each sentence.

Say, "You don't have to say 'right now.' I understand that it's right now, at the present time." When you say the word "understand," point significantly to your forehead.

Present Continuous - Written practice Do 2 more pages. **Practical English, pp. 122-123; Side by Side, pp. 27-33; New American Streamline Departures, p. 22.**

Present Continuous - Correct or Incorrect? Write on the board.

1. He is work.

2. He working.

Point to #1 and ask the class, "Is it correct?" They say, "No." Say, "You're right, it's INcorrect!! It's WRONG!!!!!" Be dramatic. Say, "Fix it!" Call on someone to come to the board and make the correction. Point to #2 and repeat. You can use this technique any time you spot common errors in written work or homework.

Verb form teaching sequence Some textbooks choose to teach the present simple form before the present continuous. The benefit of doing present continuous first is that you have already taught "to be" with questions, negative, and short answers. Since "to be" is the helper verb for present continuous, students already know how to make questions by reversing the helper verb. Teaching present continuous next allows you to review and extend their knowledge. It is also a very commonly used form which is easily demonstrated in the classroom.

If you prefer to teach present simple first, you will need to teach "do," which is a more difficult helper verb. If you do teach present simple first, it is easiest to start with verbs such as "like," "want," "need," and "have," because they are almost always used in the present simple form.

You will need to teach both forms in any case and both forms have their difficult points, so the choice really depends on your mandated text.

6. Pronunciation - Short I Sound Short I is one of the most difficult sounds in English for Spanish speakers. Give students the attached word list and sentences. Practice the short I and point out the CVC and CCVCC words.

Remind the class that some very common words have a short I followed by one consonant, for example, "is," "it," "in," and "if." The consonant cuts off the vowel and makes it short. For example,

Is it in the sink?

Read the sentence quickly with natural intonation. It should sound like, "Isitinthe SINK?" The CVC = short vowel rule extends to a VC = short rule.

Compare vowel-consonant words with consonant-vowel words.

VC = short. Vowel-Consonant words are short, following the CVC rule.
CV = long. Consonant-Vowel words are long. For example, "me," "hi," and "go."

Pronunciation - Short I

it

is

in

this

little

bit

sick

quiz

list

kitten

written

print

tip

important

zip, zipper

Where is the test? It is in this room.
Is the quiz written? Yes, it is. Is it important? Yes, it is.
Where is the list of words? It's on the board.
I feel a little bit sick. Can I go to the nurse?
A kitten is a little cat.
Give the waitress a big tip. What is the tip? It's fifteen or twenty per cent.
Zip your jacket. I can't. The zipper is broken.

Day 19

Vocabulary

NOT FOR QUIZ
door
floor
window
closet
deck
patio
balcony

FOR QUIZ
driveway
mailbox
roof (vs. ceiling)
heater
air conditioner (2 words)
inside wall
outside wall
fence
gate
toilet
microwave
freezer
stairs
pool
spa (Jacuzzi)

Agenda

1. Opening routine
2. Rooms #2 - review - pictures, flashcards
    Collect homework, quiz
3. Rooms #3 (more house and yard) - introduce with text, pictures or drawings, repeat
    Oral practice - talk about students' house or apartment complex
    Review with flashcards
    HOMEWORK - copy 20X, quiz
    Written practice, dialog, or reading
4. Present continuous - written practice - 1-2 pages

Stuff

1. Pictures and flashcards of today's quiz words
2. Pictures and flashcards showing today's vocabulary on areas of the house
3. Pictures of activities in the house and yard
4. Pictures of other action verbs (Add an action verb category to your collection of pictures from newspapers, specialist magazines, and the Web.)

Lesson Plan

1. Opening Routine

2. Rooms #2 - Review Use pictures and flashcards to review. Collect homework and do a quiz.

3. Rooms #3 - Introduce Use text, pictures, and drawings to define the new words on the vocabulary list. Repeat them and practice pronunciation.

Rooms #3 - Oral practice Talk about students' house or apartment complex with pictures to prompt answers.

> Do you have a house or an apartment?
> Do you have a driveway? Where do you park your car?
> Is there a fence? Is there a fence at our school? Point to our gate.
> Is there a pool in your apartment building? Do houses in California have pools?
> Is there a spa? Where is a pool here (in this town)? Is there a spa at that pool?
> Are there stairs in your house? Inside or outside?
> Do you have a microwave?
> Where is your freezer? In the refrigerator or in the garage?
> Is there an air conditioner in the apartment?
> How many toilets are in the house?

Rooms #3 - Reading practice Do a dialog or reading with house and furniture words. **Side by Side, pp. 46-48, 49; Composition Practice, Book 1, pp. 10-15.**

4. Present Continuous - Oral practice Talk about routine activities in the present continuous form. Model the sentences as you show the students pictures.

> They're playing video games.
> She's drinking water.

Review the verbs with this model on the board. Ask the questions.

> What is he doing right now?   He's sleeping.

Present Continuous - Written practice Do 2 more pages. See **references, Day 17 and Day 18.** Also **GrammarWork, pp. 58-59, 62-65; New American Streamline Departures, p. 25.**

Day 20

Vocabulary

come
go
talk
speak English, speak Spanish

stand
sit
walk
run
ride
write   vs. ride
erase

open
shut
close
read
study
leave
take
carry

Agenda

1. Opening routine
2. Rooms #3 - review - pictures, flashcards
        Collect homework, quiz
3. Verbs - most common - review with TPR
        Use #1#2 technique - difference between write and ride
        Review homework verbs with pictures if any, then flashcards
        HOMEWORK - copy 20X, quiz
4. Present continuous - spelling rule - introduce briefly
        Practice rule with examples from today's vocabulary
        Written practice - 1 page
        Short reading or dialog - 1 page
5. WH question words - list on board, review, give examples including "to be" and present
        continuous
        Oral practice - questions including present continuous
        Review - WH flashcards
6. Present continuous verbs with questions - written practice
IF TIME
7. LAST 15-30 MINUTES - BINGO

Stuff

1. Pictures and flashcards of today's quiz words, Rooms #3
2. Flashcards of today's vocabulary verbs, most common verbs
3. Pictures of today's vocabulary verbs
4. Flashcards of WH question words - who, what, when, where, why, how, how many, how old. Don't include which. It's too complicated and needs its own exercise.

Lesson Plan

1. Opening Routine

2. Rooms #3 - Review Use pictures and flashcards to practice. Collect homework and do the quiz.

3. Verbs - Most common - TPR review Students should know most of the verbs already.

Stand up.
Sit down.
Stand up again.
Walk to the door.
Stop! Run to the door.
Close the door.
Open the door.
Shut the door.
Come back. (Motion student to the front of the room.)
Stop! Go back to the door. Open it.
Go to your desk.

(Another volunteer)

Stand up.
Walk to the board.
Take the chalk.
Write your name on the board.
Erase it.
Go to your desk, and take the eraser.
Sit down.

(Another volunteer)

Stand up.
Walk to the door and take your books with you.
Open the door and leave.
Stop!
Come back!
Walk to your desk and sit down.

(Another volunteer)

> Stand up.
> Walk to that box.
> Pick up the box and carry it to my desk.
> Put it down.
> Oops! Don't put it down!
> Pick it up and take it to the door.

Review the verbs for homework with flashcards and pictures as available. Use the #1#2 technique to show the difference between "write" and "ride." HOMEWORK is to copy the vocabulary 20X for a quiz.

4. Present Continuous - Rules for adding "ing" - Introduce Students have problems with this rule for a long time, but introduce it now so that you can correct it in written work. Later you can give them the chart at the back of this manual as a summary of the rules.

Write headings on the board and list today's vocabulary words in each category.

Regular	CVC	ends in e	ends in y	other
talk	sit	come	study	go
speak	run	ride	carry	open
stand	shut	write		
walk		erase		
read		close (the door)		
		leave		
		take		

Pointing to each column, explain the rule for each category.

Regular - add "ing." If a verb has 2 consonants at the end or 2 vowels in the middle, it is normal and just adds "ing." Add "ing" to all the words under "Regular." Point to each and ask students to say, "Two consonants" or "Two vowels."

CVC, one syllable - A word of one syllable with Consonant-Vowel-Consonant doubles the consonant at the end, then adds "ing." Add the extra consonants and "ing" to the words in the CVC column. Don't talk about the exceptions now (W and X). Point out that "open" does not have one syllable, so it does not follow the rule.

ends in e - Take the "e" off the end and add "ing." Don't double the consonant after taking off the "e." One at a time, take the "e" off each verb on the board and add "ing."

100

ends in y - Add "ing." Do not take off the "y." Add the "ing" to "studying" and "carrying" and pronounce their 3 syllables very clearly several times. Students often write "studing" instead of "studying."

Other - Verbs ending in vowels simply add "ing." Say, "Verbs with 2 syllables have different rules." Add "ing" to "open." Underneath, split the word into "o pen." Write an accent mark over the "o." Tell students that when the accent is on the first syllable, the end consonant does not double.

Ask students to copy the chart with today's vocabulary words in the "ing" form.

Present Continuous - Spelling rule - Written practice Exercises on these rules are in **GrammarWork, pp. 58-59, 61; Lifeskills, p. 66; Skill Sharpeners, p. 59.**

Present Continuous - Rules for adding "ing" - Reading Do a reading, dialog or written practice. See **references, Day 19. Also Side by Side, pp. 49, 50-51; Lifeskills, p. 65.**

5. WH Question Words - Introduce List the WH question words on the board and review them. Give more examples for the less familiar ones.

WH Question Words - Oral practice Ask a lot of questions with WH words. Include present continuous verbs.

> Who is your English teacher?
> Who is teaching your math class?
> What is this?
> What are you looking at?
> What color is this book?
> When is our English class?
> Where is Los Angeles?
> Where are you sitting -- in the front or the back?
> Why am I drinking coffee?
> Why are you studying English?
> How are you today? (Supply answers if necessary. "Fine, great, good, so-so.")
> How much is a pencil?
> How old are you?
> How old is your mother/husband/baby?

Review the WH words with flashcards one more time.

6. Present Continuous - Written practice - Yes/No and WH questions Yes/No questions are in **GrammarWork, pp. 64-65.** WH questions are in **GrammarWork, p. 66; New American Streamline Departures, pp. 21, 22; Practical English, p. 79; Writing Practical English, p. 63.**

7. LAST 1/2 HOUR, IF TIME - BINGO

Day 21

Vocabulary

sleep
dream
wake up
take a shower
      bath

wash your hair
dry
comb
brush
brush your teeth

shave
take off
put on
tie your shoes

eat breakfast
have

kiss your wife good-bye
say good-bye
leave the house

Agenda

1. Opening routine
2. Verbs - most common - review - pictures, flashcards
      Collect homework, quiz
3. Verbs - daily routine - introduce with pictures
      Oral practice - act out routine in order and out of order
      Talk and questions about order of actions with before/after
      Review with flashcards
      HOMEWORK - copy 15X, quiz
4. Present continuous - oral practice - statements and questions with daily routine pictures
5. Present continuous - spelling rule chart - review rules, apply to today's vocabulary
      Verb List Continuous - optional - pass out
6. Present continuous - written practice - 2 pages of negative, questions, short answers
7. WH question words - oral practice - ask WH questions
      Pronunciation - how vs. who - #1#2 technique
      Review WH questions - flashcards

Stuff

1. Picture sheet or text page of daily routine words in order
2. Flashcards of daily routine verbs - simple form on front, "ing" form on back
3. Separate pictures of daily routine verbs
4. Flashcards, WH question words - who, what, when, where, why, how, how many, how old
5. Copies of "Verb List Continuous" chart from end of manual

Lesson Plan

1. Opening Routine

2. Verbs - Most common - Review Do flashcard review. Collect homework and do the quiz.

3. Verbs - Daily routine - Introduce or review Use a picture sheet or pictures in normal daily order. **Practical English, pp. 68-69, also p. 244.** (For page 244, use pictures only. Re-order for practices and quizzes.) Also **Lifeskills, p. 109; Side by Side, p. 97.**

Verbs - Daily routine - Oral practice Act out the daily routine in normal, then mixed-up order.

Before/after - Oral practice Talk about order of daily actions. Give examples.

> I take a shower before I eat breakfast.
> I take a shower after I eat breakfast.
>
> I put on my clothes before I drink coffee.
> I put on my clothes after I drink coffee.

Say "yes" or "no."

I make my bed before I get up.	NO
I dream after I eat breakfast.	NO
I dream before I get up.	YES
I brush my teeth after I eat breakfast.	YES
I brush my teeth before I eat breakfast.	NO
I take a shower after I put on my clothes.	NO
I take a bath after I take a shower.	NO
I take a shower before I eat breakfast.	Some YES, some NO
I take a shower after I eat breakfast.	Some YES, some NO
I dry my hair after I wash my hair.	YES
I put on my shoes before I tie my shoes.	YES
I put on my shoes before I put on my pants.	NO
I say good-bye after I leave the house.	NO

Review the verbs for homework with flashcards. HOMEWORK is to copy the words 15X for the quiz.

4. Present Continuous - Oral practice Use your daily routine pictures. Ask students to make a complete sentence for each picture.

He's washing his hair.

Now ask them questions with Yes/No answers.

Is he washing his hair?	Yes, he is.
Is he washing his car?	No, he isn't. He's washing his face.

5. Present Continuous - Rules for adding "ing" - Review Students look at the chart of rules with examples they copied from the board on Day 20. Review the rule for each column.

Regular - Add "ing." Verbs with 2 consonants at the end or 2 vowels in the middle add "ing."

CVC, one syllable - Words of one syllable with consonant-vowel-consonant double the consonant at the end, then add "ing."

Ends in e - Take the "e" off the end and add "ing." Do not double the consonant.

Ends in y - Add "ing" to the end. Do not take off the "y."

Other - Some verbs must be memorized because they follow a more unusual rule.

Write the category titles on the board. Ask students to read today's vocabulary list and place each word into the correct category.

Regular	CVC	ends in e	ends in y	other
sleep	put on	wake up	dry	tie
dream		take	say	
wash		shave		
comb		have		
brush				
eat				
kiss				

Write each verb on the chart. Go back and change all of the verbs into the "ing" form. "Tie" follows another unusual rule. The IE turns into Y, and then adds "ing" = tying. This is because it is very unusual in English to have three vowels together or two I letters together.

Present Continuous - Verb chart - Optional Pass out copies of the "Verb List Continuous" chart at the end of the manual. The list shows basic verbs with their present continuous forms and rules to use as a reference.

6. Present Continuous - Written practice Do 2 pages with negative, questions, and short answers. See **references, Day 17, Day 18, Day 19, and Day 20.**

7. WH Question Words - Review List the WH question words on board and ask students to give sample questions. Explain ones they are unsure of with more examples.

WH Question Words - Oral practice Ask more questions with WH words.

> When is your birthday?
> Where do you live?
> Who is your guardian/best friend?
> What is your favorite color?
> Where do you eat lunch/shop for clothes/buy your food?
> What do you do after class/after school?
> Who is your favorite teacher? (me, of course)
> What do you want for Christmas/for your birthday?
> How old am I?
> How much did your notebook cost? How much was this notebook?

WH Question Words - Pronunciation - How vs. who Use the #1#2 technique to practice this common error. (See Day 3.)

WH Question Words - Review Use flashcards.

Day 22

Vocabulary

arrive
begin
build
change
clap
clean
draw
drink
eat
erase
fill in
talk
speak
whisper

NOT ON QUIZ
I - me
you - you
he - him
she - her
it - it
we - us
you - you
they - them

Agenda

1. Opening routine
2. Verbs - daily routine - review - acting, pictures, examples
       Flashcards - read in simple and in present continuous
       Collect homework, quiz
       Write daily routine words in sentences
3. Verbs #1 - review vocabulary, introduce unknown verbs with TPR, acting, pictures
       Pronounce 2-3X with flashcards
       Practice with flashcards - change simple form to "ing" form
       HOMEWORK - copy simple form only 15X for quiz
4. Present continuous - reading practice - short reading, dialog or written exercises
5. Object pronouns - introduce - compare subject and object pronouns with examples
       Oral practice - TPR
       Jazz chant - "I'm Mad at You"
       Written practice - 1 page

Stuff

1. Flashcards and pictures of daily routine words, simple on front, continuous on back
2. Flashcards with pronouns - subject on front, object on back
3. Flashcards of homework verbs, simple form on front, "ing" form on back
4. Copies of verb chart (See Verb List Continuous chart at end of manual.) (See Day 21.)
5. Copies or projectable file of jazz chant "I'm Mad at You"

Lesson Plan

1. Opening Routine

2. Verbs - Daily routine - Review Use acting, pictures, and examples. Read in both simple and present continuous form from flashcards. Collect homework and do the quiz.

Students write the daily routine words in sentences on a separate sheet of paper. Have the words and model on the board. "He's/She's _____ ." You can prompt with pictures in regular order. Ask students to add more ideas to the sentences if they can. At the end, hear a few answers for each word. Check the papers for errors in the "ing" form.

3. Verbs #1 - Introduce Review or introduce new verbs with TPR, acting, and pictures. Pronounce them 2-3 times with flashcards. Then read each simple form and change it to the "ing" form. HOMEWORK is to copy the words 15x for a quiz on the simple form only.

4. Present Continuous - Reading practice Do a short reading, a dialog, or one page of written exercises using the "ing" form. See **references, Day 21.**

5. Object Pronouns - Introduce On the board or a poster have a list with subject pronouns and their object pronouns. Give examples.

I am your teacher. Point to me.
You are my student. (Indicate one person.) I'm looking at you.
He is Juan. (Point to a man.) I'm looking at him.
She is a girl. (Point.) I'm looking at her.
They are my students. I'm looking at them. (Point to a pair or group of students.)
You are all (indicate the whole class) my students. I'm looking at you (all).

Object Pronouns - Oral practice - TPR Place people in different parts of room. You need yourself, 1 girl or woman in a separate area from 1 boy or man, and 2 people together. Put 1 chair in 1 corner of the area in front of the students, and 2 chairs in an opposite part of the room. Do the TPR routine with the class and individual students.

Point to me.
Look at him.
Point to her and look at him.
Where are Maria and Juan? Point to them.
How many windows are in the room. Count them.

107

Look at the chair. Walk to it and sit down.
Point to Juan. Stand up and walk to him.
Look at the two chairs. Point at them. Walk to them and sit down.
Point to me.
(Walk to the girl or the boy.) Now point to us.
(Walk to the two people together.) Now point to us.
Point to a girl. Walk to her.

Object Pronouns - Jazz chant - "I'm Mad at You" Write or project the jazz chant on the board or distribute copies. Read it several times with great feeling and rhythm. Have students repeat each line after you and then with you. Since this jazz chant is a dialog, practice it several more times with a divided class, boys vs. girls, or with two sides of the room against each other. You will need to conduct the students or have a very reliable student to lead the groups. **(For information on Jazz Chant books, see "Text" section in this manual.)**

Object Pronouns - Written practice Do 1 page. **Practical English, pp. 38-39; Writing Practical English, pp. 26-27 (top); GrammarWork, pp. 96-98; Skill Sharpeners, p. 87 (bottom); Side by Side, p. 100.**

Jazz Chant - Follow-up - Optional Read the jazz chant to the class, stopping at the pronouns to see if they can provide the correct ones. The following day, give copies of the chant as a "cloze" exercise, where you replace about half of the object pronouns with a blank to fill in. You could repeat this the day after that as a quiz.

You can have students copy the jazz chant several times for homework, give them a dictation on part of it, or even have them memorize the whole thing for a grade or extra credit. These are great exercises to do with secondary students, especially a noisy class.

Day 23

Vocabulary

fix
repair

lie (say something which isn't true)
light
live (vs. leave)

paint
point

make
write
work

need
have
give

Agenda

1. Opening routine
2. Verbs #1 - review - TPR, pictures, flashcards
    Collect homework, quiz
Verbs #2 - introduce - TPR, gestures, pictures
    Repeat in simple form
    Repeat in present continuous form, except need, have, and give
    Review spelling with 2-sided flashcards
    HOMEWORK - copy 20X, quiz
3. Indirect object pronouns - oral practice - review direct object pronouns - TPR
    Practice indirect object pronouns - after "to," without "to" - TPR
    Written practice - 1 page
4. Present simple - need - introduce need/needs with reading or pictures
    Chart - S on verb with he, she, it
    Oral practice with pictures or questions - answer yes or no
    Written practice

Stuff

1. Verb List Continuous copies (See Day 21.)
2. Flashcards with pronouns - subject on front, object on back (I, he, vs. me, him)
3. Flashcards of homework verbs, simple form on front, "ing" form on back
4. Pictures of needed objects - gas pump, grocery store, money, a nice family, a pair of shoes, an air conditioner, a cell phone, a pair of jeans, a soccer ball, a big test, a lot of homework
5. Pictures of objects which are wanted, but not needed - a diamond ring, a flashy sports car, a pair of expensive sports shoes, a pet snake, a very large house, a very expensive watch

Lesson Plan

1. Opening Routine

2. Verbs #1 - Review Use flashcards, TPR, or pictures. Collect homework and do the quiz.

Verbs #2- Introduce Use TPR, gestures, and pictures. Practice all in simple form. Repeat in present continuous form except for "need," "have," and "give." Review spelling for the other verbs. Students look at the flashcards and give the rule for spelling each word in continuous. In this list, the choices are "add ing" or "drop e and add ing." Put a circle around "fix" and "lie." Refer to the "Verb List Continuous" rule sheet or simply tell the class that X does not double. Remind them that "lie" has "ie" like "tie," so it also changes "ie" to "y" and adds "ing." HOMEWORK is to copy the words 20X for the quiz.

3. Indirect Object Pronouns - Review object pronouns - Oral practice Use TPR to review object pronoun words again.

> Point at me.
> Look at Luis. Point at him.
> Look at the TV. Point at it.
> Look at the windows. Point at them.
> Look at Maria. Point at her.
> Look at Maria and Ana. Point at them.
> Look at Luis and me. Point at us.
> Look at Maria and me. Point at us.
> Look at your shoes. Point at them.
>
> (Hold up a book.) Look at this! Look at it!
> (Hold up two pencils.) Look at these! Look at them!
>
> I see you. (Point to one person.)
> I see him. (Point to a boy.)
> I see it. (Point to a desk or computer.)
> I see you, all of you. (Wave your hand around the class, indicating all students.)
> I see these books. I see them.

Review object pronouns - More oral practice - Optional Use sentence completion to review object pronoun words again. Do the above sequence again with blanks for the object pronouns. Give the command and let students finish the sentence. For example,

> Look at Luis. Point at _____.
> Look at the TV. Point at _____.
> (Hold up a book.) Look at _____.

When going on to indirect pronouns, don't use the terms "object pronoun" and "indirect object pronouns." Don't ask students to explain the difference between direct and indirect.

Indirect Object Pronouns - Oral practice - TPR Don't use the terminology indirect object and direct object pronoun. Just show how "to" comes out of the sentence and the position of the pronoun changes. The pronoun goes from the end to after the verb.

Give the pencil to me.
Give me the pencil.

I'm giving the pencil to you.
I'm giving you the pencil.

(Point to a girl.) Give the pencil to her. Give her the pencil.
(To the girl, pointing to a boy) Now give the pencil to him. Give him the pencil.

Make a group of 3 students, a group of 4 students, one girl and one boy. Ask a student volunteer to give some colored pencils to the students you point to.

> Give him a red pencil.
> Give her the green pencil.
> (Point to the group of 3 students.) Give them three blue pencils.
>
> (Point to the group of 4 students.) Give them four pencils. Give Maria a yellow pencil. Give Roberto the green pencil. Give Juan two blue pencils. Don't give Ana a pencil.

If the class is having any trouble understanding you, after you say, "Give him a red pencil," you can add, "Give a red pencil to him," and point to the person. You want the students to understand that "Give him a pencil" is the same as "Give a pencil to him."

Practice this routine with several different objects. Then write sample sentences on the board.

> Give the bag to her.
> Give your book to him.

They copy the examples. Then circle "to her" and draw an arrow to between "Give" and "the bag." Write underneath "Give (to) her the bag." Tell the class that "to her" can go between

111

the verb and the rest of the sentence. Point with one hand to "Give" and with the other hand to "the bag." Then put a big X over the word "to" and erase it. Tell the students that if you put "her" between "Give" and "the bag," you don't say "to." They repeat the sentence, "Give her the bag." Make sure they do not say, "Give to her the bag."

They repeat several times, "Give the bag to her. Give her the bag." Do the second sample sentence the same way. Write on the board a few more sentences with "to" and have students change them the same way.

Indirect Object Pronouns - Written practice Do 1 page. **Practical English, pp. 42-43, 79F, 141; Writing Practical English, p. 27 (bottom), 54; Side by Side, Book 2, p. 7.** Be sure to correct the two following mistakes.

> Give him the pencil to him. (No, they only need to say "him" once.)
> Give to him the pencil. (This sentence is never heard. It sounds antiquated.)

4. Present Simple - Need - Introduce - Reading A good introduction to "need" is found in **Practical English, pp. 159-162; Writing Practical English, pp. 111-114.**

Present Simple - Need - Introduce Write 2 sentences on board. Fill in the blanks.

> I need _____(money)_____ .
> He needs _____(work)_____ .

Ask the class what they really need. Make a list of some true needs on the board, like money, gas, food, clothes, work, a car, my family, a cell phone, an ESL class. If they have trouble thinking of ideas, add some of your pictures of true needs. Students look at the pictures and say quickly sentences like "I need _____."

> a car
> a job
> a phone

Then ask the class to repeat the sentences with the same list, but this time with "he." Make sure they put S on the end of "needs."

Need - Oral practice Write the forms of "need" on the board in sentences.

> I need food.
> You need a new pencil.
> He needs a car.
> She needs paper.
> Look at this pencil. It needs an eraser.
> We need a Bingo game.
> You need a nice teacher.
> They need a new TV.

Show that with "he," "she," and "it," you add S to the verb. I need = no S. You need = no S. He needs = S on the end of the word. Circle the S on "He needs" and make the S bigger and darker. Do the same for "She needs " and "It needs." For the rest of the sentences, point to the end of the word "need" and draw a big blank circle at the end. Ask, "Is there an S here?" NO!!!!!!

Need - Questions and short answers - Oral practice Show the class both sets of pictures, with real needs and expensive objects mixed. Give examples first.

Do you need shoes?	YES
Do you need a Mercedes car?	NO
Do you need money?	YES or YES, I DO.
Do you need a pet snake?	NO or NO, I DON'T.

Go through the pictures. If someone claims that they need a Rolex watch, ask them, "Do you REALLY need a big expensive watch?"

After doing true needs and luxuries, include some items to discuss. For example, a dog, a horse, an iPad, a backpack, a bathtub, a washing machine in the house, a swimming pool, a quiz, a lot of homework tonight. Use pictures to help them.

Need - Written practice Use **Practical English, pp. 159-162; Writing Practical English, pp. 111-114.** Use pictures and readings from **New American Streamline Departures, pp. 13 or 16** to create your own questions about what the characters need or don't need.

Vocabulary

pick
practice
put

ride
write

sleep
throw
tie
try

wait
stand
stop

wear (not use)

Agenda

1. Opening routine
2. Verbs #2 - review - gestures, flashcards, pictures
      Collect homework, quiz
Verbs #3 - introduce with TPR, gestures, acting, pictures
      Practice with questions
      Review with flashcards in simple form, then "ing" form
      HOMEWORK - copy 20X, quiz tomorrow
3. Indirect object pronouns - oral review and practice with needs - TPR
4. Present simple - need - do/does/don't/doesn't - questions and short answers
      Review questions and answers "Yes, I do." and "No, I don't." from Day 23
      Oral practice - What do you need? I need _____.
      Write 5 sentences with "I need" and 5 sentences with "I don't need"
      Hear 1 answer per student
      Written practice - continue

IF TIME

5. Alphabet - review or introduce consonants. (See Sub Work 1.) Do letter grid game.

Stuff

1. Verb #2 pictures and flashcards (yesterday's vocabulary)
2. Verb #3 pictures and flashcards (today's vocabulary)
3. Pictures of objects (See Day 23.)
4. Game rewards of candy, stickers, or small school supplies like erasers and pencils
5. Alphabet chart
6. Puzzle grids in supplementary text or paper to copy the puzzle grid. See **reference below**.

Lesson Plan

1. Opening Routine

2. Verbs #2 - Review Use gestures, pictures, and flashcards. Collect homework and do the quiz.

Verbs #3 - Introduce Use acting, TPR, pictures, and gestures to explain new words.

Verbs #3 - Oral practice

> You're wearing black shoes. Do you wear black shoes every day?
> You're wearing a blue shirt. Do you wear blue shirts every day?
> Our teacher wears _____ every day.
> When do you practice your English?
> Do you write with a black pen or a blue pen?
> Where do you put your pencils?
> Where do you carry your phone? Do you put it in your bag?
> Do you put your money in a wallet or a purse?
> Where do you sleep?
> Do you throw your clothes on the floor?
>
> Where do you wait for the bus?
> Where does the bus stop?
> Do you stand on the corner?
> Do you wait with your friend?
> Does your mom pick you up after school? Where do you wait for her?
> Who rides with you? Do you ride in the front or the back?

For a final review, use flashcards to repeat the words in the simple form and then in the "ing" form. HOMEWORK is to copy the words 20X for a quiz.

3. Indirect Object Pronouns - Oral practice - TPR

> (Point to a boy.) He needs a pen. Give him a pen.
> (Point to yourself.) I need a pen. Give me that pen.
> (Point to any one student.) I'm giving you this pen.
> (Point to a girl.) She needs a pen. Give her the pen.

115

I need some paper. Who has paper? (A student raises her hand.) Give me a piece of paper, please. Thanks.

Who needs this paper? (A student raises his hand.) Okay, I'm giving you this paper.

(Show a pencil.) Who needs a new pencil? (A student raises her hand.) Watch me, students. I'm giving her the pencil.

You can continue this longer if you have candy or small school supplies to give away.

4. Present Simple and Need - do/does/don't/doesn't - Introduce Write the models on the board.

Yes, I do.

No, I do not.
No, I don't.

Yes, he does.

No, he does not.
No, he doesn't.

Ask each student a question with your pictures of objects. (See Day 21.) Then ask his neighbor about what he just said. Stress "do" and "does" in the questions, and model the answers until the students get the idea. Nod or shake your head "no" to help them answer.

(Ask a student.)	Do you need a car?	Yes, I do.
(Ask his neighbor.)	Does he need a car?	Yes, he does.
(Ask a student.)	Do you need an apartment?	No, I don't.
(Ask her neighbor.)	Does she need an apartment?	No, she doesn't.

Ask each student, "What do you need?" They must answer with 1 thing that they really do need. "I need money." "I need a good car." Then ask the class, "What does he need?" The class answers, "He needs money." "He needs a good car."

(Ask a male student.)	What do you need?	I need a pencil.
(Ask the class.)	What does he need?	He needs a pencil.
(Ask a female student.)	What do you need?	I need a new phone.
(Ask the class.)	What does she need?	She needs a new phone.
(Hold up a Bingo card.)	What do we need?	We need Bingo.
(Point to the clock.)	What do we need?	We need a break.
(Show your coffee cup.)	What do I need?	You need coffee.
(Show your water bottle.)	What do I need?	You need water.

If students have trouble thinking of things they need, cue them with pictures or office supplies and other objects in the room, like TVs and computers.

After doing some practices with "we" and "you," do a few extra practices with "he" and "she." Because "we," "I" and "you" don't take S on the verb, many students will forget to add the final S with "he" and "she" after practicing with the other subjects.

Need - Written and oral practice Students write 5 sentences about what they need and 5 about what they don't need.

       I need a _____ (new apartment)_____.
       I need some _____(video games)_____.

       I don't need a _____(pen) _____.
       I don't need _____(paper) _____.
       I don't need _____(any paper) _____.

Each reports to the class about 1 thing he needs and 1 thing he doesn't. Try to get a different answer from each student. If student reports something interesting, the teacher can ask the class, "Who else needs money? Anybody else?"

You can use "any" in your examples, such as "any money" or "any paper." If anyone asks, just say that "any" is used in negative sentences and that you will explain in a future class.

Need with don't and doesn't - Written practice Continue. (See Day 23.)

IF TIME

5. Alphabet - Consonants - Review or introduce Consonants are introduced in "Sub Work 1" at the end of the manual as well as in Day 5.

Alphabet Grid Game Distribute game grids or have students copy a game grid with 5 squares across and 5 squares down. Dictate letters of the alphabet in mixed order. Students write each letter they hear, first across the first row, then across the second row, etc. Have them fill up all of the 25 squares and then tell you the answers row by row. Write them on the board so students can check their work. (As seen in the High Point phonics program text **Reading Practice Book. See "Text" section below.**)

Day 25

Vocabulary

No set vocabulary words today. You can announce a "quiz-free day." If you want to provide students a list for a quiz, use vocabulary taken from their text, their supplementary texts, or their next unit test. Choose words which you intend to practice and use in class.

As a substitute for the vocabulary and quiz, you can have a "dispatch activity." This is a written, self-explanatory, review quiz or activity which gives students a focus at the beginning of the class. It should take no more than 15 minutes to do and check. It should have about 6 questions such as fill-in blanks, True/False, or multiple-choice. It should not involve independent writing or a lot of reading. Some teachers have the class do a dispatch activity every day, starting without teacher direction before the opening routine.

Agenda

1. Opening routine
2. Verbs #3 - review - gestures, flashcards, pictures, questions
     Collect homework, quiz
     If vocabulary assigned (see above), introduce, practice, review with flashcards
     HOMEWORK - copy 20X
3. Present simple - need - review and oral practice
     Need - oral practice or dialog - do a dialog or hear 1 idea with need and 1 idea with don't need from each
4. Need - do/does/don't/doesn't - written practice - finish
5. Have/has - introduce or review with examples in classroom
     Oral practice - pictures from text, picture collection
6. Present simple - need and have/has - do/does/don't/doesn't - introduce
     Oral practice - optional - objects in class and pictures
7. Have/has - irregular verb - introduce and explain
IF TIME
8. Have/don't have - oral practice - negatives, questions, and short answers
     Written practice - begin
9. Which - questions with have/has - optional - ask questions about a picture

Stuff

1. Verb pictures and flashcards
2. Pictures and flashcards of today's vocabulary, if any
3. Pictures of needed and not needed objects (See Day 23.)
4. Picture collection of objects, including pictures of previous vocabulary which could fit into this lesson. For example, shoes, boots, dress, sofa, car, stove, refrigerator, garage, book, notebook, computer
5. Pictures from previous classes of furniture and rooms

Lesson Plan

1. Opening Routine Do the dispatch activity, if any.

2. Verbs #3 - Review Use gestures, pictures, and flashcards to review. Ask some questions with the words, such as those in the oral practice on Day 24. Collect homework and do a quiz.

If there is a vocabulary quiz tomorrow, introduce the words. Practice orally and assign HOMEWORK to copy the words 20X.

3. Present Simple - Need - Do/does/don't/doesn't - Oral practice Ask only volunteers to answer the following questions truthfully with "yes" or "no." If they have trouble saying what they need, offer suggestions.

> Do you need a car? No, I don't. What do you need? I need a bicycle.
> Do you need a dollar? No, I don't. What do you need? I need a million dollars.
> Do you need a pencil? No, I don't. What do you need? I need a pen.
> Do you need a house? No, I don't. What do you need? I need a car.
> Do you need a swimming pool? Yes, I do.
> Do you need a big TV? No, I don't. I need a computer.
> Do you need a cell phone? Yes, I do.
> What type of phone do you need? I need a smartphone. OR I need a cheap phone.

Need - Oral practice or dialog Hear 1 idea with "I need" and 1 idea with "I don't need" from each student, very quickly. For a dialog, **New American Streamline Departures, p. 31.**

4. Need with don't and doesn't - Written exercises Continue written pages with "need." See **references, Day 23.**

5. Have/has - Introduce or review briefly Use classroom objects and clothing.

> Juan has a white shirt. Juan has black pants.
> Maria has a brown purse. Linda has a purple backpack.

> Level 3 is a good class. They have a nice teacher.
> The girls have their homework today.

> Juan has beautiful shoes. I have ugly shoes.
> I have a red pen. You have black pens.
> We have a TV and a computer.
> We have a big classroom.
> You have a beautiful teacher. I have a wonderful class.

6. Present Simple - Need and Have/has - Do/does/don't/doesn't - Introduce Give examples.

(Hold up a pencil.) "I don't need a pencil. I have a pencil."
(Hold up a pen.) "I don't need a pen. I have a pen."
(Hold up some crayons.) "I need a red crayon. I don't have a red crayon."
(Hold up some money.) "I need a quarter. I don't have a quarter. I only have dollars."

Write on board.

> Need = doesn't have
> Have = doesn't need
>
> He doesn't need gas. He has gas.
> I don't need paper. I have paper.

Need and Have/has - Oral practice - Optional Use objects in class, pictures in text, and picture collection. Teacher makes a statement and students answer with "need" or "doesn't need." Prompt with examples to help them answer correctly. If students have problems with this practice, stop after a few examples.

I don't have any money.	You need money.
Juan doesn't have a big house.	He needs a big house.
She has shoes.	She doesn't need shoes.
He has a new car.	He doesn't need a new car.

7. Have/has - Irregular verb - Introduce Write the following chart on the board.

I have	We have
You have	You (plural) have
He has (haves) She has (haves) It has (haves)	They have

Go down the list and read "I have, you have, we have, they have." The students repeat. Then ask them to say, "He haves," "She haves," and "It haves." Pronounce the words very distinctly and clearly. Ask, "Is it easy or difficult?" Students should see that it is difficult to say "haves." Tell them that the usual rule is that with "he," "she," or "it," you must add an S to the verb. But "haves" is difficult to say, so it is IRREGULAR.

Write IRREGULAR on the board. Say, "It's different. It does not follow the rule." Put an X over the VE in "He haves" and repeat, "He haves, he has." Do the same with the next two forms, "She haves, she has. It haves, it has." "Has" should sound easier to them.

Have/has - Oral practice Write the following models on the board. Go through your collection of object pictures. Have the class, either together or individually, practice each model with several pictures. Solicit additional answers for each model.

I have (a) _____.

> I have a dog.
> I have a car.
> I have a bracelet.
> I have a phone.

I have a family. We have (a) _____.

> We have a sofa.
> We have an apartment.
> We have three cars.

I have two brothers. They have _____.

> They have a TV.
> They have a computer.

He has (a) _____.
He has a bicycle.

She has (a) _____.
She has a party dress.
She has black jeans.
She has red shoes.

8. Have/don't have - Introduce Point to the model sentence, "I have a _____, " and hold up your pencil. "I have a pencil." Look around your desk and in your pockets. Show them that you only have a pencil. "I don't have a pen."

Walk to your desk and pick up your coffee cup. "I have coffee." Look around the room and shrug your shoulders. "I don't have water." If a student has a water bottle on his desk, walk over to it and pick it up. "NOW I have water."

Show the class your marker collection. "I have a black marker. I have 3 black markers." Display all of the markers. "I don't have a green marker." Write on the board.

We have a _____.
We don't have a _____.

Each student looks at a picture and says truly what his family has or doesn't have. For each picture, ask two or three students.

shower
bathtub
swimming pool
spa (Jacuzzi)
basement
garage
dining room
dishwasher
washer and dryer
stove
microwave (a little stove in a box)
coffee table (a little table in front of the sofa)
carpet (a big rug)
television (How many?)

At the end, using pictures if necessary, students ask you about 5 things in your house.

Have/has - Questions and short answers - Oral practice Using your groups of pictures of objects, rooms, and furniture, ask each student questions.

Do you have a bathtub?   Yes, I do. OR No, I don't.
                              Yes, we do. OR No, we don't.

Have/has - Written practice Do exercises with questions, negative, and short answers. **Practical English, pp. 83-88, 94-96 top; Writing Practical English, pp. 57-62; Side by Side, pp. 102, 103; GrammarWork, p. 87; New American Streamline Departures, pp. 16-17.**

Have/Need - Optional The best exercises for "have" and "need" are in **New American Streamline Departures, pp. 13 and 16,** which have 5 stories about characters and their possessions. Compare the possessions of the characters on the page on separate T-charts. Students list on the chart what each character has and doesn't have. If not done before, extend the lesson by making sentences about what each character needs.

Which - Questions - Optional Using the pages above or another picture which shows possessions, ask questions with "which." (Don't explain "which" at this time.) **New American Streamline Departures, pp. 13 and 16.**

Which person has a swimming pool?
Which lady has a Mercedes?

Vocabulary

bank
cash machine (ATM)
market
supermarket
swap meet
dollar store
restaurant
drugstore
pharmacy
hospital
clinic
post office

Agenda

1. Opening routine
2. Place words #1 - introduce - pictures, flashcards
    Oral practice - questions with vocabulary words
    Quick review with flashcards
    HOMEWORK - copy 20X, quiz
3. Have/has - written practice, continue and 1 more written page
    More oral practice
4. Have/has - pronunciation and stress - oral practice
5. Some/any - introduce rule
    Oral practice with pencils, pens, paper, cup of coffee, bottle of water
    Written practice
6. Have/has with but - introduce, oral practice - optional
    Written practice - optional

Stuff

1. Flashcards and pictures for today's vocabulary (places)
2. Objects for some/any - pencils, pens, a few sheets of paper, a cup of coffee, a bottle of water

Lesson Plan

1. Opening Routine

2. Places #1 - Introduce Use pictures, photos, and flashcards to review or introduce places. HOMEWORK is to copy the words 20X for a quiz.

Places - Oral practice Ask questions using "have" with vocabulary words and pictures.

What do they have at the bank?	They have money. They have credit cards.
What do they have at the supermarket?	
What do they have at the swap meet?	
What do they have at the restaurant?	
What do they have at the drugstore?	
What do they have at the hospital?	
What do they have at the post office?	
Where do they have money?	They have money at the bank.
	They have money at the cash machine.
	They have money at the supermarket.
Where do they have food?	
Where do they have medicine?	
Where do they have stamps?	They have stamps at the post office.
	They have stamps at the supermarket.

3. Have/has - Written practice Do at least one page. See **references, Day 25.**

Have/has - More oral practice Using student clothing, objects in the room, or pictures of objects, practice questions with short and long answers. Give the class lots of examples and prompts to get the correct responses. If they have difficulties, help them answer as a group.

Does Juan have a white shirt?	No, he doesn't. He has a black shirt.
Does Julia have black shoes today?	No, she doesn't. She has white shoes.
Do I have black pants today?	Yes, you do.
(Hold up a water bottle.) Do I have coffee today?	No, you don't. You have water.
(Hold up a red pen.) Do I have a black pen?	No, you don't. You have a red pen.
Do we have homework?	Yes, we do.

4. Have/has - Pronunciation - Oral practice

Read several sentences with "have" and "has," breathing heavily on the H sound or making the H very raspy. Indicate "no" with your finger or give thumbs down to explain that it is wrong to make the H too strong a sound.

Write some of the above sentences on the board. Students repeat some of them after the teacher to show how the H disappears and how the stress in the sentence highlights the information.

Duz JUAN 'ava WHITE SHIRT? NO, 'e DOESN'T. 'e 'azza BLACK SHIRT.
Dz JULIA 'ave BLACK SHOES today? No, she DOESn't. SHE 'as WHITE shoes.
DoI'ave COFFEE today? NO, you DON'T. YOU'ave WATER.
D'WEE'ave HOMEWORK?
You'ava RED pen.

5. Some/any - Introduce Write the choices on the board.

a/an = 1
some = 2-10, not a lot, not a million, but 5 or 6
a lot of = 100, 1,000 or a million
any = some in questions and negatives

I have a dollar, but Bill Gates has a million dollars.
I have some money, but Bill Gates has a lot of money.
(Write $$ under your name. Write $$$$$$$$$$$$$$$ under Bill Gates' name.)

Do I have any money? Yes, I have some. (Look in your purse or pocket.)
Does Bill Gates have any money? Yes, he has a lot of money.

Is there any coffee in this cup? Yes, there is some. There is some coffee in this cup.
There is a lot of coffee at Starbucks.
I have some coffee. Starbucks has a lot of coffee.

Some/any - Oral practice Ask questions. Write model answers on the board.

Do you have any money?	Yes, I have some money.
	No, I don't have any money.
_____ paper?	
_____ water?	
Do you have a pencil?	Yes, I have a pencil. Yes, I have 2 pencils.
	No, I don't have a pencil.
Do you have any pencils?	Yes, I have some pencils.
	No, I don't have any pencils.

Do we have any gas in the car?	No, we don't have any gas. Yes, we have some gas.
Do we have any food in the house?	No, we don't have any food. We need some food.

Ask students, "When do you use 'some'?"
Answer: Some = affirmative sentences. Any = negative sentences and questions

Write the following sentences on the board without the parentheses.

Do you have (any) money?	Yes, I have (some) money.
	No, I don't have (any) money.
Do you have money?	Yes, I have money.

Tell students that "some" and "any" are very usual, but optional. Put the parentheses around the words as shown above. Erase the parentheses and the words in them, and tell students that the sentences are still okay.

125

Some/any - Written practice Many practices with "some" and "any" involve food. **Practical English, pp. 151-152; Writing Practical English, pp. 103-104; New American Streamline Departures, p. 11 (only repeat the dialog).**

6. Have/has - Oral practice with "but" - Optional "But" is used when you have 2 ideas which are contrary in some way, like "have" and "doesn't have." Write on the board.

I have a girlfriend, BUT I don't have a wife.

Repeat the sentence for the class with thumbs up for "I have," heavily stress the word BUT, and show thumbs down for "don't have."

I have a bicycle, BUT I don't have a car. (Repeat gestures.)
I have a pencil, BUT I don't have any paper.
He has work, BUT he doesn't have any money.
He has a TV, BUT he doesn't have a computer.

You can return to previous practices with characters who have or don't have things and talk about them with the word "but." Help the students use the practices and situations to make sentences similar to the model above. **New American Streamline Departures, pp. 13, 16; Practical English, pp. 87, 88; Writing Practical English, pp. 61-62; Side by Side, p. 102.**

Written practice with "but" - Optional - See **Practical English, pp. 85-86; Writing Practical English, p. 59.**

Day 27

Vocabulary

school
park
playground
basketball courts
soccer field
library
department store
beauty salon
cafe
coffee shop

Agenda

1. Opening routine
2. Places #1 - review - examples or photos of local stores, pictures, flashcards
    Collect homework, quiz
Places #2 - introduce - pictures, examples of local places, stores
    Review with flashcards
    HOMEWORK - copy 20X, quiz
3. Have/has, some/any - written practice - finish, do 1 more page
4. Helper verbs - do/does/don't/doesn't - introduce, part 1
    Introduce, part 2 - optional
    Written practice - 1 more page
5. Verbs of thinking and emotion - rule
6. Like - introduce, practice with pictures of objects

Stuff

1. Pictures and flashcards for Places #1 words
2. Pictures and flashcards for Places #2 words
3. Pictures of consumer goods, needed, ordinary, and luxurious (See Day 23.)

Lesson Plan

1. Opening Routine

2. Places #1 - Review Use examples from area and pictures. Review with flashcards. Collect homework and do the quiz.

Places #2 - Introduce Use pictures, examples, and questions about your area. You can practice with "have."

We have a _____. It's on _____ Street.

127

3. Have/has, Some/any - Written practice Finish and continue with 1 more page. (See **references, Day 25 and Day 26**.) You can do the additional written practice after the helper verb review, #4, below. Or you can start a long written practice and do the helper verb review below in the middle.

4. Helper Verbs - Do/does/don't/doesn't - Introduce - Part 1 Write on the board, leaving space between the sentences as shown.

He is working

She is working.

It is working.

They are working.

Draw arrows from "is" and "are" to a spot in front of the subject to remind students how the question reverses the subject and the verb. Flip your fingers back and forth to remind them of the rule. Add questions to each sentence on the board.

He is working.   INFORMATION
Is he working?   QUESTION

They are working.
Are they working?

Add the long and short answers.

He is working.
Is he working?   Yes, he is working. (long answer)
                      Yes, he is. (short answer)

                      No, he isn't working. (long)
                      No, he isn't. (short)
He is working.
He is not working.
He isn't working.

Point to the 2 negative sentences and remind the class that the negative adds "not" or "n't" onto the HELPER verb. The HELPER verb is "is" or "are" or "am." The MAIN verb is "work." The helper verb tells you the time of the main verb. Write the word HELPER on "is" and "are" and MAIN over "work."

Review the rule. "To make a question, you have to reverse the helper verb and the subject. (Flip 2 fingers back and forth. See Day 7.) The MAIN verb gives information. The HELPER verb makes a question."

Now write the following chart on the board.

I have	We have
You have	You (plural) have
He has She has It has	They have

Ask, "What is the main verb here?" Students should answer, "Have." Point to "has." Tell the class to remember that they need an S with "he," "she," and "it." Write "haves" next to each "has" verb. Say, "It would be 'haves,' but it is IRREGULAR." Cross out the VE. Say, "You have to remember the form (tapping your forehead) because it's NOT REGULAR."

Ask, "What is the helper verb?" Point to each sentence to show that there is no helper verb, because they don't see "is," "are," or any other helper verb in the sentences.

You say, "That's right. There is no helper verb in these sentences. You have to have the helper verb up here. (Tap your forehead.) You have to remember the helper verb. It's 'do.' You remember the helper verb 'do' and then you flip the helper with I, you, etc."

Under "I have" write, "Do I have?" Under "You have" write, "Do you have?" Do the same with "we," "you (plural)," and "they." When you come to "he has" write on the board.

has = haves (IRREGULAR)
Do he has = Do he haves

Draw an arrow from the S in "haves" to "do." Add ES to "Do." Draw a big X over the S in "haves."

Does he have

Go to "she has" on the board and add "does."

Does she has

Point to both S's. Shake your head. Say, "S two times, NO!" Cross out the S on "has" and add VE to get "have." Rewrite the sentence. Do the same for "it."

Does she have? Does it have?

As review, tell the students that "I," "we," "you plural," and "they" don't need S on the end of their verbs, so they don't use "has" and their helper is "do." "He," "she," and "it" need an S on the end of their verbs, but the S goes to the helper verb, so their helper is "does."

Write on the board.

Do I have
Do we have
Do you have
Do they have

Does he have
Does she have
Does it have

Helper Verbs - Do/does/don't/doesn't - Introduce - Part 2 - Optional If your class is exhausted, you can stop at this point, do a written page from the references above, and continue the rest of this helper verb comparison in the next class.

Write on the board.

You are working.   You have a car.
Are you working?   Do you have a car?
Yes, we are.   What is the short answer? Yes, I do.

Remind students that the helper is the same for the question and the short answer. Write "Yes, I do" and point to "do" in the question and the answer. Write on board.

No, we are not.   No, I do not.   (Add "not" after both helpers.)
No, we aren't.   No, I don't.   (Make the "not" short = "n't.")
                                        (Add "n't" to both helpers.)

We aren't working.   I don't have a car.   (Helper + negative + regular form)

Write on the board.

He is working.   He has a car.
Is he working?   Does he have a car?

Remind students that S goes to "'does" and leaves "have" not "has. " Write the "is" forms on the board. Ask students to help you fill in the answers on the "does" side by looking at the "is" side.

Yes, he is.   Yes, he _____.   Yes, he does.
No, he is not.   No, he _____.   No, he does not.
No, he isn't.   No, he _____.   No, he doesn't.
He isn't working.   He _____ have a car.   He doesn't have a car.

Go through the two lists with the class comparing each sentence one more time.

Helper verbs - Do/does/don't/doesn't - Written practice Do another page. See **references, Day 25 and Day 26.**

5. Verbs of Thinking and Emotion - Rule Say, "Present simple is used for an action that is true every day, always. I like coffee. I always like it. I like coffee every day. If I like my friend, I like her every day. If I love my children, I always love them. So some verbs are usually present simple." Write on the board.

like
love
want
hate
think
understand

Also some verbs are true every day or for a long time.

have
need

Write on the board a summary of the rule.

Present simple verbs of thinking and emotion = present simple with "do." Not continuous.
Action verbs = present simple with "do" - He walks to school. (every day)
OR   = present continuous with "is" and "are" - He is walking to school. (right now)

6. Like/don't like - Introduce When you say "like," have a big smile, thumbs up, or nod. "Don't like" is a frown, headshake, or thumbs down. With your pictures, give some examples.

I like candy. (every day)
I like shoes. (every day)
I like Coca-Cola.
I like smartphones.

With pictures, give some examples of negative things.

I don't like traffic.
I don't like vegetables.
I don't like hamburgers.
I don't like garbage.
I don't like big dogs.

With 10-15 pictures of objects from other vocabulary lists, students say,

I like _____. OR I don't like _____.

Day 28

Vocabulary

office
construction site
barber shop
garage
gas station

library
bookstore

bus stop
bus station
train station

Agenda

1. Opening routine
2. Places #2 - Review with examples, pictures, flashcards, and sentences
        Collect homework, quiz
Places #3 - Introduce with pictures, examples, practice with sentences
        Repeat with flashcards
        HOMEWORK- copy 20X, quiz tomorrow
3. Helper Verbs - do/does/don't/doesn't - introduce - part 2 - if not done
4. Like/don't like - oral practice with pictures of objects and places
        Written practice
Like/don't like - questions and short answers - oral practice
        Written practice
5. Present simple - need/want - review - optional
6. Like/want - introduce, written practice
        Rule - objects after like and want - optional
7. I'd like/ I like/I want - optional - introduce
        Optional - oral and written practice

Stuff

1. Pictures and flashcards of place words from yesterday's homework
2. Pictures and flashcards of place words for today's homework
3. About 12 flashcards of consumer goods like iPad, expensive sneakers, flat screen TV, swimming pool, lots of money, horse, new kitchen, vacation in Hawaii. Include some things which might be controversial, like an expensive dog or cat, pet snake, flashy sports car, diamond ring, Rolex watch. The pictures should be large and clear.
4. For the T-chart, big Post-it poster paper
5. Cup of coffee and bottle of water or box of cookies

Lesson Plan

1. Opening Routine

2. Places #2 - Review Use examples and flashcards to review quiz words.

Practice with questions. Write clues on board and use their own ideas also.

> Where are you going? I'm going to the school. Why? To talk to the teacher.
> Where are you going? I'm going to the park. Why? To play basketball.
> Where are you going? I'm going to the soccer field. Why? To see my friends.
> library ... get a movie.
> playground. .. to pick up my kids
> department store ... to get some shoes
> beauty salon ... because my hair is terrible

Collect homework and do the quiz.

Places #3 - Introduce Show pictures or give examples of businesses in your town to define the vocabulary words.

Practice with sentences about the homework pictures.

> Where is the library?
> Do we have a bookstore in this town?
> Is there a train station here? Is it a city train or a long-distance train?

Explain the difference between a bookstore and a library and between a bus stop and a bus station. Review all words with flashcards. HOMEWORK is to copy them 20X for a quiz.

3. Helper Verbs - Do/does/don't/doesn't - Introduce - Part 2 - Optional Finish comparing helper verbs here if it was not done in the previous class.

4. Like/don't like - Oral practice Use pictures of objects to help students complete the models. Be sure to include some pictures that students might not like.

> I like _____ .
> I don't like_____.

Like/don't like with places Show your pictures of places. Students say,

I like the dollar store.
I don't like the dollar store.

I like the park.
I don't like the park.

133

Like/don't like - Written practice - Finish Use **Practical English, pp. 105-106 (bottom), 112, 121 (discussion); Writing Practical English, p. 73; Side by Side, p. 95; New American Streamline Departures, p. 29 (questionnaire); Skill Sharpeners, p. 48 (reading and multiple-choice quiz). With "to," Side by Side, Book 2, p. 2.**

Like/don't like - Questions and short answers - Oral practice Ask the class to answer together. Use pictures to help them.

> Do you like dogs?   YES, I DO. or NO, I DON'T.
> Do you like cats?
> Do you like horses?
> Do you like snakes?
> Do you like animals?

Say to individual students, "Tell me about your wife/mom/sister/best friend."

> Does she like jewelry?   YES, SHE DOES. or NO, SHE DOESN'T.
> Does she like perfume?
> Does she like dresses?
> Does she like jeans?

Say to individual students, "Tell me about your husband/brother/cousin/friend at work."

> Does he like boots?
> Does he like suits? (business clothes)
> Does he like ties?
> Does he like hats?

Like/don't like - Questions and short answers - Written practice - See references above.

5. Present Simple - Need/want - Review - Optional

If not done previously, use a page such as **New American Streamline Departures, p. 13** or your pictures of consumer goods. Make a T-chart of NEEDS and WANTS on large poster paper. Students place the objects under the correct categories.

NEED = money, gas, food, clothes, work, a car, air, water
WANT = a swimming pool, a diamond ring, a motorcycle, a super-luxury car

Quickly going around the class, each student makes a sentence using one of the objects.

> I need _____.
> I want a _____.

6. Like/want - Introduce
Explain the meaning of "like" and "want" with gestures. When you say "like," have a big smile or nod. "Don't like" is a frown or headshake, or negative

gesture. "Want" means "give me." (Make a grasping motion. Point to something and indicate that you want it. "I want that pencil. I want your book.") Give examples of the difference.

"I like coffee." Point to your coffee cup and give thumbs up. "BUT I don't want coffee now." (Pick up the cup, but then pretend to change your mind. Gesture, "No.")

"I like water." (Repeat the routine with your water bottle or a box of cookies.)

"I like hamburgers. Do I want a hamburger now?" (Pretend to think about it.) Say, "No, I want a hamburger for lunch."

Say, "I like dogs. BUT I don't want a dog, because I have 3 cats."

Like/want - Written practice The following pages distinguish between "like" and "want." **Practical English, pp. 105-106 (top); Writing Practical English, pp. 73-74.**

Like/want - Introduce plural objects after like and want - Optional "Like" is general, so it has plural after it. If you like movies, you like all movies. If you like dogs, you like all dogs. But "want" is specific, so the object after it is usually singular.

>   I like hamburgers. Do I want **a** hamburger now? No, I want **a** hamburger for lunch.
>   I like dogs. But I don't want **a** dog, because I have 3 cats.

7. I'd like/I like/I want - Introduce - Optional First, review the rules about "like" and "want" with plural objects above. Write on the board.

I like hamburgers. (every day or always)
I want a hamburger. (right now)

I would like a hamburger. (right now) (more polite)
I'd like a hamburger. (short form) (more polite)

Tell students that "I'd like" = "I would like" = "I want," but more politely. When you are ordering food in a restaurant, you want to be polite.

Underline the "a" after "I want," "I would like," and "I'd like." Say, "I'd like" is the same as "I want," so you put one thing after it.

I'd like hamburgers.	You will get 2 hamburgers.
I'd like a hamburger.	You will get 1 hamburger.
I like a hamburger.	Not possible. You want a hamburger. OR
	You would like a hamburger.

I'd like/I like/I want - Optional - Written and oral practice Use **New American Streamline Departures, p. 15 (dialogs) or p. 11 (menu)** and add questions with "like" and "want."

Vocabulary

NO QUIZ TOMORROW
Pass out attached list of location words (optional).

Agenda

1. Opening routine
2. Places #3 - review with pictures, examples, flashcards
    Oral practice - places from all 3 lists with have/don't have
    Collect homework, quiz
Places - oral practice - why and need - optional
3. Like/love/need/want - review - dialog
4. Present simple vs. present continuous - written practice
5. Location words (prepositions) - oral practice - talk about places, write prepositions on a
    Post-it paper poster
    Location Words (Prepositions) chart - attached - pass out copies - optional
    Written practice - 1 long or 2 short pages

Stuff

1. Pictures and flashcards with Places #3 on today's quiz
2. Pictures and flashcards with places #1 and #2 (previous quizzes)
3. If possible, pictures or computer display of local or city locations with signs for businesses
on vocabulary lists Places #1, #2, and #3, continuing to Places #4, #5, and #6
4. Large Post-it paper for a chart of prepositions used in class
5. Copies of the attached Location Words (Prepositions) chart

Lesson Plan

1. Opening Routine

2. Places #3 - Oral practice Review for the quiz with pictures and flashcards. Do the oral practice below including the homework words. Collect homework and do the quiz.

Places - Oral practice Show pictures from Places #1, 2, and 3 and practice the places with "have" and "don't have." There will be 3 more lists of place words in future vocabulary. If your area has most of the locations on the first 3 lists, go into your picture collection and pull out some words from Places #4, #5 and #6 such as "hotel" and "stadium," so students can practice "don't have." Students respond,

> We have a school.
> We have a park.
> We don't have a department store.
> We don't have a stadium.

Less common locations might be airport, community college, swap meet or flea market, dollar store, hospital, department store, bookstore, bus station, or train station.

Places #1, #2, #3 - Oral practice - Optional Show a picture or flashcard and ask the class questions. Give a lot of help with answers. Encourage them to use "need" and "want."

> Where are you going? I'm going to the market.
> Why are you going to the market? I need tomatoes.
>
> Where are you going? I'm going to the supermarket.
> Why? I need soap and pantyhose.
>
> Where are you going? I'm going to the bank.
> Why are you going there? I need a money order.
>
> Where are you going? I'm going to work.
> Where? I work in an office downtown.
>
> Where are you going? To the cash machine.
> Why? I need money.
> Where is the cash machine? At the bank.
> Where is the bank? On Main Street.

Try to limit your questions to the above examples. "Where are you going? Why are you going there? Where is it?" If students give short answers, model a longer answer. For "To get tomatoes," model, "I want to get tomatoes," or "I need tomatoes." For "At the bank," model "It's at the bank."

3. Like/love/need/want - Review - Dialog Practice this dramatic dialog. **New American Streamline Departures, p. 30.**

4. Present Simple vs. Continuous - Written practice Begin written practice with pages which focus on this problem (right now vs. every day). It is very difficult for students to learn to use present simple correctly and to use present continuous as much Americans do. The following references have good practices comparing them. **New American Streamline Departures, p. 37; Practical English, pp. 145-148, 155; Writing Practical English, pp. 101-102, 127-128; Side by Side, p. 108-109, 112 and 113 (readings); GrammarWork, p. 103.**

Correct helper words in the answers. Short answers must use the same helper verb as the question, or the questioner may think that the person did not understand his question.

> Are you studying English?   Yes, I do. (WRONG)
>   Yes, I am. (RIGHT)

5. Location Words (Prepositions) - Oral practice Using the vocabulary list, students talk about one store or location near their house or near the school, practice with pictures or maps of city locations from a text, or do a puzzle with a graphic of city buildings.

Some good map activities which are cited later in this manual and which can be used here are **Skill Sharpeners, pp. 32, 33; Lifeskills, pp. 38, 39.**

Location Words Prepositions Chart Review easier location words from previous lessons. Make a big Post-it chart with the title LOCATION WORDS (PREPOSITIONS). Write the prepositions that students already know. During classwork, add new words to the chart. Don't hold the class responsible for the word "preposition." Just use it together with the term "location word." When you have used many of the words on the attached list, give the class a copy of the list as a summary of the words to know.

Location Words Prepositions Chart - Illustrate the location words - Optional Ask students to illustrate the meaning of each location word on the chart by drawing pictures or stick figures. They can also use arrows, or show letters, numbers, or objects illustrating the relative positions. For example, they can draw a picture with an A inside a box and a B outside the box. Students can also try to illustrate the meanings by moving around and positioning themselves in the room, as they do in TPR practices. You should do this as a class, with teacher or students illustrating the meanings on the board, or review their ideas as a class.

You have already done this for the easiest words on the list. The whole list should not be done at one time. You could have students do only part of the list each day over the course of a week.

Location Words (Prepositions) - Written practice Do 2 pages, continuing to add new location words to the Post-it chart. **Side by Side, pp. 55-58, 63-65 (readings and listening); Practical English, pp. 10-11, 12; Writing Practical English, pp. 5-7; GrammarWork, pp. 79, 82; New American Streamline Departures, p. 40 (puzzle); Access, pp. 71-75 (listening), 77-78.**

Location Words (Prepositions)

A preposition is a very short word which comes before a noun (person, place, or thing). It usually talks about a place or a time. The words in this list talk about locations and places. These are the words we use when we give people directions to a place. Some of the words are review.

1. in	14. behind
2. on	15. up
3. under	16. down
4. over	17. across
5. on top of	18. across from
6. next to	19. along
7. between	20. around
8. inside	21. away from
9. outside	22. toward - towards
10. into	23. near
11. out of	24. by
12. in front of	25. kitty-corner from
13. in back of	26. diagonally

Day 30

Vocabulary

Continue to add location words to the list on the poster.

Agenda

1. Opening routine
2. Have/need/want - optional - review with attached clothing worksheet, in pairs or groups
HOMEWORK - OPTIONAL - clothes at home - write about what you have, need and want
3. Pronunciation of short A - oral practice, review rule (sheet attached)
4. Places/location words - oral practice
        Map activity or dictation, add to location words list
IF TIME
5. Present simple - jazz chant - "Banker's Wife's Blues" (See Day 32.)
6. LAST 1/2 HOUR - BINGO

Stuff

1. Copies of clothing worksheets (attached) (optional)
2. Copy or projectable file of short A words (attached)
3. Post-it chart paper for list of location words.
4. Copies or projectable file of "Banker's Wife's Blues" jazz chant
5. Bingo game and rewards

Lesson Plan

1. Opening Routine

2. Have/need/want - Review - Optional - Higher group In small groups or pairs, students talk about the clothes they have at home. With help, they fill in the attached worksheet. Give examples on the board to help students write the reasons why they don't need certain garments. Part of it can be done in class as an example and the rest done for homework.

> I have a lot of tee shirts now.
> I don't like to swim.
> Los Angeles doesn't have rain.
> I don't like skirts. I like pants.
> I don't work in a uniform.
> I don't need a watch. I have a cell phone.
> I don't need a backpack. I have a purse.
> I'm a boy/girl.

OPTIONAL HOMEWORK - Look at your clothes at home. Write answers on your list to turn in.

140

3. Pronunciation of Short A Sound - Oral practice Write or project the attached list on the board and repeat it. Define the words they don't know.

Short Vowels - Memory words - Review Repeat several times - hat, get, hit, hot, hut.

Pronunciation - Short vowels - Review rule Write on the board.

     CVC = short
     CCVCC = short
     VC = short

Ask students to explain the meaning of these abbreviations. If they can't, go over the rules again. Words with these consonant-vowel-consonant patterns GENERALLY follow the rule of being short. The end consonant cuts off the length of the vowel sound. You can ask students to look at today's pronunciation list and write CVC, CVCC, CCVC, VC, etc. next to some of the words. Good examples are am, ax, map, fan, flag, hand, ramp, and classroom.

4. Places/Location Words - More oral practice Ask questions about the neighborhood. See Day 31 and Day 32 for more words to use.

    Where do you go to buy a special dress or special clothes?
    Where do you go to dance?
    Where do you go to see a soccer game? What about American football? Tennis?

    Do we have a _____ in this neighborhood? Where is it?
           movie theater
           sports arena
           airport
           big shopping mall
           swap meet
           swimming pool
           health club
           community college

Places/Location Words - Map activity Do a map activity, dialog, dictation or exercises which review places and location words. See **references, Day 29.**

IF TIME

5. Present simple - Jazz chant Do "Banker's Wife's Blues." (See Day 32.) **(See "Texts" section on how to get jazz chants.)**

6. LAST 1/2 HOUR - BINGO

Have and Need with Clothing Words

Clothes	Do you have one/any?	Do you need one?	If not, why not?
tee shirt	Yes/No		
shirt			
blouse			
jeans			
pants			
shorts			
uniform			
sweatpants			
sweatshirt			
sweater			
shoes			
sneakers			
boots			
cap			
hat			
skirt			
suit			
dress			
wallet			
bag			
backpack			
socks			
sunglasses			
bathing suit			
scarf			
gloves			
umbrella			
raincoat			
belt			
watch			
necklace			
bracelet			

Short A Sound (not "ah")

am	band
an	Band-Aid
at	can of soda
has	fan (machine, soccer lover)
classroom	ham sandwich
map	hand
flag	man
magazine	nana (grandma)
I am a fabulous teacher!	nanny (young babysitter)
I have a map and a flag in my classroom.	pan
add	Pampers (for babies)
actor, actress	ramp
after	sand, land
agriculture	tan (a color, to sit at the beach)
apple	van
ax	vampire

Day 31

Vocabulary

church
laundromat
movie theater

fast-food restaurant
coffee shop
snack bar
bar

elementary school
middle school
high school
community college

Agenda

1. Opening routine
2. Places #4 - introduce - pictures, examples from the area
   Oral practice with model sentences
   Review vocabulary with flashcards
   HOMEWORK - copy 20X for quiz
3. Clothes - extra credit - optional - collect clothing list homework. If many students have done assignment, extra credit HOMEWORK.
4. Daily routine/activities/habits - oral practice - review - pictures and flashcards
5. Present simple - reading/dialog practice - daily schedule, work schedule
   Written practice - 1 or 2 pages

Stuff

1. Flashcards and pictures of daily activity verbs
2. Flashcards and pictures of tasks and jobs

Lesson Plans

1. Opening Routine

2. Places #4 - Introduce Use pictures and examples from your area to talk about places.

Places #4 - Oral practice Use the following models to practice the vocabulary words.

They _____ to/at the _____ every _____.
We
He
She

They go to (the) church every Sunday.
They go to the laundromat every Saturday.
We go to the movie theater every Friday night.
We eat at a fast-food restaurant every Saturday.

He eats at the snack bar every day.
She eats at the coffee shop every day.
He has a drink (drinks beer or alcohol) at the bar every Saturday.

He goes to (the) elementary school (every day).
She goes to (the) middle school (every day).
They go to (the) high school (every day).
We come to (this) community college (every day, twice a week, three times a week).

Make sure students are putting S on verbs with "he" and "she." Ask them to add their own ideas.

"The" in parentheses can be left out depending on the meaning of the sentence.

Review the vocabulary with flashcards. HOMEWORK is to copy the words 20X for a quiz.

3. Clothes - Extra credit - Optional Collect homework (the clothing list).

HOMEWORK - If enough students have filled in wardrobe items, offer extra credit if they expand the list into sentences. Write these examples on the board for those students.

shirt = I have 5 shirts. I need 2 shirts. OR I want 2 shirts.
shoes = I have a lot of shoes. I don't need any shoes.
1 suit = I have a suit. I want a new suit.

It might be better to explain this homework after class to students who are interested.

4. Daily Routine - Review - Oral practice   Review the daily routine words with pictures and flashcards from Day 21.

> I brush my teeth every day.
> I wash my face every day.

Repeat with "he" and "she."

> He washes his face every day.
> She brushes her teeth (every day)(two times a day).

5. Present Simple - Reading or dialog practice   Do a short reading or dialog about a person or family's daily schedule or work schedule. Read several times and answer oral questions, making sure to include the S in third person singular. Do the written exercises that come with the reading or use the reading to create questions, short answers, and negatives. **New American Streamline Departures, p. 33; Practical English, pp. 129-130, 131-132, 137-138; Writing Practical English, pp. 91-96, 121-122; Side by Side, pp. 79-85, 90-94.**

Present Simple - Written practice   Do 1 or 2 pages on what people do every day. **GrammarWork, p. 82 (previous reference), 84 (more daily routine); Lifeskills, p. 91.**

When orally reviewing answers, make sure you hear the S. You should also stress the S, but then repeat the sentence naturally so that students can hear that "does" becomes "dz" and that "doesn't" is more stressed than "does." Students need to understand that S is in the sentence, but that they will not hear it very well.

Day 32

Vocabulary

hotel
motel

parking lot   parking garage   parking structure

tennis courts
baseball field
track
drinking fountain   water fountain

disco nightclub
police station
fire station

apartment building   apartment complex

stadium
arena

elevator
escalator

Agenda

1. Opening routine
2. Places #4 - review with pictures, examples, flashcards
      Collect homework, quiz
Places #5 - introduce with pictures, oral questions, local examples.
      Choose most common words for oral practice and Places #5 quiz tomorrow
      Review chosen quiz words with flashcards
      HOMEWORK - copy 20X, quiz
3. Jazz chant - Banker's Wife's Blues - introduce, copy, oral practice
4. Present simple - oral practice
5. Present continuous - helper verbs review - optional
6. Present simple vs. present continuous - review - optional
7. Present simple - written practice with do, does, don't, doesn't

Stuff

1. Flashcards and pictures for places quiz and homework words - entire list
2. Pictures of workers and job sites
3. Copies or projectable file of "Banker's Wife's Blues" jazz chant

Lesson Plan

1. Opening Routine

2. Places #4 - Review Practice Places #4 words with pictures, examples, and flashcards. Collect homework and do the quiz.

Places #5 - Introduce Explain Places #5 with pictures, oral questions, and local examples. Ask students to choose 10-12 of the words most commonly used in your area for the quiz tomorrow. Focus on those words and continue oral practice. The remaining words will be the Places #6 list.

Review with flashcards only tomorrow's quiz words. HOMEWORK is to copy them 20X for a quiz.

3. Jazz Chant - "Banker's Wife's Blues" - Introduce, copy, oral practice This is a very good practice for present simple. Project it on the board or hand out copies. Teacher reads the poem at least once. Ask students to explain the chant. Who has a problem? What is her problem?

Students read the chant several times, trying to get a good rhythm, and then copy once to use for homework. Then the class can practice the chant in two competing sections, as a class, in pairs, or in groups. (See Sub Work 1 and Day 22.)

HOMEWORK - Students copy the chant 1-3 times, making sure to include the final S. Give 1 homework point per copy.

4. Present Simple - Oral practice Talk about workers and where they work. Try to make a few sentences for each location.

> Bankers work in banks.
> Security guards work in banks.
>
> Doctors work in hospitals.
> Nurses work in hospitals.
>
> Mothers work at home.
> Housewives work at home.
> Housekeepers work in the houses or homes of other people.

Present Simple - Oral practice Use your pictures of workers at job sites to fill in blanks.

He works at the _____ every day.
She works at a _____ every day.
She goes to _____ every day.

Stress the S on the end of verbs with "he" and "she."

A good written practice for jobs with locations is **GrammarWork, p. 82**, if not already done. Also **GrammarWork, pp. 88-89.** For job names, see **Skill Sharpeners, pp. 64-66.** You can do those pages before the oral practice.

5. Present Continuous - Helper verbs - Review - Optional Write quickly on the board.

SUBJECT, PERSON   MAIN VERB

He   is   a student.

Flip your fingers to show a question. Draw arrows between subjects and verbs. (See Day 7.)

Is   he   a student?

Yes, he is.
No, he isn't.
He isn't a student.

(In these three sentences, show the verbs flipping back to regular order for the answer, because you are giving information, not asking a question.)

"Is" is the MAIN VERB in these examples. It reverses to show questions and it adds "n't" to show negatives. (Point to the question form and the negative forms.) This "special verb" is the only verb to do this. All other verbs use a helper verb for questions and negatives.

"Is," "am," and "are" are also helper verbs, but not in this example. (Ask the class if they see another verb in the above sentences. There is no other verb, so "is" is the main verb.

In British English, "have" is also a special verb which can reverse to make questions and add "not" to make the negative. In American English, "have" and "has" use "do" and "does" as helper verbs, just like other verbs.

Present Continuous - Use helper verbs to make a question Say, "Now you want to ask a question about an action which is happening right now." Point to the floor.

SUBJECT, PERSON	HELPER VERB	MAIN VERB
He	is	walking.

Flip fingers and draw arrows between "he" and "is" to make the question.

Is	he	walking?

> Yes, he is.
> No, he isn't.
> He isn't walking.

(Show the three verbs flipping back to regular order because the answers are information. Only questions can reverse order.)

No, he isn't walking. He is sitting. (right now)

Underline "isn't walking" and "is sitting" and write COMPLETE VERB over them.

The MAIN VERBS which carry the information are "walk" and "sit." Circle them and write MAIN above them. The HELPER VERB is "is." It tells you that the action is happening right now. Circle them and write HELPER above.

The "ing" part of the verb never changes. All changes (like adding "n't") go on the helper verb. Remind students that you can write out the word "not" if you separate it from the main verb.

6. Present Simple/Present Continuous - Review - Optional Present simple verbs talk about every day or regularly, not right now. You do the action every day, three times a week, every year, etc.

He walks to school. (every day)
Every day he walks to school, but he isn't walking right now.

(Indicate a student in the front row.)

Mrs. Garcia sits in the front in every class.
She sits in the front.

Is she sitting in the front right now?	YES, SHE IS.
Does she sit in the front every day?	YES, SHE DOES.

150

(Write a few words on the board.)

Am I writing on the board right now?   YES, YOU ARE.

(Go to your desk and sit down.)

Am I writing on the board right now?   NO, YOU AREN'T.
Do I write on the board in every class?   YES, YOU DO.
Do I write on the board on Sunday?   NO, YOU DON'T.

Put on the board.

He walk + s to school. S means he does this every day or regularly.
He work + s at a bank. He works there 5 days a week.
She sit + s in the front. She sits there for every class.

Say, "Now you want to make a question. Where is the helper verb? There isn't one. So you
have to remember to use 'do' for the helper verb."

Say, "You can use 'do' as a main verb."

     I do my work every day.
     You do your homework every night.

Remind the class to add S to "do" with "he," "she," and "'it."

     He does his job.
     She does a lot of work.
     I have a computer. It does everything.

     We do
     You (plural) do
     They do

Remind students that they can use "do" as a helper verb also.

Do they work every day?
     Yes, they do.   SHORT ANSWER, REGULAR ORDER
     No, they don't.
     They don't work every day. They work 3 days a week.

Does she work here?

     Yes, she does.
     No, she doesn't.
     No, she doesn't work here. She works in the city.

Point to "work" in the negative sentence above. Move your finger from the end of "work" to "doesn't." Remind students that the "s" came off "work" and went onto "doesn't."

Point to the affirmative sentence, "She works in the city."

Ask students where "does" is in the affirmative sentence. If nobody can explain it, repeat the rule that you only need "does" for questions, short answers and negative sentences. (Point to each example above.)

Now point to the word "works" in "She works in the city." Remind students that you took out "does" so the S goes back on "work."

7. Present Simple - Do, does, don't, doesn't and questions - Written practice Use **New American Streamline Departures, pp. 30, 32; GrammarWork, pp. 90-95.** Walk around room checking papers to catch errors with S.

Day 33

Vocabulary

On Day 32, students chose 10-12 vocabulary words from a list of 20. Use the remaining words for the vocabulary quiz tomorrow.

Agenda

1. Opening routine
2. Places #5 - review homework words with pictures, examples, flashcards
   Collect homework, quiz
   Places #6 - review and oral practice with words not used yesterday - pictures, questions, examples, flashcards
   HOMEWORK - copy 20X, quiz
3. Present simple - do, does, don't, doesn't and questions - written practice - continue
4. Pronunciation - Short E words (list attached)
5. Jazz chant - Banker's Wife's Blues - collect homework
   Oral practice - do chant 2-3X

Stuff

1. Flashcards and pictures for quiz and homework words
2. Copies or projectable file of short E words (attached)

Lesson Plan

1. Opening Routine

2. Places #5 - Review Review Places #5 words with pictures, examples, and flashcards. Collect homework and do the quiz.

Places #6 - Review With remaining words from yesterday, review with pictures, questions, examples, and flashcards. Review differences between similar words, like "parking garage" and "parking structure," "stadium" and "arena," "escalator" and "elevator." HOMEWORK is to copy these words 20X for a quiz.

3. Present Simple - Do, does, don't, doesn't and questions - Written practice Continue. Focus on errors with S. See **references, Day 31 and Day 32.**

4. Pronunciation - Short E Sound Most of these words are from previous vocabulary lists. After practicing as a class, listen carefully to individual students reading the words. This is a very difficult sound for them.

5. Jazz Chant - "Banker's Wife's Blues" - More oral practice Practice the poem a few more times with homework copies. Collect homework.

Short E Sound
CVC or VC = short ("eh")

seven, ten

pen, pencil, desk

man, men

when

bed, television

necklace, dress, belt

elegant

Jell-O (gelatin) vs. yellow

yellow, red

tell me, address

send, letter, envelope

memory, memorize, mental, remember

elbow

egg

elephant

next

Tell me your address.
Remember to send the letter.
Send the rent in the envelope on the desk.
Put the dress, the necklace, and the belt on the bed.

Day 34

Vocabulary

No quiz tomorrow. The list of location words attached to Day 35 will be on future quizzes.

Agenda

1. Opening routine
2. Places #6 - review with pictures, examples, flashcards
   Collect homework, quiz
3. Location words (prepositions) - oral practice - talk about town or photos of local places
   Give directions to places, prompt with words on Post-it chart, add words to chart
4. Places - map activity #1 with directions
   Written practice - 1 or 2 pages
   Reading or dialog with places in city
5. Location words (prepositions) - written practice - 1 long or 2 short pages
IF TIME
6. Frequency words with present simple - read story or dialog

Stuff

1. Pictures and flashcards with places on quiz
2. If possible, pictures or computer display of places and signs in local area which illustrate words on Places lists #1, #2, #3, #4, #5, and #6
3. Large Post-it paper for the Location Words chart

Lesson Plan

1. Opening Routine

2. Places #6 Review with pictures, examples, and flashcards. Collect homework and do the quiz.

3. Location Words (Prepositions) - Oral practice or review Students talk about stores or places near their houses and school OR discuss map of places and buildings from a text. (See activities, Day 29.) Add new location words to the Post-it chart if necessary.

Ask questions.

> Where is there a movie theater around here?
> Is there a movie theater in Glendale?
> Which restaurant around here is a coffee shop?
> What is the name of that elementary school across the street?

If available, use projections or photos of local locations to prompt ideas. Ask students to give directions to the places in your town. Help them by pointing to words on the Post-it chart.

155

4. Directions - Vocabulary - TPR Use TPR routine to review or introduce "go left," "go right," "go straight," "continue," and "stop." (See Day 2.)

Directions - Vocabulary - Oral practice Also **Skill Sharpeners, p. 11 (left and right); GrammarWork, p. 80; Side by Side, Book 2, pp. 61-65 (directions with place names), 66-67 (subway); New American Streamline Departures, pp. 31, 40; Practical English, pp. 50-51 and 180-181.**

Places - Map activity #1 with directions Do one activity with a diagram of a city, or dictate city places to fill in a map. If not done before, **Skill Sharpeners, pp. 32, 33.** On page 33, dictate sentences while they fill in a blank map. Check and then copy the sentences. Or **Lifeskills, pp. 38, 39.**

If you have a cartoon or picture showing places in a city, you can copy and modify it to create many different additional dictation exercises and oral practices. **Side by Side, Book 1, pp. 64 and 65; Side by Side, Book 2, pp. 64, 63.**

5. Location Words (Prepositions) - Written practice Do 2 pages which continue written practices from Day 29. For additional exercises, **Practical English, p. 183; Writing Practical English, p. 117.** Add any new location words to the chart as you check the work.

IF TIME

6. Frequency Words with Present Simple Read a story or dialog with present simple and frequency words. Discuss the story or dialog without writing the answers. Copy the story. **Composition Practice, Book 1, pp. 20-27 (Unit 3).**

Day 35

Vocabulary

The Location Words/Prepositions List (by difficulty) is attached. The quiz on group 1 will be a dictation of sentences with group 1 words. Sentences for the quiz are attached to Day 36.

Agenda

1. Opening routine
2. Location words #1 - introduce new list of location words (prepositions), review
   Illustrate first group of words with little pictures. Review if done Day 11.
   HOMEWORK - copy group 1 location words 10X - quiz will be dictation of sentences with these words
3. Places and location words - map activity #2 with a city map or blank map (or dictation from yesterday's map activity #1)
4. Places - reading practice
5. Directions - oral and written practice
6. LAST 1/2 HOUR - BINGO

Stuff

1. Flashcards or sheets with blank maps or cartoons of places for classwork
2. Bingo supplies with reward candy
3. Copies of list - location words sorted by difficulty

Lesson Plan

1. Opening Routine

2. Location Words - Review Give students the attached list of prepositions. Review the known words. Have the students illustrate each location word next to the word on their papers. (For example, show an A next to a B, or over it, or under it. See Day 11, where the easiest words were done.) Remind them to show spaces between words. Review spelling of "of." HOMEWORK is to copy 10X the words in the first group only. Dictation of sentences with these words will be the quiz. (Quiz sentences for teacher's use are attached to Day 36.)

3. Places - Directions - Map activity #2 Use a text exercise or map with place names to practice directions and locations. If no new activity is available, give a dictation from yesterday's map activity. See **references, Day 34.**

4. Places - Reading Read about places. **Side by Side, Book 1, pp. 63, 64, 65.**

5. Directions - Oral practice Do 1 page from **Side by Side, Book 2, pp. 61-67.**

6. LAST 1/2 HOUR - BINGO

157

Location Words/Prepositions List (divided by difficulty)

Basic (already done by Day 33)

1. in
2. on
3. under
4. next to (2 words)
5. between
6. in back of (3 words)
7. in front of (3 words)
8. up
9. down
10. out of (2 words)

More difficult

1. inside (1 word) (in)
2. outside
3. across
4. behind (in back of)
5. over
6. near

Most difficult - may need for text or testing

1. into (1 word)
2. along
3. around
4. above (over)
5. beside (next to)
6. by (near)
7. below (under)

Vocabulary

Location words, second group on list attached to Day 35. Test sentences attached.

Agenda

1. Opening routine
2. Location words #1 - review list of location words, group 1, with flashcards, give quiz with group 1 of sentences (attached)

Location words #2 - review location words, group 2. Give examples, illustrate meanings.
> HOMEWORK - copy 20X words in group 2. Dictation of sentences with these words will be quiz.

3. Directions - oral practice
4. Locations - reading practice - 2 pages
5. Frequency words - finish any work from Day 34
> Oral practice
> Written practice - activity verbs - start
> Rule - where to place frequency words - review
> Written practice - "to be"
> Rule - where to place frequency words - written practice

Stuff

1. Flashcards of location words (prepositions) from list given out Day 35
2. Copies of list of Location Words/Prepositions List (divided by difficulty)
3. Flashcards of frequency words

Lesson Plan

1. Opening Routine

2. Location Words, group 1 - Review Use flashcards.

Dictate the first group of sentences from the attached Locations Dictation Quizzes. Dictate the complete sentence, but give credit for prepositions with correct spelling and spacing.

Location Words, group 2 - Review Review meanings and examples. Stress necessity to show spaces between the words correctly, as some location words are 2 or 3 words long, while all of group 2 words like "inside" must be only 1 word.

HOMEWORK is to copy 20X the location words in group 2. Dictation of sentences with these words will be tomorrow's quiz.

3. Directions - Oral practice Do 1 page. See **references, Day 34 and Day 35.**

4. Locations - Reading and practice Practice with more difficult location words. See **references, Day 34 and Day 35.**

5. Frequency Words - Introduce Write on the board.

always = 100%
usually = 85%
often = 70%
sometimes = 40%
rarely = 5%
never = 0%

once = 1 time
twice = 2 times
3 times

a lot = always, usually, often
sometimes = so-so (Wave hand to show both sides and look noncommittal.)
rarely = not much
never = NOT

When do you watch TV?   I usually watch TV at night.
When do you go to sleep?   I always go to sleep at 10.
When do you go to clubs?   I never go to clubs.

Frequency Words - Oral practice For examples, talk about your own habits. Have students ask the questions and choose the correct answer from the choices you give.

Mrs. Lockwood, do you ever drink coffee in class?
        Yes, I always drink coffee in class. OR
        Yes, I sometimes drink coffee in class.

Do you ever bring cookies to class?
        Yes, I usually bring cookies to class. OR
        Yes, I sometimes bring cookies to class.

Do you ever wear running shoes to class?
        I often wear running shoes to class. OR
        I rarely wear running shoes to class. OR
        I never wear running shoes to class.

Do you ever wear jeans to class?
        I always wear jeans to class. OR
        I usually wear jeans to class. OR
        I often wear jeans to class.

Frequency Words - More oral practice Ask the following questions and students write only the frequency word on their paper. Don't make them answer in a complete sentence. Point to the list with percentages to remind them of the meaning while they are writing.

How often do you take the bus?
How often do you eat out? (eat in a restaurant)
How often do you drink beer?
How often do you go to the beach? (or the park, or a local attraction)
How often do you shop for food?
How often do you ride a bicycle?
How often do you go to the movies?
How often do you go to the mall?
How often do you get a new cell phone?
How often do you leave work early?

Check the questions by asking 1 or 2 students what they answered. Compare class answers by asking other students to raise their hands. "Who else said/answered that they never take the bus/always take the bus?"

6. Frequency Words - Written practice with activity words Do 3 separate pages. Most written exercises practice frequency words with either activity words first or "to be" words first. Then they will practice the other type. For activity words, see **Practical English, pp. 133-34, 140-141; Writing Practical English, pp. 97-98; New American Streamline Departures, pp. 35, 36; Side by Side, p. 101; GrammarWork, p. 85.**

Frequency Words - Rule review Frequency words come BEFORE an action verb, but AFTER the verb "to be."

Mrs. Campbell always drinks coffee in class.
Mrs. Campbell is always nice to students.

Juan never comes to class on time.
Juan is never on time to class.

Frequency Words - Written practice with "to be" For practice with "to be," **Practical English, pp. 135-136; GrammarWork, p. 28.**

Frequency Words - Written practice with activity words and "to be" words To choose where to place frequency words with both types of verbs, use **Composition Practice, Book 1, p. 34.**

Locations Dictation Quizzes

(Use names of your own students.)

1. Luis is in Room 100.
2. Mrs. Lopez is in front of the students.
3. William is walking up the stairs.
4. I'm riding down the escalator.
5. Michael is walking out of the cafeteria.
6. The book is on the table.
7. The carpet is under the table.
8. Michael is between Ramon and Joshua.
9. Mrs. Ramirez is in back of Ramon.
10. Sit next to the door.

1. The students are inside the room.
2. Gabriel is walking across Main Street. (Dictate capital letters. Spell out "Main.")
3. The tree is outside the room.
4. Mrs. Ramirez is behind Ramon.
5. The flag is over the desk.
6. Luis is next to Gabriel.
7. He is sitting near him.

1. The trash can is beside the teacher's desk.
2. Mrs. Smith is walking into Room 100.
3. He is walking along the street.
4. The trees are around the house.
5. The trash can is by the door.
6. The basement is below the house.
7. The attic is above the house.

Day 37

Vocabulary

The quiz tomorrow is on the group 3 location words, from the list attached to Day 35.

Agenda

1. Opening routine
2. Location words #2 - review list group 2 with flashcards, dictate quiz sentences (attached to Day 36)

Location words #3 - review location words, group 3. Give examples, review meaning with little pictures

HOMEWORK - Copy 20X the location words in group #3. Dictation of sentences with these words will be quiz.

3. Directions - oral practice - continue
4. Frequency words - oral practice
   Written practice - continue, finish if possible (3 pages in total)

IF TIME

5. Start next jazz chant (See Day 38.)

Stuff

1. Copies of list of location words by difficulty
2. Flashcards of location words (prepositions) from list given out Day 35

Lesson Plan

1. Opening Routine

2. Location Words - Review Use flashcards or list to review location words, group 2.
Using the sentences attached to Day 36, give the quiz. Dictate complete sentences, with credit only for prepositions perfectly spelled with correct spaces.

Review location words, group 3. Give examples and illustrate meanings with little pictures. Point out that all the prepositions in this group are only one word.

HOMEWORK - Copy 20X the location words in group 3. Dictation of sentences with these words will be the quiz.

3. Directions - Oral practice Continue. See references, Day 34 and Day 35.

4. Frequency Words - Oral practice Write the list on the board as a reminder.

always = 100%
usually = 85%
often = 70%
sometimes = 40%
rarely = 5%
never = 0%

once
twice
three times

With action words

Remind students that frequency words come **before** action words. Practice the rule with sentence completion. Point to the list of percentages to help students complete their ideas or choose answers. Write the models on the board.

What do you eat in the morning?
    I always/usually eat _____.
    I often/sometimes eat _____.
    I rarely/never eat _____.

How often (how much) do you go to the movies?
    I go to the movies about _____ times a week/a month/a year.
So you often/sometimes/rarely go to the movies.

Do you ever smoke cigarettes?
    Yes, I sometimes/often smoke a cigarette.
    No, I never smoke.

Do you wear jeans to work?
    Yes, I always/often/usually wear jeans to work.
    No, I never wear jeans to work.

    I _____ wear jeans to work on Friday.

Review rule Review the examples from Day 36 if necessary. Frequency words come BEFORE an action verb, but AFTER the verb "to be."

Mrs. Campbell always drinks coffee in class.
Mrs. Campbell is always nice to students.

Juan never comes to class on time.
Juan is never on time.

With "to be"

Write the models on the board.

Are you ever tired in my class?

Yes, I am.
I'm _____ tired in your class.
   always
   usually
   often
   sometimes

No, I'm not.
I'm _____ tired in your class.
   never
   rarely

Are you ever hungry at night?

I am _____hungry at night.
   always
   often
   usually
   sometimes

I am _____hungry at night.
   never
   rarely

Are you ever bored at work?
Are you ever angry at a supermarket?
Are you ever sad at movies?

Frequency Words - Written practice To practice with both types of verb. See **references, Day 36. Also GrammarWork, p. 104 (with seasons and weather).**

5. IF TIME, start the next jazz chant. (See Day 38.)

165

Day 38

Vocabulary

No vocabulary homework today

Agenda

1. Opening routine
2. Location words #3 - review location words group 3, use flashcards
   Collect homework, give quiz (sentences attached to Day 36)
3. Frequency words - oral practice - jazz chant "On the Rocks"
   HOMEWORK - copy jazz chant 1-3X
4. Frequency words - written practice - continue
5. Directions - reading and practice
6. Party flyer - read model in text or teacher-made example, explain
   Make a flyer - pairs, small groups, or alone
   HOMEWORK - finish party flyer

IF TIME

7. Share party invitation with whole class or small group

Stuff

1. Copies of list of location words by difficulty
2. Flashcards of location words (prepositions) from list given out Day 35
3. Sample of teacher-made party flyer for teacher's birthday party
4. Blank paper and colored pencils or crayons for party flyers

Lesson Plan

1. Opening Routine

2. Location Words - Review Practice group 3 location words. Give quiz on group #3 by dictating sentences from list attached to Day 36.

3. Frequency Words - Oral practice - Jazz chant Use "On the Rocks," if available. (For practice procedure, see Day 22.) Make sure everyone is pronouncing the S on the end of present simple verbs.

HOMEWORK is to copy the jazz chant 1-3 times for 1-3 points, minimum 1 time.

4. Frequency Words - Written practice Continue. See **references, Day 36 and Day 37.**

5. Directions - Reading and practices Use **Side by Side, Book 2, pp. 68-69** for party flyer sample (difficult) and listening practice. Directions practice, **Side by Side, Book 2, pp. 62-67.**

6. Party Flyer - Explain and create   Review an example in a text or look at the teacher's birthday party flyer. In pairs, small groups, or alone, each person makes a party flyer. Include a reason for the party, date, time, address, and name of the host. Also include a small map with directions from the nearest big street or highway. Students check each other's flyers against the list on the board and make sure all necessary information is there. Explain RSVP, BYOB, and "potluck" to the class. Sample party information, see above, #5.

Write on board.

Name of host
Reason for party
BYOB or potluck?

Date
Time
RSVP phone number or email
Address

Directions to house
Map

HOMEWORK is to complete the party flyer if it's not finished in class.

IF TIME

Party Flyer - Speech   When most students are finished, ask volunteers to show their party invitations to the whole class or have students share them in small groups. Explain the occasion, give information about the party, and give general directions to the location. They shouldn't report numbers, such as phone numbers or times.

Day 39

Vocabulary

No vocabulary homework. There is spelling work in class.

Agenda

1. Opening routine
2. Repeat jazz chant "On the Rocks" 1-2X, collect homework of chant copies
3. Present simple - more spelling rules - introduce (chart attached)
     Written practice
4. Pronunciation - short O (list attached), consonant-vowel-consonant rule review
5. Locations - if not already done, volunteers give short speeches with information from their party invitation flyer to whole class or small groups. Collect flyers.
6. Locations and directions - written practice - another written practice or map activity

Stuff

1. Copies or projectable file of difficult verb spelling rules
2. Copies or projectable file of list of short O words

Lesson Plan

1. Opening Routine

2. Frequency Words with Jazz Chant Repeat "On the Rocks" a few times. This is a great jazz chant, especially for adults. Collect homework of chant (copied 1-3 times).

3. Present Simple - Spelling rules - Introduce Write or project the attached chart of present simple spelling rules. Review the rules.

Present Simple - More spelling rules - Written Do exercises on with difficult spelling. **GrammarWork, p. 83.** For pronunciation and review of spelling, **Side by Side, p. 101; Practical English, p. 142 (bottom); Writing Practical English, p. 108 (bottom).**

4. Pronunciation - Short O Sound Introduce the sample words with short O sound. (See list attached.) It sounds like "ah" which in other languages might be spelled with the letter A. Review rule that Consonant-Vowel-Consonant and Vowel-Consonant = short O. Use the #1#2 technique to compare short O with short A in some common words on the list.

5. Location Words and Places If not done, students give short speeches with information from their party invitation flyer to the whole class or small groups.

6. Locations and directions - Written practice - Optional Do another written practice or map activity. See **references, Day 34 and Day 35.**

Present Simple Spelling Rules

Verbs ending in consonant or in E - Add S

leaves
closes
eats
runs

Verbs ending in CH, SH, S, SS, X - Add ES

watches
kisses
relaxes

Verbs ending in consonant plus Y - Change Y to I and add ES

studies
tries

Verbs ending in vowel plus Y - Just add S

plays
says

Short O = Ah!

on

hot

not

lot

mop

pop

top

cop

hop

jog

Mom

on top of

pot

parking lot

The hot pot is on top of the stove.
There are not a lot of joggers in the parking lot.

"Minimal Pairs" = Two words exactly the same except for one sound. Use the #1#2 game to practice the difference between each pair of words. Define the words that students don't remember or know.

      on - an
      hot - hat
      mop - map
      top - tap
      cop - cap
      pot - pat

Day 40

Vocabulary

nice
hot
warm
cold
cool
sun - sunny
wind - windy
rain - rainy - raining
snow - snowy - snowing
ice - freezing

Agenda

1. Opening routine
2. Weather #1 - introduce with pictures, questions, acting
        Oral practice - sentences
        Review - flashcards
        HOMEWORK - copy words 15X, quiz
3. Frequency words - review rule, written practice
4. Pronunciation - short U sound (attached list)
5. LAST 1/2 HOUR - BINGO - replace "BINGO" with "WACKY"

Stuff

1. Pictures and flashcards for weather words
2. Copies or projectable file of short U word list
3. Bingo game and rewards

Lesson Plan

1. Opening Routine - Weather For the rest of the course, review weather by writing a 1-sentence weather report with the agenda and discussing it as part of the opening routine, especially when local weather changes.

        It's cloudy today.
        What's the weather like today?
        It's nice outside.

2. Weather #1 - Introduce Use pictures, questions, and acting. Review with flashcards and assign homework after the oral practice.

Weather - Oral practice Write the sentences on the board and repeat them in pairs, so that the ideas "a lot of sun" and "sunny" are said together.

There's a lot of sun today.   It's sunny today.
There's a lot of wind today.   It's windy today.
There's a lot of rain today.   It's rainy today.
There's a lot of snow today.   It's snowy today.
It's very, very cold out there. It's freezing out there.

Weather - Oral practice #2 The teacher says the first sentence and students respond with the second sentence. Explain that when you say, "It IS sunny," you are agreeing with the first sentence. Students should repeat the second list several times after the teacher before doing the entire practice.

There's a lot of sun today.   It IS sunny.
There's a lot of wind today.   It IS windy.
There's a lot of rain today.   It IS rainy.
There's a lot of snow today.   It IS snowy.
It's very, very cold out there. It IS freezing out there.

Review all of the weather words with flashcards. HOMEWORK is to copy the words 15X for the quiz tomorrow.

3. Frequency Words - Review rule - Optional Sometimes you will hear the frequency word before the verb "to be," although it is much more common for the frequency word to come after it. However, the frequency word never comes after the action word. Review this rule on the board if you are hearing errors.

She is always late. (correct)
She always is late. (Sometimes you hear this.)
She always comes late. (correct)
She comes always late. (never correct)

Frequency Words - Written practice For exercises with weather and seasonal clothing, **GrammarWork, pp. 104-105.** Continue written pages with "to be" and location of frequency words.

4. Pronunciation - Short U Sound - Oral practice Repeat the attached list. Explain the meanings of unknown words briefly. Modify the #1#2 game to a #1#2#3 game to compare words with 3 different vowel sounds.

5. LAST 1/2 HOUR - BINGO Replace the title of "BINGO" with "WACKY" to practice new consonants. Have the students place a piece of paper with the letters W A C K Y over the B I N G O on their Bingo game boards and use those letters when calling the numbers. The idea is to practice letters other than just B I N G O.

Short U Sound

Show students how to make this sound by letting their jaw drop and saying "Uh. . ."

Cartoon sounds: "Uh. . .Duh. . .Yup!"

bug
but
cut
hut
mud

nut
butter
peanut butter

sub - when your teacher is absent

tub (bathtub)
duck
I have a rubber ducky in my bathtub.

dull (opposite of sharp)
dumb
dump
dust
judge
jump
gas pump
tummy
yummy

Compare the following words with only one vowel changed.

mud - mad
nut - not
bug - bag - bog
hut - hat - hot

Use the #1#2 game (and now the #1#2#3 game) to practice the different vowel sounds in the above words.

Day 41

Vocabulary

sandals
shorts
bathing suit
sunglasses

rain boots
rubber boots
raincoat
umbrella

scarf
wool hat
wool sweater
heavy jacket
coat

Agenda

1. Opening routine - today's weather
2. Weather #1 - review - pictures, questions, acting, flashcards
      Collect homework, quiz
Weather #2 - introduce with pictures, questions, acting
      Oral practice with sentences
      Flashcard review
      HOMEWORK - copy 15X, quiz
3. Weather - written practice
4. Direction words - introduce east, west, etc. using classroom maps
      Oral practice
5. Verb List - Harder Verbs - review or introduction of more difficult verbs (list attached)

Stuff

1. Pictures and flashcards for weather words
2. Large classroom maps with world, U.S., your state, your town
3. Copies of list of more difficult verbs

Lesson Plan

1. Opening Routine Talk about recent changes in local weather.

2. Weather #1 - Review Use pictures, questions, and flashcards. Collect homework and give the quiz.

Weather #2 - Introduce Use pictures and questions to talk about the vocabulary. Discuss clothes worn or never worn by the class. Define "wool" and "coat."

Weather - Oral practice Write the model on the board.

When it's _____, I wear (a) _____.

> When it's hot, I wear sandals.
> When it's hot, I wear a hat.
> When it's raining, I wear a raincoat.
> When it's raining, I take an umbrella.

Practice all of the vocabulary words, but take most of the examples from your local weather. Review with flashcards. HOMEWORK is to copy the words 15X for a quiz.

3. Weather - Written practice Write about weather and activities or weather and clothing. **GrammarWork, pp. 67, 104-105; Lifeskills, pp. 25-26 OR Skill Sharpeners, pp. 24, 102-103; Side by Side, pp. 40-41, 42-43, 113.**

4. Direction Words - Map - Introduce Write "north," "south," "east," and "west" on the board. Using a U.S. or world map, make sentences and questions with the words. Start with your class location. Help students by pointing to directions and locations on the maps as you practice.

> Mexico is south of Los Angeles. San Francisco is north of Los Angeles.
> What is west of Los Angeles? The Pacific Ocean is west of L.A.
> What is east of Los Angeles? How about Las Vegas? Is it east or west?
> Is Guatemala north or south of L.A.?
> If I want to go to New York, which way do I go? North, south, east, or west?
> What about Canada?
>
> Where is the hot weather? (to the south)
> Where is the cold weather? (to the north)

Ask students to show their countries on the world map and say which direction they are in.

Direction Words - Oral practice Use **Skill Sharpeners, p. 85 (time zones, directions).**

5. Verb List - Harder Verbs - Review or introduction Pass out copies of the attached verb list for student notebooks. These are verbs the class has already seen in texts or worksheets. Ask students to mimic or explain each action. Work in groups to put a check next to the verbs they know well. Write the remaining verbs on a poster sheet and use that list to create vocabulary quizzes for the next day without one, such as Day 48.

Verb List - Harder Verbs

bake
cook
plant
wash the car
wash clothes
iron clothes
clean

try
relax
rest

play guitar
skate
park the car

like
love
hate

eat out

take the bus
miss the bus

chase
catch a ball
catch a cold
exercise

enjoy
hang around
sit around

call
visit
stay

turn on
turn off

pick
choose (vs. shoes)
ask a question
answer a question
ask for

learn
pass
pass up (papers)
raise your hand

deliver
add

take a walk
take a break
take a vacation

give a party
have a party
throw a party

water the plants
water the grass
cut the grass
mow the lawn

Day 42

Vocabulary

weather
temperature

sun - sunny

clouds - cloudy
dark

rain - rainy - raining
wet

snow - snowy - snowing
wind - windy
blowing

fog - foggy
smog - smoggy

Agenda

1. Opening routine - today's weather
2. Weather #2 - review with pictures, flashcards
        Collect homework, give quiz
Weather words #3 - introduce with pictures, acting, drawings, examples
        Explain the different word forms with chart
        Review with flashcards
        HOMEWORK - Copy 15X all words, quiz tomorrow, choose 12 most relevant words
3. Weather - written practice - continue
        Oral practice with clothes - yes or no
        Oral practice - talk about weather in home countries - optional
4. Pronunciation - long vowels vs. short vowels (list attached)
        Review rule CVC = short
        Introduce rule CVC + e = long with pairs, lots of examples

Stuff

1. Pictures for weather and weather clothing
2. Flashcards for weather and weather clothing
3. Copies or projectable file of the attached pronunciation list of CVC+e words
4. Projectable file of the weather words chart

Lesson Plan

1. Opening Routine Include today's weather.

2. Weather #2 Review weather words #2 with pictures, drawings, acting, and flashcards. Talk briefly about the weather and seasons in your current location. Collect homework and do the quiz.

Weather #3 - Introduce Use pictures, gestures, drawings, words, examples. Use pictures only, **Practical English, pp. 188-189. Also Side by Side, p. 54 (listening).**

Many students will be unclear on the difference between rainy and raining, snowy and snowing, etc. Write on board or project the chart below. Briefly define "noun," "adjective," and "verb." After defining the words, which they will see in their texts and written practices, you can edit the quiz list to leave out rainy, snowy, blowing, or other words which aren't common in your area. Test the class only on words which they will need to use a lot.

Noun	**Adjective**	**Verb**
(thing)	(tells what something is like)	(action)
	Comes before a noun	Subject is "It"
		Changes like other verbs
I hear rain.	This is a very rainy day!	Is it raining right now?
rain	rainy or wet	raining
snow	snowy	snowing
wind	windy	(blowing)
sun	sunny	
cloud - clouds	cloudy	
fog	foggy	
smog	smoggy	

HOMEWORK - Students should copy all of the words 15X, but give the quiz tomorrow on only about 12 of them. Don't use more than one form of each word. For instance, choose snow, snowing, or snowy.

Review with flashcards the words you choose for the quiz.

3. Weather - Written practice Continue practice on weather, activities, clothes, and seasons. Include activities with frequency words. See **references, Day 41.**

Weather - Oral practice Say yes or no. You could also do this in writing.

Do you wear rain boots with a bathing suit? NO
Do you wear sandals with a heavy coat? NO
Do you wear socks with sandals? NO (Or YES in Los Angeles, Hawaii, and Australia!)
Do you wear shorts with sunglasses? YES
Do you wear rain boots with a raincoat? YES
Do you wear a scarf with a heavy coat? YES
Do you wear a wool sweater when it's freezing? YES
Do you wear a bathing suit when it's raining? NO
Do you wear shorts when it's cold? NO
Do you wear a heavy coat when it's sunny? NO (You may have to explain to students in warm states that "coat" is a very long jacket.)
Do you wear a scarf and a wool hat when it's windy? YES

Weather - Oral practice (more difficult) - Optional This might be too difficult for your students. Talk about weather in their home countries. Try to get them to use frequency words. Ask questions.

Is it ever cold in your country? Is it cold in the summer or in the winter?
Is it usually rainy in Los Angeles? When is it rainy? Is it raining right now?

Try to get students to make a complete sentence. "In my country, _____."
> It's usually cold.
> It's never cold.
> It's cool and rainy in the winter.

4. Pronunciation - Short vowels vs. long vowels with E at end - Introduce Review the rule that CVC and VC = short. The new rule says, "But when a word ends in E, the vowel becomes long." Give lots of examples. Use the attached sheet to practice words with the pattern Consonant-Vowel-Consonant-Final E, or CVCe.

If students ask why words with the vowel E in the middle are not on the list, explain that E is different because usually the E sound is written with 2 vowels together. It's very unlikely that anyone will ask the question.

Short vowels vs. long vowels with E at end

at vs. ate
hat vs. hate
can vs. cane
cap vs. cape
tap vs. tape
app vs. ape
man vs. mane

bit vs. bite
sit vs. site
tip vs. type (Note the Y.)

hop vs. hope
mop vs. mope
not vs. note
Pop vs. Pope

cut vs. cute
hug vs. huge
fun vs. June

Pronounce the following words: bat, gate, mat, tape, kite, kit, biker, wife, bomb, hope, top, sock, but, dune, nuts, gun, June.

Use the #1#2 game to compare the following pairs:

cap - cape
app - ape
bit - bite
hop - hope
cut - cute

Day 43

Vocabulary

season
fall
autumn
winter
spring
summer

sky
clear
air
freeze
freezing
ice
icy

flowers
picnic
beach

NOT ON QUIZ
go on vacation
take a vacation
need a vacation (no s on vacation)

Agenda

1. Opening routine - today's weather
2. Weather #3 - review weather #3 - pictures and flashcards
    Collect homework, do quiz
Weather #4 - introduce seasons - pictures
    Oral practice with all words
    HOMEWORK - copy 15X, quiz (10-12 words)
3. Weather - with have, a lot of, much - introduce rule, oral practice
4. East/west - written practice
5. Capital letters - written practice - 1 page - finish for HOMEWORK
6. Weather and vacations - reading or dialog - start

Stuff

1. Flashcards divided into quiz words and homework words
2. Pictures showing seasons, seasonal activities and sports
3. Capital letter practice sheets - copies that students can write on to change small letters to capitals

Lesson Plan

1. Opening Routine Talk about today's weather and possible changes.

2. Weather #3 - Review Use pictures and flashcards to review. Collect homework and do the quiz.

Weather #4 - Introduce seasons Practice words with pictures and flashcards, especially words which apply to your location. HOMEWORK is to copy words 15X for the quiz. Edit the word list to the 10-12 words best for your location.

Point out that "vacation" has no S. Also, if necessary, tell students that in American English, "holiday" means a special non-work day like Christmas, not a summer vacation.

3. Weather - Have/a lot of/much - Oral practice Introduce the use of "much." The rule is to use "much" only for negatives and questions with words that you can't count and which do not end in S, such as sun, rain, snow, and fog. Don't teach all the rules of "much" vs. "many" here. It's too complicated. Simply practice the pattern. Only mention the rule if someone tries to use "much" in a positive sentence.

Students hear and repeat all of the examples.

> Los Angeles has a lot of sun.
> Does it have much rain?
> No, it doesn't have much rain.

> Seattle has a lot of rain.
> Does it have much snow?
> It has some snow, but it doesn't have much.

> San Francisco has a lot of rain.
> It has a lot of wind.
> It has a lot of fog.
> It doesn't have much ice or snow.

> Las Vegas has a lot of sun.
> It doesn't have much rain.
> It doesn't have much snow.

> How about New York City? It has a lot of rain.
> It has a lot of snow and ice.
> It has a lot of wind.

Weather - Have/a lot of/much - Oral practice - Optional Students follow the patterns above to make sentences describing their home city. Help them or have them repeat complete sentences after you if necessary. It may be too difficult for them.

4. East/west - Written practice See **Skill Sharpeners, pp. 85, 34; Lifeskills, pp. 86-87.**

5. Capital Letters - Introduce Write on the board a list of common nouns vs. proper nouns. Do not ask students to remember this terminology.

Common Noun (general)	**Proper Noun** (specific)
girl	Maria
weekday	Monday
weekend	Saturday and Sunday
month	December
the new year	New Year's Day
school	Carver High School
city	Seattle
lake	Great Salt Lake
state	California
the president	President Barack Obama
my mother	Mom
a street	Milton Avenue

Tell students that a common noun is a general thing and a proper noun is the name of a person, place, or thing. You give one person, place, or thing a name with a capital letter. Proper nouns don't need "a" or "the" because they are names.

Capital Letters - Written practice Give students several short paragraphs or a series of sentences where they have to change incorrect small letters into capitals, or use **Lifeskills, p. 18; Skill Sharpeners, p. 40.** If many students have trouble making capital letters, use **Access, pp. 51-52, 124.** If the exercises for practicing capitals are long, students can finish for HOMEWORK, or you can spread the exercises over several days.

6. Weather and Vacations - Reading or dialog practice Read about vacations and weather. **Side by Side, pp. 40-41 (dialog), 42-43 (reading a letter).**

Day 44

Vocabulary

Who
What
When
Where
Why
How
How much
How many
How old

Agenda

1. Opening routine - today's weather
2. Weather #4 - review with pictures, flashcards, collect homework, quiz
3. Capital letters - review with capital/no capital
    Written practice - finish in class or check homework
4. Weather and vacations - written practice - finish
5. WH question words - review - to be/present simple/present continuous
    HOMEWORK - copy 15X and quiz tomorrow - optional
6. Pronunciation of long A sound with 2 letters (list attached)

Stuff

1. Pictures and flashcards for quiz words on weather
2. Capital letter practice sheets (See Day 43.)
3. Flashcards of WH question words - who, what, when, where, why, how, how much, how old (See Day 21.)
4. Copies or projectable file of the list of long A sound words (attached)

Lesson Plan

1. Opening Routine Talk about weather in your town.

2. Weather #4 Review with pictures and flashcards. Collect homework and do the quiz.

3. Capital Letters - Review Using examples from Day 43, read a list of common and proper nouns to class in mixed order. Students say, "Capital letter" or "No capital letter." Add some new examples.

a cup	the World Cup
the doctor	Dr. Crawford
the pope	Pope Francis
a city	New York City

Capital Letters - Written practice Continue, finish in class, or check homework.

4. Weather and Vacations - Reading or dialog Begin or continue reading about vacations and weather. See **references, Day 43. Also (with was/were) Practical English, pp. 188-191 and p. 250; New American Streamline Departures, p. 43.** If you use exercises with "was" and "were," briefly explain that they are the past forms of "to be."

5. WH Question Words - Review and oral practice List WH question words on the board and review. Explain the ones students don't remember with examples. Ask more questions.

Who is your English teacher?
Who is your math teacher?
What is this? (Hold up a common object.)

When is (Thanksgiving, Christmas, New Year's Day, Valentine's Day, etc.)?
When is class finished?
Where is Los Angeles?

Why am I drinking coffee?
Why are you studying English?

How many students are in this class?
How much is a pair of sneakers?
How old are you?
How old is your (mother, husband, brother, baby)

What is the homework page?
What do you have in your bag?
What are you looking at?
What are you doing?

When do you go to bed?
When do you leave for school?
Where does your mom work?
Where is the soccer game?

How do you come to school, in a car or in the bus?
How do you write - with a pen or a pencil?
How many children do you have?
How much does a hamburger cost at McDonald's?

WH Question Words - Quiz - Optional Review with flashcards. HOMEWORK is to copy the words 15X for an optional quiz. Or, you can give an ungraded quiz and check it in class.

6. Pronunciation of Long A Sound with 2 Letters Practice the sounds with the attached list. Explain that the sound is a single long "ay," like "day," not "ah-ee."

Long A Sound with 2 Letters

AI

chair
hair
air
stairs
pair
fair (street fair)
sailboat
train
railroad
tail
braid
rain
paint
pail
jail
wait

AY

tray
gray
play
today
May
okay
stay
away

EI

neighbor
eight
weigh
weight

EY

Hey!
They

EA

Great!
break
steak
tear (Pretend to rip paper.)
wear
pear
bear (animal)

Today is a great day to stay away from school!

Our neighbor is painting his house gray.

Does she have her hair in braids or a pony tail? (Illustrate these hairstyles on the board.)

Saturday they went sailing in the rain.

Day 45

Vocabulary

family
mother
father
sister
brother
husband
wife
child, children
kid
son
daughter

NOT FOR QUIZ
his
her
their

Agenda

1. Opening routine
2. WH question words - review with flashcards, collect homework, quiz
3. Yes/No and WH questions - review the difference - optional
    Review the difference - more oral practice
4. WH questions with do/does - written practice
5. Yes/No and WH questions - review question form - optional
6. Yes/No and WH questions with do/does - review question form - optional
7. Family #1 - introduce nuclear family only, with pictures, words "his," "her," "their," and
    family tree with labels
    Written practice
    Oral practice
    HOMEWORK - copy 20X, quiz
8. Family #1 - possessives - review - optional
9. LAST 1/2 HOUR (maximum) - BINGO - Title is "FRESH"

Stuff

1. Flashcards of WH question words - Who, what, when, where, why, how, how much, how
    old (See Day 21.)
2. Copies or projectable file of family tree of nuclear family (parents and children only)
3. Pictures of families and flashcards of family vocabulary, nuclear family only
4. Bingo game and rewards

Lesson Plan

1. Opening Routine

2. WH Question Words - Review Use flashcards to review. Collect homework and do quiz if assigned.

3. Yes/No and WH Questions - Review the difference - Optional Compare these question forms. Write two lists on the board.

YES/NO	WH
Are you my teacher?	Who is my teacher?
Is this a pen?	What is this?
Are we in class now?	Where are we?
Is English class at 8:00?	When is English class?
Are we in school?	Where are we?
Are you studying English?	Why are you studying English?
Is this pencil $1.00?	How much is this pencil?
Are you 16?	How old are you?

Students answer all of the questions, first Yes/No questions with "yes" or "no" and then WH questions with information. Then you ask, "Who is my teacher?" and give an answer, "Yes." They see that this doesn't make sense. Then you tell them that Yes/No questions have an answer of "yes"' or "no" but that WH questions need information in the answer. Give more examples if necessary. Then circle all of the WH words in column 2 individually. Ask students, "Where are all of the WH words?" They should see that the WH words are all at the beginning of the sentence or that they are the first words in the sentence. Then point out that after the circled WH words, the subject and verb are reversed.

Yes/No and WH Questions - Review the difference - More oral practice
Say, "Answer with a short answer OR information. WH questions need information."

Do you live here?
Where do you live?

Do you have a pet?
What do you have?
How many pets do you have?

Do you need a pencil?
What do you need?

Is it 10:00?
What time is it?

Do we go home at 10:00?
When do we go home?

Is it Wednesday?
What day is it?

Are you going home at 3:00?
When are you going home?

Is your name Juan?
What is your name?

Is Maria here?
Where is Maria?

Are we studying Spanish now?
What are we studying?

4. WH Questions with do/does - Written practice See GrammarWork, pp. 100 and 101; Side by Side, pp. 100, 83-84; Practical English, pp. 137-139. For questions after readings, **Composition Practice, Book 1, pp. 12 and 22.**

5. Yes/No and WH Questions - Review question form - Optional

Write these questions and answers on the board. Review the difference between Yes/No answers and information answers.

Are you my teacher?	Yes, I am.
Who is my teacher?	Your teacher is Mrs. Lockwood.
Are we in Room 5?	Yes, we are.
Where are we?	We are in Room 5.

Write on the board,

You are my teacher.	INFORMATION
Are you my teacher?	QUESTION

We are in Room 5.	INFORMATION
Are we in Room 5?	QUESTION

Review the rule that you flip the verb and the person for a Yes/No question. (Use fingers reversed or crossed. See Day 7.) Give more examples if necessary.

Go on to the WH questions. Write the sentences on the board with space in between.

My teacher is who?

Who is my teacher?

We are where?

Where are we?

Circle the WH words and draw arrows to show how they move to the beginning of the questions. Then draw arrows between "my teacher," "is," "we," and "are" to show that the subjects and verbs in the questions are now reversed.

Go back to the 4 sentences in your first examples. Point out to the class that the short answers after the Yes/No questions are in regular sentence order. Point out that the answers to the WH questions are also in regular order.

6. Yes/No and WH Questions with do/does - Review - Optional Review question words with "do" and "does." Write on the board.

She lives in Los Angeles.

Does she live in Los Angeles?   Yes/No question
Where does she live?   WH question

Pointing to the sentence, ask students what they need to make the question. Ask them what happens to the "s" in lives when they add "does." Write "does" before "she lives" and then X out the S on "lives." Recopy the sentence correctly. Make sure to include the question mark.

(Does) She liveX in Los Angeles.
Does she live in Los Angeles?

Ask students for the short answers and add them to the board.

Yes, she does.
No, she does not.
No, she doesn't.

To make a WH question, the helper word is added after moving the WH word to the front. Write on the board.

She lives in Los Angeles.

190

Ask the class, "What is the WH question word for this sentence?" They should answer that it is "where." Draw a line through "in Los Angeles" and write the word "Where?" over it.

She lives where

Draw a circle around "where" and draw an arrow from "where" to the beginning of the sentence. Write "where" before "She."

Now you have

where she lives

Ask students what you need to do next. They should tell you that you need to reverse the subject and the verb. Write on the board.

where lives she?

Ask, "Is this okay?" They should answer that it is not okay. Erase it.

Point to the original sentence and ask, "What is the helper verb for she lives?" Hopefully someone will answer that the helper verb is "does."

Say, "That's correct! You have the helper word 'does' in your brain (tap your forehead significantly) and you use it to reverse the subject and the verb." Flip your fingers to show that the 2 words reverse order. Write on the board as follows.

where she lives
   does she

where + does she + live

Add a capital letter and a question mark and rewrite the question. Write the answer in regular sentence order. Circle "Where" and draw an arrow to show that the answer to "where?" returns to the end of the sentence.

Where does she live?
       She lives in Los Angeles.

Even if students understand this at the time you explain it, they will probably not make these questions correctly in beginning ESL. This grammar has to be practiced for a long time. You can include it in multiple-choice tests, but don't be frustrated if you hear students asking, "Where she lives?" Just model the correct answer for them.

7. Family #1 - Introduce To introduce the family vocabulary, use **Skill Sharpeners, p. 53; Lifeskills, p. 41; Side by Side, pp. 53 and 45; GrammarWork, p. 22.** Or, explain the family words with pictures. Then draw on the board a family tree with two parents and only one boy and one girl.

Pointing to the man and the woman, say,

> He is the father. She is the mother.
> She is the wife. He is the husband.

Pointing to the boy and the parents or parent, say, "He is the son."

Indicating the girl and the parents or parent, say, "She is the daughter."

Indicating the boy and the girl, say, "He is a brother. She is a sister."

Avoid using "his," "her," and "their" in this exercise. This will confuse Spanish speakers, where the possessive word "her" would be used with female words such as "mother" and "sister," while the possessive word "his" would be required for male words like "son" and "brother." (See below in this lesson plan for a review of this problem.)

Pointing to the boy and the girl, say, "He is a child. She is a child. Those are the children."

Say, "They are the kids. He is a kid. She is a kid. The family has two children. How many kids are in the family?"

Possible answers are,

> They have two kids.
> They have two children.
> They have one son and one daughter.

Add one more boy and two more girls to the graph on the board, for a total of five children. Ask, "How many kids do they have?"

The answer is, "They have five."

Ask and answer. "How many children do they have? They have five children."

(Ask a trick question.) Ask, "How many sons do they have?"

(Spanish speakers often answer, "Five.") "No, not five. In English, sons are only boys. You have to say that the family has two sons and three daughters."

You now have a picture of two boys and three girls on the board. Point to one girl and ask, "How many brothers does she have?"

Students should answer, "Two (the two boys)." Spanish speakers may think the answer is four, because in Spanish "brothers" can mean all the siblings.

Ask, "How many sisters does she have?" The answer is two.

Ask, "How many brothers are in the family?" Two. The girls are sisters.

Ask, "How many brothers and sisters does she have?" She has four, two brothers and two sisters.

Family #1 - Written practice See **references above and in Day 46.** For a good listening practice, also see **Access, p. 58.**

Family #1 - Oral practice Ask class members these questions.

> How many children do you have?
> How many sons? How many daughters?

If Spanish speakers say, "I have four sons," ask how many are boys and how many are girls. Explain again if necessary that they can say, "I have four children," or "I have two sons and two daughters."

Practice with more questions, but limit them to today's vocabulary.

> Is this your wife?
> Is that your son?
> Who do you live with? (I live with my mother.) Where is your mother right now?
> Do your children live with you? Where do your kids live?
> Do you come from a big family?
> How many sisters and brothers do you have? Where are your sisters now?
> Does your brother live here? Where does he live?

You can put students into small groups to ask each other these questions. In that case, write sample questions on the board to help them.

HOMEWORK is to copy the words 20X for a quiz.

8. Family #1 - Possessives - Review - Optional Students sometimes match possessives to the object owned instead of the owner. This is a difficult point. You could practice the rule only orally now, or save it for a later unit as review. Pointing to the man and the woman, say,

She is his wife. He is her husband.
He is their father. She is their mother.

Pointing to the boy, indicate the parents together and then point to each parent individually. Say, "He is their son. He is his son. He is her son."

Pointing to the girl, indicate the parents together and then each parent individually. Say, "She is their daughter. She is his daughter. She is her daughter."

Pointing to the boy, say, "He is her brother."

Pointing to the girl, say, "She is his sister."

Pointing to both parents and both children, say,

> These are their children.
> Those are their kids.
> He is their kid.
> She is their kid.

9. LAST 15-30 MINUTES - BINGO For the title, use "FRESH."

Vocabulary

aunt
uncle
cousin
parents (only father and mother)
relatives (the whole family)
grandmother
grandfather
grandparents
niece
nephew

Agenda

1. Opening routine
2. Family #1 - review nuclear family words with pictures, family tree, flashcards
      Collect homework, do quiz
Family - written practice - reading, dialog, or written exercise
Family #2 - introduce extended family words with pictures, family tree, questions in context,
      definitions using English
      Review with flashcards
      HOMEWORK - copy 20X and quiz
Family - written practice
3. Was/were - introduce
      Written practice with weather
4. Family #2 - review - oral practice - optional - teacher's family tree

Stuff

1. Pictures and flashcards of family list #2
2. Two family tree graphs including grandparents and nieces and nephews. See **Lifeskills, pp. 42 and 43; Skill Sharpeners, p. 54; Side by Side, p. 53.**
3. Copies or projectable file of teacher's own family tree. Don't show more than 4 in each category, for example, only 2 brothers, 2 sisters, 2 aunts, 2 uncles. If the gender of the names is not obvious, change them or write "girl," or "boy," after the name. See examples in recommended texts above. You should have one filled in with names only and the same one with no names or relationships. For easier exercises, you can also have one with both names and relationships filled in.

Lesson Plan

1. Opening Routine

2. Family #1 - Review Review family words with pictures, family tree, and flashcards. Collect homework and do the quiz.

Family - Written practice Do a reading or dialog and written exercises. See **references, Day 45** or use **Practical English, pp. 94-95 top.**

Family #2 - Introduce Explain members of the extended family with pictures, a family tree, questions in context, and definitions using English. HOMEWORK is to copy the words 20X for a quiz. Review for quiz with flashcards now or at the very end of class.

Family - Written practice Do a reading, dialog, or written exercise. Copy reading or dialog in class when finished. **Lifeskills, p. 42; Skill Sharpeners, p. 54; Side by Side, pp. 45-48 and 50-53; GrammarWork, pp. 4-5, 42, 87.**

3. Was/were - Introduce If necessary to do the above pages, briefly explain that "was" and "were" are the past forms of "to be." Write on the board.

PRESENT	PAST
I am	I was
You are	You were
He is	He was
She is	She was
It is	It was
We are	We were
You (plural) are	You (all) were
They are	They were

Explain that "was" and "were" do not have short forms, but are pronounced "wz" and "wr" and do not have a lot of stress.

Note that past weather and past time are usually expressed with "was."

It's raining.
It was raining.

It's eight o'clock.
It was eight o'clock.

Was/were with Weather - Written practice Do a written page, or review with focus on "was" and "were." **Practical English, pp. 188-190, 250; New American Streamline Departures, p. 43.**

4. Family #2 - Review - Optional Students look at copies or a projection of your family tree with 4 generations. It should show names but no relationships. Ask students questions about your family using the graph. Explain "Jr." and "Sr." For example,

> Who is my grandfather?
> Who is his wife?
> How many brothers do I have?
> What are their names?
> Do I have any sisters? How many?
>
> Who are my nieces?
> Who are my nephews?
>
> Which family members are married?
> Which family members have children?
>
> Do I have any aunts or uncles?
> Who has more sisters and brothers, my mother or my father?

To make the practice easier, you can give them or show them your family tree with both names and relationships labeled.

Day 47

Vocabulary

stepfather
stepmother
stepsister
etc.

half sister
etc.

mother-in-law (Show them how to include the hyphen without spaces. See Day 3.)
brother-in-law
etc.

friend
girlfriend
boyfriend

Agenda

1. Opening routine
2. Family #2 - review for quiz with flashcards, family tree, pictures, text
        Collect homework, do quiz
Family #3 - introduce with family tree, questions in context, definitions
        HOMEWORK - copy 10X, quiz
        ADDITIONAL HOMEWORK - write names of relatives on blank family tree or list
        Oral practice - answer questions (attached list)
3. Family - written practice - continue
        Reading practice
4. Was/were - pronunciation - stress of was, were, wasn't, weren't
        Oral practice
        Oral practices - optional
        Written practice - questions, negatives, short answers

Stuff

1. Pictures, graphs, and flashcards of family words, sorted into the 3 vocabulary groups
2. Worksheets with blank graph of a general family tree. **Lifeskills, p. 43.**

Lesson Plan

1. Opening Routine

2. Family Words #2 - Review Go over the second group of family words for a quiz with pictures, flashcards, and a family tree. For pictures, **Side by Side, pp. 45, 53.** Collect homework and do the quiz.

Family Words #3 - Introduce Use the list below to help you explain these terms to the class. There will be confusion, because these terms mean different things in some other languages.

parents - Parents are your father and mother, and usually your stepmother and stepfather.
relatives - Everybody in your extended family is a relative.
stepfather - You don't say this unless it is important. "Step" means that the person is related because one of your parents married again. Maybe the new parent has children.
half sister, half brother - You don't say this unless it is important. "Half" means that you and the other person have one parent the same.
mother-in-law - She is your mother by the law (a marriage ceremony), not by blood. "In-law" means the person is related to you because you married their family member.
girlfriend - romantic or friendship
boyfriend - romantic relationship

HOMEWORK is to copy the words 10X for the quiz.

ADDITIONAL HOMEWORK - Students ask at home about the names of grandparents and other relatives. They make a list or fill out a blank family tree graph. If the person is deceased, they still include the name. If family members do not know the name, they put ? on the family tree. Tomorrow they will fill in their own graph with the information that they found out. There will be a limit of 3 names in each category. Give out copies of the blank graph if you think your students can fill it out at home. Make sure everyone understands it. If not, they can write the family member's name next to the word on their vocabulary list. **Lifeskills, p. 43** is a blank family tree.

Family Words #3 - Oral practice When students hear the questions or words from today's vocabulary, they write only names as answers. See attached questions. If they don't have a certain type of family member (for example, they don't have a stepfather), they write "none."

3. Family - Written practice - Continue See **references, Day 46.**

Family - Reading Do a dialog or story with a family situation. See **references, Day 46 and Side by Side, p. 54.**

4. Was/were - Pronunciation When doing the practices and going over the written work, remind the class that "was" and "were" in positive sentences and questions have very little stress. The negative forms and "was" and "were" in short answers are spoken more clearly.

Was/were - Oral practice - Continue Practice questions and negatives.

Were you here yesterday?
      Yes, I was. No, I wasn't.
      Yes, we were. No, we weren't.

Were we here last week?
      Yes, we were. No, we weren't.

Were they here last week?
      Yes, they were. No, they weren't.

Was he here yesterday?
      Yes, he was. No, he wasn't.

Was/were - Oral practice - Optional Show how the meaning of the sentence changes when you put emphasis on each word. Act out the emotions to show the meaning.

WAS he here yesterday?	(I don't believe you. OR I'm not sure.)
Was HE here yesterday?	(he, not she, we, or somebody else)
Was he HERE yesterday?	(I thought he wasn't here.)
Was he here YESTERDAY?	(I thought he was here on a different day.)

Was/were - Oral practice - Optional Students must give a short answer first. Then you try to get more information.

Is it sunny today?   Yes, it is.
Was it sunny yesterday?   No, it wasn't.
What was the weather like yesterday?   It was dark and cold.

Were you in the cafeteria at 12:30?   No, I wasn't.
Where were you at 12:30?   I was in the lunch area.
Who was there with you?   The girls from my math class were there.

Was/were - Written practice For practice with questions, negatives, and short answers, use **GrammarWork, pp. 114-118; Practical English, pp. 190C-193; Writing Practical English, pp. 133-138; Side by Side, p. 160; New American Streamline Departures, p. 42.**

Your Family - Oral Practice

Students listen to questions about their families and write only names to answer.

1. Mother's name

2. Father's name

3. Stepfather or stepmother

4. Brothers

5. Sisters

6. Stepbrothers or stepsisters

7. Grandparents who are alive now

8. Aunts on mother's side OR father's side

9. Uncles on mother's side OR father's side

10. How many aunts and uncles do you have total?

11. How many cousins do you have? (boys and girls)

12. Who is your favorite niece/nephew?

13. What name will you give your son?

14. What name will you give your daughter?

15. Who is your best friend?

16. Who is your girlfriend/boyfriend?

17. Which relatives live in your house now?

Day 48

Vocabulary

No vocabulary tonight. Or use less familiar verbs from the Day 41 list.

Agenda

1. Opening routine
2. Family #3 - review with flashcards, answer any questions
   Collect homework, quiz
3. Family - fill out blank family trees if not done for homework, as a class, pairs or group
   Oral practice - Students give information about 1 family member to class or group
   Written practice - finish family reading, dialogs, and exercises
4. Was/were - written practice - finish or do 1-2 pages more

IF TIME

5. Present continuous and present simple - written practice
6. Present continuous - spelling rules - review
   Written practice

Stuff

1. Pictures, family trees, and flashcards with family words
2. Worksheets with blank family tree

Lesson Plan

1. Opening Routine

2. Family Words #3 - Review Use flashcards to review family words #3. Answer any questions. Collect homework and give the quiz.

3. Family - Oral practice With homework (names of family members), students fill out their family trees in pairs, small groups, or as a class. Then as a class or in small groups, each student gives some information about a family members. Ask them questions.

> My sister is Alma.
> How old is she? Is she here in Los Angeles now? Is she married?

> My grandmother's name is Ana.
> Does she live with you? Where does she live?

Family - Written practice Finish family reading, dialogs, and written exercises. See **references, Day 45, Day 46, and Day 47.**

4. Was/were - Written practice Finish questions and negatives. See **references, Day 47.** When previewing and reviewing the written work, remind the class of stress rules. (See Day 46 and Day 47.)

IF TIME

5. Present Continuous - Written practice Continue with present continuous, present simple, or both. See **references, Day 29 and Day 49.**

6. Present Continuous - Spelling rules - Written practice Review spelling rules with written practices. **GrammarWork, p. 61; Lifeskills, p. 66; Skill Sharpeners, p. 59.**

Day 49

Vocabulary

salesperson
store clerk
cashier

waiter
waitress
server

custodian OR janitor
gardener

doctor
psychologist

teacher's aide

Agenda

1. Opening routine
2. Jobs - introduce - ask students about their jobs or family jobs
      Oral and written practice with job titles
Jobs #1 - pictures of workers at job sites - introduce and practice
      Pronounce 2-3X with flashcards to review
      HOMEWORK - copy 20X, quiz
3. Present simple - written practice - 1 or 2 pages about work routines
      Review written practice using short answers
      Reading practice
4. Present simple vs. present continuous - matching helper verb - oral practice
      Written practice (right now vs. every day)
5. Family - oral practice - "family opposites" quiz, go over in class
6. Family - guided composition - 2 family pictures with T- chart and paragraph
HOMEWORK - finish pictures

Stuff

1. Flashcards of family words
2. Pictures and flashcards of workers and job sites
3. Blank white paper for T- charts and composition - prefer 8 1/2 x 14

Lesson Plan

1. Opening Routine

2. Jobs - Introduce Ask students what jobs they or their family members do. Write the jobs on the board, including the workplaces.

Jobs - Introduce - Oral and written practice Remind students to use "a" or "an" with job titles. **New American Streamline Departures, p. 4B; GrammarWork, pp. 8-9; Writing Practical English, pp. 41-42; Lifeskills, pp. 64-65.**

Jobs #1 - Introduce Use pictures of workers at job sites. Say the names of jobs and work sites. Pronounce the vocabulary list several times and review it with flashcards. HOMEWORK is to copy the words 20X for a quiz.

3. Present Simple - Oral practice Ask questions about work routines with "do" and "does." **New American Streamline Departures, p. 34.**

Present Simple - Reading practice - Family jobs In **Skill Sharpeners, pp. 61, 66, 70; Lifeskills, p. 67.**

4. Present Simple vs. Continuous - Matching helper verb - Oral practice

When students have learned both present simple and present continuous, they start to mix up the two forms. Stress the helper verb when asking questions. Check their knowledge with the following questions.

Are you a student?	Yes, I am. (Not "Yes, I do.")
Am I your teacher?	Yes, you are.
Do I come to class every day?	Yes, you do.
Do you come to school on Wednesday?	Yes, I do. OR Yes, we do.
Are you in school now?	Yes, I am. OR Yes, we are.
Do you come here Thursday nights.?	No, we don't.
Are we studying English now?	Yes, we are.
Are we talking now?	Yes, we are.
Are we watching TV now?	No, we aren't.
Are you a teacher?	Yes, I am.
Do you work in a school?	Yes, I do.

If the students answer, "Yes, I do, " when they should have said, "Yes, I am," review the verb forms again. (See Day 29.) Repeat and show by correcting that they must answer with the same helper verb that is in the question. Continue to review the rule.

Does your dad (husband, brother, etc.) work?	Yes, he does.
Does your mom (wife, sister, aunt, etc.) work?	No, she doesn't.
Is she working now?	No, she isn't.
Is your dad working right now? (at 6:00 p.m.)	No, he isn't.
What is he doing?	He's eating.
Where does your dad work?	He works in San Diego.
Does he work in construction?	No, he doesn't.
Is your dad an auto mechanic?	No, he isn't.
What is he?	He's a doctor.
Is he a good doctor?	Yes, he is.
Does he work in a hospital?	Yes, he does.

NOTE: "What does your mom do?" means "What is your mom's job?" Avoid asking questions in this form. Students will be confused by the use of "do" twice in a sentence.

Present Simple vs. Present Continuous - More written practice - If not done before, **New American Streamline Departures, p. 37; Practical English, pp. l53-l54; Side by Side, pp. 112-113; Lifeskills, p. 65; Skill Sharpeners, pp. 64-65; GrammarWork, pp. 88-94.**

5. Family - Oral practice Do non-graded family opposites quiz. If you give the male word, they write the opposite (the female equivalent) and vice versa. For example, when you say "uncle," they write "aunt."

1. mother
2. grandfather
3. brother
4. aunt
5. daughter-in-law
6. nephew
7. stepson
8. cousin (trick question - same word)
9. wife
10. boyfriend
11. parent (trick question - same word)

Make sure to explain the trick questions when you review the answers.

6. Family - Writing practice - Guided composition With teacher help, students put pictures and words on a T-chart and use them to write a guided composition. (See attached instructions.) They can also finish the pictures for HOMEWORK and do the guided composition on Day 50.

Family - Guided Composition T-Chart

Draw the T-chart on the board for students to copy on unlined paper. They divide page into two parts with the names of two family members, one male and one female. For example,

My Brother Ramon   **My Aunt Sonia**

First, students draw a full-length picture under each title showing things typical of the person, like a beard or curly hair, running shoes, or a soccer ball. Second, they label the person's qualities with words like "tall." Some students will do this part better than others.

Do 2 "guided compositions." (This means that the teacher dictates the paragraph to help the students with structure.) Give or suggest a title. Then dictate the indent and margins. The teacher dictates sentences and students finish them with their own information. They should use their T-charts to help them with ideas and write on separate lined paper.

This is my _____. He is _____ years old. He goes to

_____ every day, and then he goes _____. He likes to wear

_____ and _____. His

favorite color is _____, and his favorite food is _____.

He has a _____ (friend, wife, son, etc.) named_____. He

is _____ (a nice guy, a good father, my favorite brother). I love my

_____ very much.

Do the second dictated paragraph with the female character. Be sure to say "she" and "her."

Day 50

Vocabulary

veterinarian (vet)

bartender
restaurant manager
cook
busser

computer technician
IT guy
(Geek Squad)
(Apple Genius)

bank teller
bank clerk
executive

housekeeper vs. housewife

Agenda

1. Opening routine
2. Jobs #1 - review - practice with pictures and flashcards
   Collect homework, do quiz
Jobs #2 - introduce, pronounce words several times
   Ask if anybody knows someone with these jobs.
   Review with flashcards
   HOMEWORK - copy 20X, quiz
3. Present simple vs. present continuous - oral practice with company and workplace pictures
   Correct/Incorrect quiz, correct in class
   More written practice - continue IF TIME
4. Family - guided compositions using T-chart pictures - begin or finish (See Day 49.)
   Collect pictures, charts, and paragraphs.
5. LAST 1/2 HOUR - BINGO or short grid game with CVC

Stuff

1. Pictures and flashcards of workers
2. Photos or advertisements with large company names - UPS, McDonald's, Walmart, Target, Macy's, Bank of America, etc. or pictures of workplaces
3. Bingo game and rewards

Lesson Plan

1. Opening Routine

2. Jobs #1 - Review Use pictures and flashcards. Collect homework and give the quiz.

Jobs #2 - Introduce Pronounce the vocabulary words several times. Ask if anybody knows someone with these jobs. If so, where do they work? What is the work at that job? Review with flashcards. HOMEWORK is to copy the words 20X for a quiz.

3. Present Simple vs. Present Continuous - Oral practice Use photos or advertisements with names of large, well-known companies or use pictures of workplaces. Follow the model.

Where does your sister/mom/husband work? What is his/her job?	He/she works at McDonald's. He cooks the food. He's a cashier. He takes the money. He's the manager.
Where does your husband/brother/dad work? What is his job there?	He works at the Walmart. He's the boss. He's a computer technician. He fixes the computers.

Present Simple vs. Continuous - Correct or Incorrect? You can use this as a class practice or as an ungraded quiz. Give the class copies or examples on the board of incorrect sentences like the ones below. Ask them to say "Correct" or "Incorrect." Tell them there is only 1 correct answer in the 10 sentences.

Go over the answers orally. Have students put a big check mark if their answer is right and a big X if it is wrong. If the sentence is incorrect, ask, "What's wrong with it? Why is it incorrect?"

These are very common errors. If students seem too confused, see Day 29 to review and explain the rule.

1. He work every day. INCORRECT You need to put an S on "work."

2. He working. INCORRECT You need to use "is" with an "ing" word.

3. He's is working. INCORRECT The sentence has "is" two times. You only need it one time.

4. He's work now. INCORRECT You need to have an "ing" on "work."

209

5. He's working now. CORRECT

6. Hes working. INCORRECT There is no apostrophe. (Go to the board and write a very big, dark apostrophe in the correct place between "He" and the S.)

7. Is she work now? INCORRECT There is no "ing" on "work."

8. Does she work here? Yes, she is. INCORRECT The short answer must match the question. It should be "Yes, she does."

9. Is she working? Yes, she does. INCORRECT The short answer must match the question. It should be "Yes, she is."

10. Is she working? Yes, she Is. INCORRECT There is a capital I in the middle of the sentence. It should go back to small I when you reverse the subject and verb.

NOTE: Don't use the verb "going" for creating examples and questions with present continuous. Because "going" is used for future time with "going to" and future time using present continuous, it could be confusing. Try to use only activity words.

Present Simple vs. Present Continuous - More written practice Continue IF TIME. See **references, Day 49.**

4. Family - Guided compositions Use T-chart with words and pictures. Begin or finish. See Day 49. Collect pictures and compositions.

5. LAST 1/2 HOUR - BINGO Use "PALMS" as the title word instead of "BINGO."

OR

Short Vowel Grid Game You dictate a list of words with a CVC pattern and students write each in one square of a 25-square grid. Give students a list of 25 Consonant-Vowel-Consonant words to use as a reference. Show them how to check off the words they have used. See Day 24 for how to play and check a grid game. **(As seen in the High Point program Reading Practice Book. See reference in "Text" section.)**

Day 51

Vocabulary

carpenter
plumber
tile guy
construction worker
truck driver

engineer
architect

dancer
singer
actor, actress
soccer player, football coach

journalist
reporter
TV host
radio host

Agenda

1. Opening routine
2. Jobs #2 - review with flashcards, pictures
        Collect homework, quiz
Jobs #3 - introduce with pictures, gestures, acting
        Oral practice - What is a good job?
        Point out spelling -or, -er, -ist = a person who does an action
        HOMEWORK - copy 20X, quiz (10-12 words)
3. Jobs - oral practice #1 - what family members do - write jobs and job sites on board
4. Jobs - written practice
IF TIME
5. Jobs - oral practices #2 (job info), #3 (job likes), #4 (dream job)

Stuff

1. Pictures and flashcards of workers in job sites for homework
2. Pictures or advertisements with large company names - UPS, McDonald's, Walmart, Target, Macy's, Bank of America. (See Day 50.)
3. 3x5 or 5x7 index cards
4. Big Post-it paper for lists

Lesson Plan

1. Opening Routine

2. Jobs #2 - Review Review with flashcards and pictures. Collect homework and do a quiz.

Jobs #3 - Introduce Use pictures, gestures, acting, and company pictures. Point out spelling "-or," "-er," and "-ist" for a person who does an action. Repeat job titles with pictures and work sites. Ask what is a good job. Pronounce homework vocabulary several times and review it with flashcards. Choose the most relevant words for the quiz. HOMEWORK is to copy all of the words 20X all words for a quiz of 10-12 words.

3. Jobs - Oral practice #1 Continue to ask students about family work. Write the most usual workplaces on one large Post-it paper and write job names on another. Make a set of flashcards for these jobs, and try to get pictures of them for the picture collection. Ask,

> Who works in your family?
> Where does he/she work?
> What's the name of her company?
> What's his/her job?

school - teacher, secretary, teacher's aide
day care center - teacher, helper
store - store clerk, salesperson, cashier, bagger
market - cashier, stocker
supermarket - supervisor, baker, meat cutter, butcher
swap meet - vendor
construction site - construction worker, equipment driver, mason, carpenter, plumber
hospital - doctor, nurse, physician's assistant, technician, clerk
office - executive, manager, clerk, secretary, receptionist, security guard
beauty salon - hairdresser, stylist, manicurist (does nails)
restaurant - server, bartender, hostess, waiter, waitress, busser, cashier, manager, owner
gas station - garage - body shop - auto mechanic
bank - teller, manager
at home - housewife, mother

When listening to oral work and checking written work, make sure to stress the "a" in each sentence, so students will hear it and use it. "He's A doctor." "She's A lawyer." Don't let them say, "He is doctor."

4. Jobs - Written practice Some of these references may have been done before. If so, skip them or review them orally. **Side by Side, pp. 82, 117, 119, 139; New American Streamline Departures, p. 4B; GrammarWork, pp. 10, 11, 17, 23-24; Skill Sharpeners, pp. 66, 70.** For basic jobs and the employment process, **Access, pp. 101-106.**

IF TIME

5. Jobs - Oral practice #2 - Companies Write the questions on the board and have students respond using pictures of companies and their advertisements.

Who do you work for?	I work for	_____.
When do you work?	I work	part-time
		full time
		8-5
		at night
		3 days a week
		when they call me
		every day
		sometimes

Jobs - Oral practice #3 - Likes Write questions and examples on the board. Help students copy and fill in the sentences on 5x7 cards. For younger students, write about a dream job.

My job is _____
I am a _____
I work for _____ (name of company)
I work in _____ (area or city where you work)

I like my job a lot/pretty well/okay.
I don't like my job.
I hate my job!!!

Why do you like your job?	I like the money.
	I like the people.
	I like the work.
	It's near my home.
	It's easy.
	My brother works there.
Why do you hate your job?	It's difficult.
	It's boring.
	It's very far from my house.
	I work at night.
	The money is bad.

Discuss in groups, or volunteers can stand up and report their answers to the class.

Jobs - Oral practice #4 - What's your dream job? Volunteers talk about their ideal job in front of the class.

213

Day 52

Vocabulary

head
hair

ear
eye
nose
mouth

tooth - teeth

neck (outside)
throat (inside)

lip
tongue

NOT FOR QUIZ
eyebrows
eyelashes

Agenda

1. Opening routine
2. Jobs #3 - review with flashcards, pictures
      Collect homework, quiz
3. Jobs - oral practice (about 15 minutes) - finish oral practices from Day 51
      Oral practice - optional - show business dialog
      Written practice - 1-2 pages
4. Pronunciation -
      Compare CVC and VC to CVCe
      Review long vowels with CVC + e
      New rule - CV = long, CVe = long
5. Body Words #1 - introduce body words with a picture of a head and body
      Oral practice with TPR, pointing, pictures, questions - head
      Illustration - with a blank piece of 8 1/2 x 14 paper, copy the picture or use a blank
      form and label the words for tomorrow's quiz on the parts of the head
      HOMEWORK - copy 20X (vocabulary for head), quiz. Will also collect the copied
      graphic of body words for credit after second quiz
      Review for quiz with flashcards, tomorrow's quiz words only
6. Dentist dialog

Stuff

1. Pictures and flashcards of workers on job sites for homework words
2. Pictures and flashcards of workers on job sites in your local area. For example, police officer, news reporter, cameraman
3. Pictures and advertisements with large company names - UPS, McDonald's, Walmart, Target, Macy's, Bank of America (See Day 50.)
4. Picture or cartoon with body vocabulary words on worksheet or in text - see **Access, p. 88 (simple); Lifeskills, p. 103; Skill Sharpeners, p. 100.**
5. Graphic of the head and body with blanks to label body words
6. 8 1/2 x 14 blank white paper to copy the body words chart
7. Pictures and flashcards of body words

Lesson Plan

1. Opening Routine

2. Jobs #3 - Review Use pictures and flashcards. Collect homework and do the quiz.

3. Jobs - Oral practice Continue oral practices from Day 51, for 15 minutes maximum. When listening to oral work, remind students to say, "He's A doctor," not "He is doctor."

Oral practice - Optional For a dialog and picture with show business words, see **New American Streamline Departures, p. 50.** (The dialog is in past form. Don't do the exercises.)

Written practice Do 2 pages. See **references, Day 49 and Day 51.**

4. Pronunciation - Review Compare CVC and VC with CVCe. (See Day 16 and Day 42.) Use examples from previous work to review the rule that E at the end of the word makes the vowel long.

Pronunciation - CV = long, CVe = long - Introduce Remind students that in CVCe words, the E at the end usually makes the vowel long. If a word is a CV (long vowel), like "be," and it has one more E on the end, it is probably long also (bee).

Pronunciation - CV = long Practice the pronunciation of single words. Remind students that VC is short, but that CV is almost always long. (Remember rules only apply to about 80% of words in English.) Give examples: he, she, we, me, hi, my (Y usually same as I here), cry, sky, Ho ho ho! (Santa Claus), no, go, yo-yo, so-so, tutu, Hulu (TV channel).

Pronunciation - CVe = long Give examples - bee, see, hee hee! (laughing), knee (point to yours), toe, hoe, lie, tie, die, dye, bye-bye, true, glue

Remind students that CVC and VC words are short because the final consonant cuts off the vowel - hi vs. hit, be vs. bed, no vs. not. If there is no final consonant, the vowel can continue for a long time. Repeat some of the words stressing the length of the vowels.

5. Body Words - Introduce Use a labeled picture of a body. Practice the parts of the head only. **Access, p. 88 (simple); Lifeskills, p. 103; Skill Sharpeners, p. 100.**

Body Words - Oral practice Use TPR, pointing, gestures, and questions to practice.

> Point to your eye.
> Point to your eyes.
> How many eyes do you have?
> Point to your head.
> How many heads do you have?
> Point to your neck. (Point outside.)
> Point to your throat. (Point inside.)
> Point to your mouth.
> Point to your lips.
> How many lips do you have? (Students should point to 2 lips.)
> Point to your tooth. (Open mouth and point to 1 tooth.)
> Point to your teeth. (Point to many teeth.)
> Point to your tongue. (Open mouth and point to tongue.)
>
> Point to your ear.
> Point to your hair. (Students should indicate their whole head.)

Use the #1#2 technique to practice the difference between "ear" and "hair." (See Day 3.)

> Point to my eye.
> Point to your eye.
> Touch your eyes.
> Point to both your eyes.
> Point to his ear.
> Point to her ears.
> Touch your eyebrows.
> Touch your eyelashes.
> How many eyelashes do you have? (We don't know.)

On a blank piece of 8 1/2 x 14 paper, copy the head and body chart with labels. Or use a cartoon of the head and body with blanks and fill in the words for tomorrow's quiz on the head words only. Pronounce the homework vocabulary several times with flashcards. HOMEWORK is to copy only the parts of the head 20X for the quiz.

6. Dentist Dialog - Practical English, pp. 58-61.

Day 53

Vocabulary

shoulder
arm
elbow
hand
finger

leg
knee
ankle
foot - feet
toe

waist
stomach

Agenda

1. Opening routine
2. Body Words #1 - review with pictures, pointing, flashcards
      Collect homework, do quiz
Body Words #2 - introduce with the body chart, pointing, pictures
      Oral practice with TPR
      Copy remaining body words on a picture or cartoon for notebooks
      Review for quiz with flashcards
      HOMEWORK - copy 20X for quiz, will also collect chart of body words for credit
3. Health - visit the doctor - oral practice - dialog in pairs, then as a class
4. Health - illness words - written practice
5. Pronunciation - long I sound with more than 1 letter (list attached)

Stuff

1. Pictures and flashcards of body words
2. Graphic of body words on a worksheet or in text with vocabulary words
3. Body words graphic with blanks for words
4. 8 1/2 x 14 blank white paper for their body words drawing
5. Copies or projectable file of the attached list of long I words

Lesson Plan

1. Opening Routine

2. Body Words #1 - Review Use pictures, pointing, and flashcards. Collect homework and do a quiz.

Body Words #2 - Introduce Use the body words chart, TPR, and pictures.

Body Words #2 - Oral practice Use TPR and questions.

> Point to your shoulder.
> Point to your shoulders.
> Point to your arm. (They should indicate the whole length of the arm.)
>
> Point to your hand.
> How many hands do you have?
> Point to your head.
> How many heads do you have?
> How many hands do you have?

(Do a quick #1#2 game to practice the difference between "head" and "hand.")

> Point to your neck. (Point to your neck outside.)
> Point to your throat. (Point inside your mouth.)
>
> Point to your tooth. (Open your mouth and point to one tooth.)
> Point to your teeth. (Point to many teeth.)
>
> Point to your foot.
> Point to your feet.
>
> Point to your left foot.
> Point to your right foot.
> How many feet do you have? TWO
> How many teeth do you have? I DON'T KNOW.
>
> Point to your leg. (They should indicate the whole leg.)
> Point to your knee.
> Point to your knees and then point to your legs.
>
> Point to your ankle.

Do a quick #1#2 game to show the difference between "ankle" and "uncle." Write the words on the board first.

Point to your ankles.
Point to your elbows.
Point to your fingers.
Point to your toes.
How many fingers do you have?
How many toes do you have?

Point to your belt.
Your belt is on your waist. Point to your waist.
Your pants are on your stomach. What is inside your stomach? (Your lunch.)

Point to your ear.
Point to your hair. (They should indicate the whole head.)
Point to your ears.
How many ears do you have?
How many hairs do you have? (I don't know. It's impossible!!!)

Separate out 1 hair on your head and show the class what 1 hair looks like. Tell them that "hairs" is 3 single hairs, not all of the hair on the head.

He has brown hairs.	NOT OKAY
He has brown hair.	OKAY
She has a blonde hair.	NOT OKAY
She has blonde hair.	OKAY

Students finish labeling their body chart with non-head body words. HOMEWORK is to copy the words 20X for a quiz. You will collect the chart before the quiz for homework credit. Pronounce the homework words 2-3 times with flashcards.

3. Health - Doctor visit - Oral practice Use **Side by Side, pp. 141-142, 145; Access, pp. 87-90.**

Health - Dialog #1 Practice the following dialogs in pairs and deliver them to the class.

Doctor, can you help me?
What's the problem?
My _____ hurts.
    head
    ear
    tooth
    shoulder
    elbow
    knee
    ankle
    stomach

Nurse, I don't feel good.
What's wrong?
My _____ is sore.

      mouth
      neck
      throat
      arm
      toe
      foot
      leg

Health - Dialog #2 Ask the students the following questions with the models on the board.

My _____ hurts.
My _____s hurt.

What happens when you play soccer too much?
My leg/knee/ankle hurts.

What happens when you play tennis too much?
My arm/elbow/knee hurts.

What happens when you talk too much?
My throat hurts.

What happens when you work in the garden/yard too much?
My neck/shoulder/arm/knee/back hurts.

What happens when you drink beer too much?
My stomach/head hurts.

What happens when you smoke too much?
My throat/head hurts.

What happens when you text too much?
My arms/fingers/hands/shoulders hurt. (no S on verb)

What happens when you walk too much?
My feet/legs hurt. (no S on verb)
My back hurts. (S on verb)

4. Health - Illness words - Written practice Use **GrammarWork, p. 86; Side by Side, pp. 143-145; Lifeskills, pp. 105, 110.**

5. Pronunciation - Long I Sound with more than 1 letter See the attached list.

Long I Sound

It's unusual to see I alone. "Hi" is one common word. In longer words, with 2 syllables, it's long because the syllable follows the rule of CV = long.

    sci - ence
    bi-ol-o-gy
    bi-og-ra-phy

Most of the time, long I is spelled in other ways.

IE	Y	IGH or IGHT
pie	cry	sigh (Demonstrate.)
tie	my	right
die	by	light
lie	fry	night
	try	fight
	dry	bright

Remember rules of vowels

CV = long vowel
CVe = long vowel

Remember the rules of GHT = T.

You cannot change to GTH or HGT or THG
(Write these combinations. Then X them out.)

Remember that the GH is silent.
bought
brought
thought
taught
caught

The GH is there but you don't hear it. (Cross out the GH on the OUGHT example words.)

After crossing out the GH on the OUGHT example words, go back and circle the GH on the IGHT example words above. Repeat those words again.

NOTE: A single I sometimes spells the long "ee" sound as in "ski" and "taxi." Most words pronounced "ee" but spelled with a single I are words from Italian like "graffiti," "paparazzi," "panini" and "spaghetti.")

Day 54

Vocabulary

NOT FOR QUIZ

sick - ill - fine
ache
headache
toothache
backache
stomachache (Note spelling.)
sore throat
sore toe
stiff knee
stiff neck

I feel _____
I have _____
     a cold
     a fever = I am hot.
     chills = I am cold. I am shaking.
     a cough

My _____ hurts.

FOR QUIZ

sick
ill
fine
ache
headache
sore
stiff
feel
a cold
fever
chills
cough
hurt, hurts

Agenda

1. Opening routine
2. Body Words #2 - review with pictures, pointing, flashcards
   Collect the body words picture chart
   Collect vocabulary homework, quiz
3. Illness Words - introduce with acting, pointing, pictures
   Written practice
   Review for quiz with flashcards
   HOMEWORK - copy 20X, quiz
4. Healthy eating chart - introduce food vocabulary and terms like meat, dairy, poultry
   Put foods in categories
   Healthy eating chart - go over 1 recent food recommendation chart as a class
5. Healthy habits - oral practice - good and bad habits
   Written practice
6. Healthy eating chart - optional - compare different healthy eating charts as a class or in groups

Stuff

1. Text or workbook illustration of health problems
2. Most recent healthy eating chart or use one from a mandated text
3. Copies of several different healthy eating charts - optional

Lesson Plan

1. Opening Routine

2. Body Words #2 - Review
Use pictures, pointing, and flashcards. Collect the pictures with body words for credit. Collect the vocabulary homework and do the quiz.

3. Illness Words - Introduce
Use pointing, pictures, acting or text illustrations to define the words briefly before doing the written practice.

Illness Words - Written practice Use **GrammarWork, p. 86; Side by Side, pp. 141-142; Lifeskills, pp. 103-104; Skill Sharpeners, p. 100; Access, p. 87.**

After doing the written practice, review and pronounce the vocabulary 2-3 times with flashcards. HOMEWORK is to copy the words 20X for the quiz.

4. Healthy Eating Chart - Practice foods and food categories
Do several pages of practice with food names. Place foods into categories. **Skill Sharpeners, pp. 44, 49, then p. 47; Lifeskills, pp. 54, 61.**

Healthy Eating Chart - Introduce Start with the most recent chart of food groups. Review terms like "meat," "poultry," and "dairy." Ask students to give examples. Fill in the chart with examples of foods in each group.

5. Healthy Habits - Oral practice Continue with good and bad habits.

She feels good because _____.
>   she always exercises.
>   she runs every day.
>   she goes to the gym.
>   she doesn't drink much alcohol.
>   she never smokes.
>   she eats a lot of vegetables.
>   she doesn't eat candy.

He doesn't feel good because _____.
>   he never exercises.
>   he doesn't go to the gym.
>   he drinks a lot of beer.
>   he smokes cigarettes.
>   he never eats vegetables or fruit.
>   he only eats meat and potatoes.
>   he eats Cheetos and chips for lunch.
>   he eats a lot of candy.
>   he drinks 10 sodas a day.

Bad Habits - Oral practice Ask each student to confess to a bad habit.

>   I smoke.
>   I like to eat candy.
>   I drink a lot of soda.
>   I don't like to exercise.
>   I don't like to walk.
>   I eat too many Cheetos.
>   I watch TV too much.
>   I don't sleep because I play too many video games at night.

Healthy Habits - Written practice Use **GrammarWork, p. 85; Lifeskills, p. 109.**

6. Healthy Eating Chart Comparison - Optional Bring in several different healthy eating graphs. The class or small groups discuss differences in the recommendations. Briefly explain the terms "more" and "less."

MORE = 5 is more than 2
LESS = 6 is less than 10

>   This chart has more bread.
>   This chart has more vegetables.
>   This chart has less meat.

Vocabulary

Students choose 10-12 favorite activity words for quiz tomorrow.

Agenda

1. Opening routine
2. Illness words - review with acting, pictures
       Finish written practice from Day 54
       Review for quiz with flashcards
       Collect homework, do quiz
3. Activity words - introduce activities and sports with pictures
       Ask about student activities, write favorites on Post-it paper
       Students choose 10-12 activities for quiz
       Review with flashcards
       HOMEWORK - copy 15X, quiz
4. Can/can't - introduce
Can/can't - pronunciation - Students hear sentences, say affirmative or negative
       #1#2 game with can and can't
       Dialog and written practice
5. Pronunciation - Long U sound with 2 letters (list attached)
6. LAST 1/2 HOUR - BINGO

Stuff

1. Pictures and flashcards of hobbies, sports, and activities which require skill or talent
2. Post-it giant paper for chart of favorite student activities
3. Copies or projectable file of list with long U sound

Lesson Plan

1. Opening Routine

2. Illness Words - review Use acting, pictures, and flashcards for quiz review. Collect the homework and do the quiz.

3. Activity Words - Introduce Ask about activities and sports. Prompt with pictures. Talk about student activities and write them on big Post-it paper. Students choose 10-12 for the quiz. Review the activities with pictures, the chart, and flashcards. HOMEWORK is to copy the words 15X for the quiz.

Some common hobbies and activities - play soccer (football), play basketball, baseball, American football, ride a bicycle, ride a motorcycle, watch TV, lift weights, work out at the gym, cook, dance, play video games, play cards, walk in the park, garden, go to the movies, watch movies at home, shop at the mall, shop at the discount store, visit the family, go to the beach, swim, surf, sew (make clothes), play the guitar, play the piano, sing, skateboard, speak two languages, drive a car, drive a truck

4. Can/can't - Introduce - Questions Using pictures as prompts, ask students about their ability to do activities which require skill or talent.

Can you speak English? YES, I CAN. NO, I CAN'T.
Can you dance?
Can you play soccer (football)?
Can you speak Chinese?
Can you cook?
Can you swim?
Can you play basketball?
Can you drive?

Can/can't - Pronunciation Write on the board,

can + not = cannot (FORMAL)

Cross out the second N and the O and put in the apostrophe = can't. Rewrite "can't" and write (CASUAL) next to it.

Point to the word "can't" and say, "A lot of people can't hear the T. Listen to these sentences and show thumbs up for 'can' and thumbs down for 'can't.' " (Make sure this gesture is okay with all of your students.)

I can speak English.
I can't swim.
I can ride a bicycle.
I can't drive a car.
I can't understand the teacher.
I can't fly.

Show the class that "can" is usually weak. Give examples.

HE k'n fly!   No, he CAN'T fly.
They'k 'n TALK!   No, they CAN'T talk!

Practice the difference between "can" and "can't" with the #1#2 technique.

Can/can't - Dialog or written exercises Use **Practical English, pp. 163-166; Writing Practical English, pp. 115-116, 124; New American Streamline Departures, p. 14; GrammarWork, pp. 106-107, 110-113; Lifeskills, p. 94.**

5. Pronunciation - Long U Sound with 2 Letters Use the attached list.

6. LAST 1/2 HOUR - BINGO Use "QUIET" for the title.

Long U Sound with 2 Letters

UE	EW	OO	UI
blue	new	noon	suit (not "sweet")
true	a few	moon	fruit (not "froo-eat")
due	view	room	juice (not "joo-ees")
glue	blow - blew	school	
clue	grow - grew	spoon	
clueless	draw - drew	food	
rescue	chew - chewed	pool	
argue		boots	

bamboo
cool
too
zoo
broom
Whoo-hoo!
Ooh!
Boo!

Does not follow rule

you
who
to and two (same as too)

NOTE: QU = KW

question
quiet
queen
quarrel

Day 56

Vocabulary

You can give another set of activities for the vocabulary quiz tomorrow or replace the vocabulary quiz with a dispatch activity. (See Day 25.)

Agenda

1. Opening routine
2. Activity words - review - pictures, chart, flashcards
   Collect homework, quiz
Activity words - optional - assign second group of activity words for homework and quiz
3. Can/can't - introduce - continue with dialog, reading, written practice
Can/can't as modal helper verb - compare modal helper verb to regular helper verb
Can/can't - stress and pronunciation difference, sentences and short answers
   Repeat a dialog practicing pronunciation
4. "Too" + adjective - introduce - explain problem of "too" instead of "very"
   Written practice
5. Can/can't - more oral and written practice
6. Can/can't - problems - optional

Stuff

1. Post-it large chart paper and marker to add vocabulary suggestions
2. Pictures and flashcards for words posted yesterday on Post-it chart

Lesson Plan

1. Opening Routine

2. Activity Words - Review   Use pictures, chart, and flashcards to review. Collect homework and do the quiz.

Activity Words - Optional Assign another group of activity words for homework and quiz.

3. Can/can't - Introduce with dialog   Read the dialog several times and copy 1 or 2X. Answer oral questions. Add written exercises for further practice. See **references, Day 55.** For an additional dialog, **New American Streamline Departures, p. 22.**

Can/can't - Modal helper verbs - Introduce Explain that "can" is a helper verb, but it is also a "modal" vs. a regular helper verb like "do," which makes a question, or "am," "is," and "are," which show the time of the action. "Can" has an extra meaning. It means that you have the ability to do the action of the main verb or that it is possible. "Can" and "can't" show present or future time, depending on the sentence. Show that the base verb does not change. Explain that "can" does not take "s" or "ed" or "ing."

228

Don't explain other meanings of "can" at this time, just the meaning of ability. Do not explain "is able to" at this point. Write on the board.

I walk to school. (every day)
I am walking to school. (right now)
I can walk to school or I can take the bus. (right now, today, or any time)

I walk	I am walking	I can walk
You walk	You are walking	You can walk
He/she/it walks	He/she/it is walking	He/she/it can walk
We walk	We are walking	We can walk
They walk	They are walking	They can walk

First, pointing to the different forms in the chart, note that the present simple does not have a helper verb in the present form, but present continuous has "am," "are," and "is." (Circle them.) "Can" is also a helper verb. (Circle it.)

Second, underline the main verb in each example. Underline "walk" in the present simple form, the "walk" part of "walking" in column two, and "walk" after "can" in the third column.

Read each column, emphasizing the differences in the forms. In the present simple column, say the S very loudly when you read "he walks, she walks, it walks." Say, "The S is the only change in the present simple form." Dramatically, heavily circle the S.

Remind the class that with "ing" forms, the main verb "walking" is always the same, but the helper verbs "am," "is" and "are" change with the subject. Go back and dramatically re-circle each helper verb and read it very loudly with each person. I AM, you ARE, he IS, etc. Then read all of the forms, loudly emphasizing the "ing" in each verb.

Pointing to "can" and "walk," explain that "can" is a different type of helper verb, called "modal." Like every modal helper verb, "can" does not change and the main verb does not change either. Circle the "can" again more heavily in each sentence, and write "MODAL HELPER" next to that list.

Write the following bad examples on the board.

I can walks.	WRONG	I can walkX.
I can walking.	WRONG	I can walkX.
He can is walking.	WRONG	He can X walkX.

Write WRONG next to each bad example and then put a big X over the mistakes.

Can/can't - Pronunciation Again explain the stress and pronunciation differences between "can" and "can't."

> I can see it. = Ikn SEE it.
> I can't see it. = I can't SEE it. OR I CAN'T SEE it!
> Can you see it? = Kin ya SEE it?
>
> Yes, I can. = Yes, I CAN.
> No, I can't = No, I CAN'T.

Give other examples of positive and negative sentences and short answers.

> Can he help me? = Kinnee HELP me?
> He can go there later. = Heekn GO there LATEr.
> No, he can't go there until tomorrow. = NO, ee CAN'T GO there 'til toMORrow.

Do another dialog or repeat a dialog and questions one more time focusing on pronunciation. See **references above and Day 55.**

4. "Too" + Adjective - Dialog - Optional Using "too" to mean "very" is common with Spanish speakers. It should be corrected every time they say it. It's easier to explain this with a text page illustrating characters in an impossible situation, where they can't do a certain action.

Explain that in English, "too" does not mean "very" or "extremely." Explain that too + adjective means "too much." It means something is impossible or bad about the situation or something bad will happen to you if you have this quality. Write examples on the board.

He is too thin. = I think he is not healthy.

He is too tall. = He is funny because he is tall.
> He can't walk through the door because he is tall.
> Tall is bad.

BETTER

He is very thin.
He is really thin.
He is extremely tall.

"Too" + Adjective - Written practice Use **GrammarWork, pp. 108-109 (with can/can't); Side by Side, Book 2, pp. 14 (food) and 94-95.** (Use only the pictures for oral practices with "can" and "can't" in the present time.) Also **New American Streamline Departures, p. 64.**

5. Can/can't - Written practice Continue. See **references, Day 55.** Also **Side by Side, pp. 118-119, 120, 121 (includes listening).**

6. Can/can't - Problems - Optional It's hard for beginning students to understand explanations. Don't explain the following problems with "can" to the class unless you hear these mistakes.

"Can" and "can't" refer to actions at present, in the future, or in general. If you can do something now, you can do it later. For the past, you must use "could."

> I can swim. (now and in the future)
> I can go to the movies with you Friday. (It's possible in the future.)
> Cats can't fly. (in general)

Unlike other helper verbs, "can" is never a main verb. When "can" appears alone, the main verb is understood.

You cannot use 2 different helper verbs together.

> I do can speak English. IMPOSSIBLE

"Do" and "can" are both helper verbs. Choose one. The main verb is "speak."

BUT you can use "can" when the other helper verb is used as a main verb.

> I can do the homework. POSSIBLE

In this case, "can" is the helper verb because it comes first. The main verb is "do."

> I do my homework every day.
> I can't do my homework tonight because I'm busy.

Day 57

Vocabulary

NOT FOR QUIZ
good - well
bad - badly
poor - poorly

careful - carefully
careless - carelessly
fashionable - fashionably (Point out the spelling change.)
slow - slowly
quick - quickly

IRREGULAR
fast - fast
hard - hard
loud - loud, loudly

Agenda

1. Opening routine
2. Activity words - review favorite activities on Post-it paper chart, pictures, flashcards
      Collect homework and do quiz if assigned
OR
      Dispatch activity instead of vocabulary quiz
3. Can/can't - written and oral practice - 5 things can do and 5 things can't do - write first,
      report to class
      Student abilities with "but" - written and oral - optional
4. Can/can't with adverbs - written practice - good vs. well and "but"
5. Adverbs - introduce adverbs
      Written practice
6. Adverbs - vocabulary - introduce
      Compare forms in vocabulary words
      No quiz on this list
Adverbs - rules - introduce - compare adjectives with adverbs
      Spelling
      Irregular forms
7. Adverbs - optional - more reading - funny drama

Stuff

1. Pictures and flashcards of fun activities, hobbies, and sports which require skill or talent
2. Post-it giant paper with chart of favorite student activities
3. Flashcards with adjective on one side and adverb on the other

Lesson Plan

1. Opening Routine

2. Activity Vocabulary #2 - Review
Read favorite activities from big Post-it paper chart. Review with pictures and flashcards. Collect homework and do the quiz if assigned.
OR
Do dispatch activity instead of vocabulary quiz. (See Day 25.)

3. Can/can't - Written and oral practice - Easy
Students write 5 things they can do and 5 things they can't do. They can write in pairs, groups, or individually. If they have time, they can compare lists within their group. Report one of each to class.

> I can dance.
> I can't swim.

Can/can't - Oral and written practice - Student abilities with "but" - Optional
After students have written 5 sentences with "can" and 5 with "can't," they put them into one sentence with "but." Explain that "but" means you have two sentences and one is the opposite of the other or different in some way. The sentences should be about a similar idea.

> I can dance, BUT I can't swim.

Both are physical activities, but you can't do both.

> I like him, BUT I don't like his brother.

The two boys are in the same family, but you only like one of them. Maybe that is strange, or it's a problem.

> I can bake, BUT I can't cook.

Both activities involve preparing food, but for some reason, you can do only one of them well.

When giving examples, stress BUT loudly and point finger, wave, or make faces to indicate that BUT is a very important word. You can show thumbs up for the positive part of the sentences, say, "BUT" very loudly, and then show thumbs down for the negative part.

Students will probably not be able to do this without teacher help, but it is good to introduce the idea. Most ESL students at higher levels do not use "but" in sentences where they should use it. They only use "and," which is not the same idea.

4. Can/can't with Adverbs - Written practice
Briefly explain the difference between "good" and "well." **GrammarWork, pp. 106, 113 (with "but").**

233

5. Adverbs - Introduce Introduce adverbs vs. adjectives with examples from class. Ask,

Do you pass in your papers quickly? No, you pass them in very slowly.
Do I speak slowly or quickly? Yes, I speak slowly.
Do I speak loudly or softly? Yes, I speak very loudly.

Ask students for a short list of their favorite sports or entertainment stars. Use the most well-known for your examples. Explain that adverbs tell HOW someone does an action.

"How does (Insert a famous person here.) (Insert action.)?"

(Their favorite star) is a good singer. She sings very well.

(Their favorite star) has very fashionable (modern) clothes.
She is very fashionable. = She dresses fashionably.

(Their favorite soccer/football star) is a great player.
He plays very well. He runs very quickly.

Adverbs - Written practice Use texts with pictures to explain the idea of adverbs and to introduce more adverbs. **Practical English, pp. 227-231, 235 (bottom); Writing Practical English, pp. 164-166, 175 (top); New American Streamline Departures, p. 38 (short paragraphs); Side by Side, Book 2, p. 72.**

6. Adverbs - Vocabulary - Introduce Review adverb forms with the vocabulary list. Give more sample sentences. Practice the forms with flashcards having adjectives on one side and adverbs on the other. No homework or quiz tomorrow.

Students may understand these rules but probably won't remember them very well. At this level and at higher levels, they rarely use adverbs, but they will find them in reading. Don't use these worksheets for homework or give a lot of test questions on adverbs.

Adverbs - Rules - Introduce Many adjectives become adverbs by adding "ly." Compare the regular adverbs on the vocabulary with the adjectives. Point out the extra L.

careful - carefully
He is a careful driver. He drives very carefully.

beautiful - beautifully
She is a beautiful dancer. She dances beautifully.

Adverbs - Spelling One L becomes a double L. LE becomes LY.

Adverbs - Irregular Some adverbs are irregular, like "well."

> He is a good player.
> He plays very well.

Some are the same in both adjective and adverb. The most common examples are "hard," "fast," and "loud."

> My father is a hard worker.
> He works very hard every day.
> How hard does he work?
> He works 12 hours a day.

> My brother is a very fast driver.
> He drives too fast all the time.
> How fast does he usually drive?
> He drives 80 miles an hour.

7. Adverbs - Optional For a dialog which is a little more difficult, **New American Streamline Departures, p. 50.**

235

Day 58

Vocabulary

NOT FOR QUIZ

SAME WORDS AS DAY 57

good - well
bad - badly
poor - poorly

careful - carefully
careless - carelessly
fashionable - fashionably (Note the spelling change.)
slow - slowly
quick - quickly

IRREGULAR

fast - fast
hard - hard
loud - loud, loudly

Agenda

1. Opening routine
2. Adverbs - review list from Day 57 (above) with flashcards
   Oral practice - answer questions
   Oral practice - choose adverb or adjective
   Rules - review briefly - adjectives vs. adverbs, spelling, irregular forms
   Hardly - explain - optional
   Reading and written practice - continue
3. Can/can't - written and oral practice - finish
4. Can and Have to - Introduce with oral practice
   More oral practice
   Written practice
5. Can and Have to - reading and dialog - optional
6. Can/can't - permission - reading practice - optional

Stuff

1. Flashcards with adjectives on one side and related adverbs on the other
2. Post-it large poster with only the adverbs on the list above.

Lesson Plan

1. Opening Routine

2. Adverbs - Vocabulary - Review
Read the list from Day 57 (shown in Vocabulary above) with flashcards. Repeat rules briefly about "ly" and irregular forms. Compare adjectives with adverbs using flashcards with adjectives on one side and adverbs on the other.

Adverbs - Oral practice Point to the adverbs on the Post-it poster to help students answer the questions. If necessary, give them the sentences to complete. Ask,

How does your mom dance?	She dances well.
She dances well or she dances very well?	Very well!
How fast does (your favorite soccer player) run?	He runs very fast.
	He runs very quickly.
How does your baby cry?	He cries very loudly.
	He cries very loud.
How hard does your ESL teacher work?	She works very, very hard.

Adverbs - Oral practice Repeat each sentence twice. Students choose adverb or adjective.

Pass in your papers quickly.	ADVERB
My sister is very fashionable.	ADJECTIVE
He runs really fast.	ADVERB
My kid is a really slow eater.	ADJECTIVE
He is such a fast player.	ADJECTIVE
Please don't eat so fast.	ADVERB
Your son is a very good student.	ADJECTIVE
He drives so carelessly that I get scared.	ADVERB
He likes to yell very loudly at the soccer game.	ADVERB

Adverbs - Review rules

An adjective describes a person, place, or thing, and comes before the thing. An adverb describes how an action is done. It can come before or after the verb.

She is a fashionable girl. OR She is very fashionable.

How does she dress?
  She dresses fashionably.
  She dresses well.

Give other examples.

He is a good English speaker.   He speaks English well.
(What kind of thing or person is he?)   (How does he speak?)

He is a great soccer player.   He plays soccer very well.
(What kind of player is he?)   (How does he play?)

Remember, "play" = the action (verb), "player" = the person who plays (noun).

Hardly - Explain - Optional Explain "hardly" only if someone uses it incorrectly. "Hard" is irregular because "hardly" has a different meaning. It means almost not at all.

She hardly works. = She almost doesn't work. She doesn't work much.
She hardly eats. = She doesn't eat much food. She eats very little.

Adverbs - Written and reading practice Continue. See **references, Day 57.**

3. Can/can't - Written and oral practice Finish written work. See **references, Day 55, Day 56, and Day 57.**

4. Can and Have to - Introduce For oral practice only, use **Skill Sharpeners, p. 92 (chores); Side by Side, pp. 122-123 (excuses); Access, pp. 113, 115, 116.**

Have to - Introduce "Have to" means that you need to do something. It's necessary. Write examples on the board.

> We have to eat lunch, because I'm very hungry.
> You (plural) have to study for the test.
> They have to pay for the shoes at the cashier.
> I have to go home at 4:00.
> I have to clean my house tomorrow.
> He has to buy food at the store.
> She has to go to work at 7.

Make sure students understand the idea by defining it in different ways.

It's important.
I can't say, "No."

Have to - Oral practice Ask students the questions and write their answers on the board. Encourage them to use "hafta." It should sound like "I'afta." However, do not allow them to write "hafta."

To pass ESL 1, what do you have to do? ("Whaddaya hafta do?")

> I have to study.
> I have to speak English.
> I have to listen to the teacher.
> I have to come to class.
>
> I have to do the homework.
> I have to watch TV in English.
> I have to read the book.
> I have to pass the final exam.
> I have to pay attention.

Using "have" twice - Optional Write these examples separated from the others. Explain that "have" is the main verb here, and "have to" is a helper verb.

> I have to have a book.
> I have to have a pencil.
> I have to have a teacher.

Can and Have to - Written practice Write the pages done orally in #4 above. **Skill Sharpeners, p. 92 (chores); Side by Side, p. 122-123 (excuses). Also Access, pp. 113 and 116 (dialogs).**

5. Can and Have to - Dialog and reading practice - Optional Use **Side by Side, pp. 124-125 (at the Department of Motor Vehicles); New American Streamline Departures, p. 58 (spy dialog).**

6. Can/can't - Permission - Reading practice and road signs - Optional Use **Practical English, pp. 174-177, 178 (funny dialog); Skill Sharpeners, pp. 97-98; Lifeskills, pp. 95-96; Access, pp. 107-109.**

Vocabulary

Regular past verbs are introduced below, with no vocabulary quiz tomorrow. A list of regular verbs is attached to Day 60, and regular past verb homework and quizzes will start then. Write regular verbs from the exercises on charts for the classroom titled REGULAR VERBS.

Agenda

1. Opening routine
2. Can/can't, have to/has to - helper verbs - review - optional
      Oral practice - okay/not okay - optional
3. Have to/has to - more oral practice, pronunciation
4. Excuses - good and bad - oral practice
      Written practice
5. Can/can't, have to /has to - readings, dialog, written practice - finish
6. Regular past verbs with "ed" - introduce with reading, list regular verbs on charts
      Written practice, IF TIME
7. Pronunciation - long E sound with 2 letters, spelling rule I before E (attached list)
      Review on Day 60

Stuff

1. Large Post-it paper for Regular Verbs list
2. Copies or projectable file for list with long E words

Lesson Plan

1. Opening Routine

2. Can/can't, Have to /has to - Helper Verbs - Review - Optional
Write the examples on the board.

> He can leave.
> Can he leave?
> > Yes, he can.
> > No, he can't.

"Can" is a helper verb. It does not need "to." It reverses to make the question. (Flip the fingers to indicate a question. (See Unit 7.)

> He has to leave.
> Does he have to leave? ("Has" goes back to "have," just like any other verb.)
> > Yes, he does (have to).
> > No, he doesn't (have to).

"Have to" has the meaning of a helper verb, but it needs "do" or "don't" to make a question, negative, or short answer, similar to "have." It needs "to" after it.

Do you have to work tomorrow?
Yes, I do.
No, I don't.
I don't have to work tomorrow.

Do we have to take the test today?
 No, we don't (have to take it today).
Yes, we do.

Does he have to work tomorrow?
Yes, he does.
No, he doesn't.
He doesn't have to work tomorrow.

In the above sentences, circle the S on "does" and "doesn't" and point to "have" to explain that the S goes onto "does," not "have." Write on board.

He doesn't has to.	INCORRECT
He doesn't have to.	CORRECT
Does he has to?	INCORRECT
Does he have to?	CORRECT

Can/can't, Have to/has to - Oral practice - Okay/not okay - Optional The verb after "can" is always regular form. Write examples on board and students say "Okay" or "Not okay."

I can't to go.	NOT OKAY
He can see her.	OKAY
He can sees her.	NOT OKAY
He can to see her.	NOT OKAY

The verb after "to" is always regular form.

I have to go.	OKAY
He has study.	NOT OKAY
He has to study.	OKAY

After "to," you always have the basic form of the verb.

3. Have to/has to - More oral practice Practice the rule that with "he," "she," "and "it" you use "has."

Ask students questions and write their answers on the board.

To help at home (your mom or your wife), what do you have to do?

   I have to clean my room.
   I have to wash the dishes.
   I have to wash the car.
   I have to sweep/vacuum the floor.

   I have to cook.
   I have to go to the store.
   I have to take out the garbage.
   I have to wash the clothes/do the laundry.

   I have to babysit/take care of the other kids.

After each student tells what they have to do, ask another student about the answer. Use "hafta" and "hasta."

   Juan, what do you have to do to help at home?
   I have to wash the dishes.

   Maria, what does Juan have to do at home?
   He has to wash the dishes.

4. Have to/has to - Excuses - Good and bad Explain excuses. Write on the board.

   Can you come to my party Saturday night?

   I'm sorry. I have to _____.
                     babysit
                     work
                     go to a family party
                     pick up my uncle at the airport

It's nice if you give a reason if you can't do something (an "excuse"). You don't have to give an excuse. You can say, "I'm sorry. I can't go. Thank you for the invitation."

Say, "BUT, if you give an excuse, it has to be a good reason! 'I can't come to your party because I don't want to go' is a reason, but it's not a good excuse. An excuse is a good reason why you CANNOT go to the party." Give students the excuses as a class and they say, "Good excuse" or "Bad excuse."

I can't go to your party. I have to wash my hair.	BAD
I can't go to your party. I have to babysit.	GOOD
I can't go to your party because I think your hair is funny.	BAD
I can't go to your party because I want to play video games.	BAD
I can't go to your party. My mother said no.	GOOD
I'm sorry. I can't go. I have to go to a family party.	GOOD
The students can't study for the test because they have to party.	BAD
The students can't study for the test because they have to work.	GOOD
We can't play Bingo right now because we have to finish our work.	GOOD
We can't play Bingo because the teacher forgot the candy.	?

Have to/has to - Excuses - Written and oral practice If not done, **Side by Side, pp. 122 and 123.** Good and bad excuses with the past form, **Side by Side, p. 153.**

5. Can and Have to - Written practice and dialogs Finish. See **references, Day 58.**

6. Regular Past Verbs with "ed" - Introduce Begin past verbs with reading and oral practice only. Make a list of regular verbs from the readings on large Post-it charts for the room under the heading "REGULAR VERBS." Students will receive copies of a similar list on Day 60. **Side by Side, p. 143; Practical English, pp. 206, 208 top, and 210C; Writing Practical English, pp. 145-146.**

Regular Past Verbs with "ed" - Written practice IF TIME, start writing regular past verbs only. See **references above. Also, Side by Side, p. 144.** (Review orally if done before.)

7. Pronunciation - Long E Sound with 2 Letters Go over the examples and spelling rule. (List is attached.) Review on Day 60.

Long E Sound with 2 Letters

EE	EA	EY	WEIRD (doesn't follow famous rule)
beer	fear	key	weird
peer	tear (cry)	chimney	
see	gear	monkey	
"sweet sixteen"	hear		FAMOUS RULE
feel	near		
green	beard		receive
foot - feet	real		
tooth - teeth	seat		BUT
need			
bee	year		believe
coffee	team		achieve
tree	sea		relief
cheer	beach		
	clean		
	peas and beans		
	tea		

The Famous Rule

I before E, except after C, or when sounding like A as in "neighbor" or "weigh."

SO

"I believe you."

BUT

"You will receive a free gift."

One important word which doesn't follow rule = weird (different, strange)

Day 60

Vocabulary

Create vocabulary lists for quizzes from the attached list of regular verbs. Choose 10-12 verbs that students do not know well for quizzes on Day 61, Day 62, and Day 63. Continue to add regular verbs from the readings to the large classroom charts.

Agenda

1. Opening routine
2. Can/have to - oral practice and written practice - finish
Can/have to - oral practice and reading practice - optional - a spy drama
3. Regular past verbs - oral practice and written practice - finish easy oral and written
practices from Day 59
   Read regular verbs from classroom chart
Regular past verbs #1 - check off most familiar verbs from list (attached)
   Create 3 vocabulary lists, write 10 words for quiz on board, define. Include past
   forms of verbs which do not simply add "ed" to make the past.
   HOMEWORK - copy 15X including different past forms, for quiz
   Oral practice - optional - use better-known verbs from list in past
Regular past verbs with "ed" - reading and written practice
4. Pronunciation - long E sound with 2 letters - review and repeat (See Day 59.)

IF TIME

5. LAST 1/2 HOUR - BINGO - "JOKER" instead of "BINGO"

NOTE: AT SOME TIME ON DAYS 60 TO 63 - The following rules should be covered during one of the classes where you practice regular verbs. If necessary, do regular verbs for an extra day to include this material before beginning irregular past verbs.

6. Regular past verbs - did - explain rule and pronunciation
7. Regular past verbs - rules for adding "ed" to certain verbs - introduce, explain
   Written practice

Stuff

1. Copies of the Regular Verb List of verbs with regular past forms
2. Flashcards for all verbs on the list
3. Continue to add to your picture collection the regular verbs on the list in the category "Regular Verbs."
4. Post-it paper and marker for large chart of regular verbs
5. Copies or projectable file for list with long E words attached to Day 59
6. Bingo game and rewards

Lesson Plan

1. Opening Routine

2. Can/have to - Oral practice and written practice Finish oral and written work. See **references, Day 58 and Day 59.**

Can/have to - Oral practice and reading practice - Optional Perform a spy drama if not done before. **New American Streamline Departures, p. 58.**

3. Regular Past Verbs - Oral practice and written practice Continue easy oral and written practices from Day 59. See **references, Day 59.** Continue to note regular verbs from the reading on the big classroom chart. When finished, read and repeat that list.

Regular Past Verbs - Vocabulary #1 Pass out the attached Regular Verb List (Review) and go over. Eliminate verbs they know well. Create 3 vocabulary lists from the rest. Choose and review 10-12 words for tomorrow's quiz. Write on board. If the chosen word does not simply add "ed" for the past, include both present and past forms on the list. HOMEWORK is to copy the chosen words 15X for a quiz on the present and past forms which are not completely regular.

Regular Past Verbs - More oral practice - Optional Practice past form with better-known verbs from the list. Make up sentences about the class and the school year. Write the verb on the board. For example,

> We started school in September.
> We started the class at 7:00 p.m.
> When did class start?   It started at 7:00.
> Did we continue class after the break?   Yes, we did.
> Did we continue after 9 p.m.?   No, we didn't.
>
> What time did we start our break?   We started at 7:45.
> What time did we finish break?   We finished at 8:00.
> What did we study last week?   We studied the body. (Note spelling of "studied.")
> Did you study the words at home?   Yes, I did.
> How long did you study (how many minutes)?   I studied for 15 minutes.
> What time did you finish?   I finished at 6:00.
>
> What did we do on February 14?   We celebrated Valentine's Day.
> What did we do on October 31?   We celebrated Halloween.

Regular Past Verbs - Reading and written practice More dialogs, paragraphs, and written practice. **Side by Side, pp. 150, 146-148 (reading); GrammarWork, pp. 121-131.**

4. Pronunciation - Long E Sound with 2 Letters - More oral practice Repeat and practice. See Day 59.

5. IF TIME - LAST 1/2 HOUR - BINGO Use "JOKER" instead of "BINGO."

NOTE: DO THE FOLLOWING SECTIONS AT SOME TIME DURING DAY 60, DAY 61, DAY 62 or Day 63. You should explain the following rules during one of the classes where you cover regular verbs, before you begin the irregular past form. If necessary, add time to regular verb lesson plans to include these rules.

6. Regular Past Verbs - Did - Rules and pronunciation Introduce with questions and answers.

Did we start class at 8:00?
>Yes, we did.
>No, we didn't.

Did we study verbs yesterday?
>Yes, we did.
>No, we didn't.

Did you attend class last night?
>Yes, I did.
>No, I didn't. I was absent.

Did we finish the work yesterday?
>Yes, we did.
>No, we didn't.

The verb "do (does)" means to work or complete a job or a chore. It is also the helper word for action verbs. The past form for "do" and "does" is "did." It is not regular, because it does not make the past with "ed." All verbs use "did" as a helper verb to talk about the past. (You don't need to add S in the past form.)

Write the following on the board.

>Did I work?
>Did you work?
>Did he work?
>Did she work?
>Did it work?

>Did we work?
>Did you (more than 1 person) work?
>Did they work?

Circle "Did" in all of the above sentences and point out that it is the same for all of the subject pronouns. Ask the questions and have the class answer each question positively. ("Yes, you did. Yes, I did.")

247

Write on the board with spacing as shown.

did
did not

didn't

Tell students that the short form of "did not" is "didn't." It's pronounced "didint" or "dint." (Have them repeat it both ways several times.) The apostrophe represents the O in "not."

Draw an arrow from the O in the word "not" to the apostrophe in "didn't." Show students that there is no space in "didn't." (Some students will leave a big space around the apostrophe or will not attach the "n't" to "did." See Day 3 for techniques to help with these problems.) When correcting written work, make sure that "didn't" is one word. Encourage students to use "didn't" instead of "did not." "Did not" may sound too emphatic and even angry.

7. Regular Past Verbs - Rules - Adding "ed" to certain verbs On the board, write examples of the rules for adding "ed" to words with certain spellings.

Regular verbs	**Verbs ending in E**
Add ed	**Add only d**
cleaned	danced
walked	shaved

Some students will try to add "ed" to verbs ending in E ("decideed," "arriveed"). Write and pronounce the incorrect version ("danceed," "shaveed") so that students can hear that the pronunciation will be wrong.

Some students drop the Y and add IED to a verb with vowel plus Y ("plaied"). Many drop the Y from study ("studed").

Verbs ending in consonant + Y	**Verbs ending in vowel + Y**
Change y to i and add ed	**Simply add ed. Do not change y to i.**
try - tried	play - played
study-studied	
carry - carried	

Regular Past Verbs - Adding "ed" - Rules - Written practice Use **GrammarWork, pp. 121-123.**

Regular Verb List (Review)

add	hate	play an instrument
answer	hug	point
arrive		practice
ask	iron	
ask for		raise your hand
attend	joke	relax
	jump	repair
bake		rest
brush	kiss	roll
call	laugh	shave
carry	learn	skate
celebrate	lie (say what is not true)	smile
change	light (a fire)	start
chase	like	stay
clap	listen to	stop
clean	live	study
close	look at	
comb	look for	talk
continue	love	tie
cook		try
cry	miss the bus	turn off
	mow the lawn	turn on
dance		
deliver	open	visit
enjoy	paint	wait
erase	park	walk
exercise	pass	wash
	pass in	water the lawn
fill	pass up	whisper
finish	pick	work
fix	plant	

Day 61

Vocabulary

You are using a list of regular verbs attached to Day 60 to create a quiz list of lesser-known regular verbs. Add regular verbs from classwork if you don't have enough for 3 quizzes. Continue to add regular verbs from the classwork to a Post-it poster list in the classroom.

Agenda

1. Opening routine
2. Regular past verbs #1 - Review vocabulary for quiz with pictures, acting, flashcards
    Collect homework, quiz
Regular past verbs #2 - use 10-12 less familiar verbs from list, Day 60
    Introduce and repeat with pictures, flashcards
    HOMEWORK - copy 15X for quiz
3. Regular past verbs - dialog
    HOMEWORK (OPTIONAL) - copy a dialog
4. Regular past verbs - "ed" sound - pronunciation and exercises
5. Regular past verbs - written practice - continue
    Rules - continue

Stuff

1. List of regular past verbs with flashcards for all (attached to Day 60)
2. Pictures if available and flashcards for vocabulary words for today's quiz
3. Pictures if available and flashcards for vocabulary words for tomorrow's quiz
4. Post-it paper and marker for large chart of regular verbs

Lesson Plan

1. Opening Routine

2. Regular Past Verbs #1 - Review Review for quiz with pictures, acting, and flashcards. Collect homework and do the quiz.

Regular Past Verbs #2 - Introduce Use the next 10-12 less familiar verbs from list, Day 60. Introduce and practice with available pictures and flashcards. HOMEWORK is to copy them 15X for the quiz. An option is to add to the quiz words regular verbs from the readings.

3. Regular Past Verbs - Reading or dialog Read a longer story or dialog and answer oral questions. **New American Streamline Departures, pp. 46 (office dialog), 47 (cartoon about outlaws), 53 (twins separated at birth).** Do only one longer dialog per class.

Regular Past Verbs - Copy a dialog - Optional If you have done a dialog or story orally in class, copy it for HOMEWORK. See **references, above.** Many students don't hear the sound of the "ed" at the end of verbs. It's good for them to copy dialogs and do writing practices with the "ed" form, so they understand that the ending is present in a lot of words even if they can't hear it.

4. Regular Past Verbs - Pronunciation with "ed" The "ed" sound on the end of past regular verbs has 3 different sounds, a D sound, a T sound, and an extra syllable. You add the extra syllable with verbs ending in D or T to make the past form audible. You can introduce this concept, but don't test students on it. However, when students speak, you should correct them if they don't add the extra syllable to words like "planted" or "decided." For written work, see **Practical English, p. 220; Writing Practical English, p. 154J; Side by Side, p. 148 top.**

5. Regular Past Verbs - Written practice and rules Continue written practices. See **references above and from Day 59 and Day 60.** Include unfinished rules from Day 60.

Day 62

Vocabulary

The quiz tomorrow will be the last from the list of lesser-known regular verbs attached to Day 60.

Agenda

1. Opening routine
2. Regular past verbs #2 - review for quiz with pictures, acting, flashcards
    Collect homework, quiz
Regular past verbs #3 - practice for quiz with pictures, acting, flashcards
    HOMEWORK - copy 15X, quiz
3. Regular past verbs - written and oral practice - finish dialogs, stories, and written exercises
    from Days 59, 60, 61, including rules with "did"
4. Much/many - introduce with reading - optional
    Summarize rule - optional
    IF TIME, additional dialog - optional

Stuff

1. List of regular verbs with flashcards
2. Pictures if available and flashcards for vocabulary words on today's quiz
3. Pictures if available and flashcards for vocabulary words on tomorrow's quiz
4. Post-it paper and marker for large chart of regular verbs

Lesson Plan

1. Opening Routine

2. Regular Past Verbs #2 - Review Practice words for quiz with pictures, acting, and flashcards. Collect homework and do the quiz.

Regular Past Verbs #3 - Practice Practice the vocabulary with pictures, acting, and flashcards. HOMEWORK is to copy the verbs 15X for a quiz tomorrow.

3. Regular Past Verbs - Written and oral practice Finish dialogs and story work. Finish written exercises. See **references, Day 59, Day 60, Day 61**. Finish "did" rules from Day 60.

4. Much/many - Introduce - Reading - Optional If available, **Practical English, Book 2, pp. 3-5. Also New American Streamline Departures, p. 17.**

Much/many - Summarize rule - Optional Introduce with reading and then go over the rule. Continue to correct students on these rules, which take students a long time to internalize. Don't test them on them too much, or expect them to use "much" correctly. Many

252

texts avoid "much" and "many" until the second level except for "how much" and "how many." Give the basic rule and read the examples. Add examples relevant to your students.

A lot of

Use "a lot of" in all sentences.

AFFIRMATIVE   I have a lot of friends.
NEGATIVE   I don't have a lot of friends.
QUESTION   Do you have a lot of friends?

Many

Use "many" in all sentences, but only with things that you can count.

AFFIRMATIVE   I have many friends.
NEGATIVE   I don't have many friends.
QUESTION   Do you have many friends?

You can count your friends. "Friends" has an S on the end. (Point to the S.) S on the end of a thing means more than one. S means that you can count the number of friends.

Much

Use "much" only when it talks about noncount nouns (things you cannot count) in negative sentences and questions.

AFFIRMATIVE   I have much money.   NOT OKAY
NEGATIVE   I don't have much money.   OKAY
QUESTION   Do we have much money?   OKAY

Remind students of the rule. You can't say "moneys." If you have a quarter, you have money. If you have two dollars, you have money. If you have a million dollars, you have money. You cannot count "moneys." You have to count dollars. You can put an S on dollars, but you never put an S on money. So you have to use the word "much" with money, BUT not in an affirmative sentence! Use "a lot of" instead.

Spanish speakers will have a lot of problems with this. Continue to review and practice the rule. Don't explain the exceptions to the rule at this time.

Much/many - Oral and reading practice - Optional Read and answer questions orally only. **New American Streamline Departures, p. 49.**

253

Day 63

Vocabulary

is - am - are - be - was - were
bring - brought
buy - bought
come - came
cut - cut
do - did
drink - drank
eat - ate

Agenda

1. Opening routine
2. Regular past verbs #3 - review - pictures, acting, flashcards
    Collect homework, quiz
3. Regular past verbs - written and oral practice - finish grammar practices, stories, and dialogs and complete rules with "did" from Day 60
4. Much/many - review rule, finish dialogs - optional
5. Past form of to be - compare am/is/are and was/were - review
    Introduce "be"
6. Irregular past verbs - introduce - short readings
7. Irregular past verbs - introduce - verbs with same meaning, regular and irregular
    Compare regular verb form with irregular
    Distribute irregular verb list
8. Irregular past verbs #1 - using vocabulary list, repeat several times, practice with pictures, TPR, acting
    HOMEWORK - copy 20X, present and past forms together, class writes both on quiz
    Review homework words with flashcards, front and back
9. Bought/brought - pronunciation, spelling
    Rules for ought
    Practice with #1#2
IF TIME
10. Irregular past verbs - reading or written practice

Stuff

1. Photocopied list of irregular verbs from text or other source. (Most texts have a list, which is shorter or longer depending on the level of the text. For example, **Practical English, p. 255; New American Streamline Departures, back pages; Side by Side, p. 172.**) Longer lists have about 75 verbs.
2. Pictures and flashcards for today's quiz vocabulary (regular)
3. Pictures and flashcards for tomorrow's quiz (irregular)
4. Flashcards of all irregular verbs with the present form on one side, irregular past on the other.

254

Lesson Plan

1. Opening Routine

2. Regular Past Verbs #3 - Review Practice vocabulary for quiz with pictures, acting, and flashcards. Collect homework and do the quiz.

3. Regular Past Verbs - Written and oral practice Finish any grammar practice and do 1 final dialog or story. See rules and **references, Day 59, Day 60, Day 61, and Day 62.**

4. Much/many - Review - Optional Review rule. Finish dialogs. See **references, Day 62.**

5. Past Form of "to be" - Am/are/is and was/were - Review On tomorrow's quiz, for "to be," students will need to write six words, including "be." This is difficult for students to understand. "Be" is the basic form, but they don't see it much because it's completely irregular in present and past. Write on board and explain.

be irregular in present form	IRREGULAR MEANS NOT REGULAR
irregular in past form	or DIFFERENT

Then write on board.

I am	I was
you are	you were
he is	he was
she is	she was
it is	it was
we are	we were
they are	they were

This is a review. ("Was" and "were" were introduced and practiced on Day 46, Day 47, and Day 48.) Remind the class that "I" also uses "was," the same as "he," "she," and "it." If necessary, repeat previous explanations and practices, maybe just orally.

Point to the verbs on the list above and tell the class that you see "am," "is," "are," "was," and "were," but that you don't see "be" anywhere. Tell them that "be" is used as a command, after helper verbs or with "to." Give and write on board the following examples.

Be nice. Be here early tomorrow.	affirmative command
Don't stand up. Don't be a bad student.	negative command with "don't"
I have to be here tomorrow.	after "to"
I can swim. You can be a good student.	with "can"
I want to be a good student.	with "to" after "want"
You need to be here early.	with "to" after "need"

6. Irregular Past Verbs - Introduce Use easy stories with short paragraphs and questions to introduce the irregular past form. Go over answers. **Practical English, pp. 207, 208 bottom, 210 D and bottom; Writing Practical English, pp. 147-148.**

7. Irregular Past Verbs - Compare irregular with regular Give examples.

close the door	REGULAR
shut the door	IRREGULAR
look at someone	REGULAR
see someone	IRREGULAR
walk to school	REGULAR
go to school	IRREGULAR

Compare the regular and irregular forms.

I walk to school every day.	I go to school every day.
I walked to school every day.	I went to school every day.
SIMILAR FORM	DIFFERENT FORM - HAVE TO REMEMBER
He walks to school every day.	He goes to school every day.
He walked to school every day.	He went to school every day.
S ON PRESENT - ED ON PAST	S ON PRESENT - NO ED ON PAST

Show students that in both regular and irregular verbs, "he," "she," and "it" have S on the end in the present time, but in the past, the forms are all exactly the same.

I walk (present)	I go (present)
He walks	He goes

I walked	I went
you walked	you went
he walked	he went
she walked	she went
it walked	it went
we walked	we went
you (plural) walked	you went
they walked	they went

Explain that students have to remember the past form of each irregular verb. They are the most common verbs, so it's important. Pass out a list of irregular verbs for students to use as a reference. **Practical English, p. 255; New American Streamline Departures, back pages; Side by Side, p. 172.** Inform students that soon they will play a game with these forms for rewards, so they need to learn them as soon as possible. (Optional - Just for fun, teach "ASAP" = "as soon as possible." Repeat several times, "ay-sap.")

8. Irregular Past Verbs #1 - Introduce With verb list #1 (for tomorrow's quiz), repeat the words several times and practice with pictures, TPR, and examples. Use time ideas like "yesterday," "last week," or "When we lived in Mexico" to help them remember that you are talking about the past. Work on pronunciation for all of tomorrow's quiz words.

Repeat, "It's important to remember both forms, because irregular verbs are the most common verbs and you will use them a lot. That's why you need this list. That's why you will have a lot of tests on these words. On your homework, you should write the present and past forms together. Like this." Write an example on the board.

drink-drank
drink-drank
drink-drank

HOMEWORK is to copy the vocabulary words 20X with present and past forms written together as in the example. On the quiz the teacher will dictate the present form and the class will write the present and past. Both must be correct to get credit. Review with flashcards.

9. Bought/brought - Pronunciation and spelling Give rules for the two verbs with "ought."

Spelling of "ought" Write "buy" and "bring" with their past forms "bought" and "brought" on the board. Underline OUGHT in each word. Circle the remaining letters B and BR and show that "bought" has a B only but "brought" has BR to match the BR in "bring." Draw an arrow from the BR in "brought" to the BR in "bring." Circle the BR in "bring."

Repeat that the combination is GHT, not GTH, HGT or THG. Draw a box around the GHT in both words and underline them 2 or 3 times.

Pronunciation of "ought" Use the #1#2 technique to focus on the difference between "bought" and "brought." (See Day 3.)

IF TIME

10. Irregular Past Verbs - Written practice Begin reading or written practice. See **references, Day 64 and Day 65.**

Day 64

Vocabulary

drive - drove
feed - fed
find - found
fly-flew (not flow)
forget-forgot
get-got
give-gave (not have)
have-had
go-went (not "whent")

NOT FOR HOMEWORK
I - me - my - mine
you - you - your - yours
he - him - his - his
she - her - her - hers
it - it - its - its (They will never hear the last one.)
we - us - our - ours
they - them - their - theirs

Agenda

1. Opening routine
2. Irregular past verbs #1 - review - pictures, TPR, acting, flashcards
        Collect homework, do quiz
        Collect quiz, review spelling, review GHT sound if necessary
Irregular past verbs #2 - introduce, repeat, practice with pictures, acting, TPR, flashcards
        HOMEWORK - copy 20X with forms together
3. Irregular past verbs - reading practice - mark irregular and regular, put on T-chart
        What is a verb?
4. Irregular past verbs - questions - compare irregular to regular - optional
        Negatives - compare irregular to regular - optional
        Ask questions from readings - positive and negative answers

IF TIME

5. Irregular past verbs - written practice - begin practices from Day 65

LAST 1/2 HOUR

6. Possessive pronouns - introduce - jazz chant
7. Possessive pronouns - introduce - TPR
        Oral practice - TPR, questions

Stuff

1. List of irregular verbs, if not given on Day 63
2. Flashcards of irregular verbs on list with present on one side, irregular past on the other
3. Pictures, if any, and flashcards for today's quiz. Add pictures to picture collection.
4. Pictures, if any, and flashcards for tomorrow's quiz
5. Copies of reading practice with yellow markers so students can mark up their copies
6. Large Post-it paper and marker to make T-chart
7. Copies of jazz chant "This is Mine, That's Yours"

Lesson Plan

1. Opening Routine

2. Irregular Past Verbs #1 - Review Review vocabulary #1 with pictures, TPR, acting, and flashcards. Collect the homework.

Do the quiz. First remind students with a free example on the board that they need to write both the dictated present form and the memorized past form next to each number.

Bought/brought - Pronunciation and spelling - Optional Review collected quizzes quickly to check spelling of "bought" and "brought." If there are errors, review spelling rules.

Write "buy" and "bring" with past forms "bought" and "brought" on the board. Repeat the explanation from Day 63. Give further examples.

> fight - fought
> think - thought

Underline OUGHT in each word. Repeat all the pairs together.

Review the rules about GHT. For each example, underline the GHT. Then cross out the GH, telling students that this sound used to be a rough, throat-clearing sound but it is now silent. Repeat the past forms on the list one more time.

Irregular Past Verbs #2 - Introduce Repeat and practice with pictures, acting, and TPR. Review with flashcards. HOMEWORK is to copy both forms 20X for a quiz.

3. Irregular Past Verbs - Reading Use **New American Streamline Departures, p. 48 (foreign vacations), Practical English, pp. 239-242A (or part of it), or any paragraphs with irregular and regular verbs.** Individually or in small groups, students underline or mark with yellow markers all of the verbs in a story. Check the answers orally. If there was a verb they didn't recognize, ask them to guess the meaning. Ask how they knew that certain words were verbs. Review the meaning of each verb. As you check the answers, make a T-chart of regular and irregular verbs, including both forms of the irregular verbs. Ask questions with affirmative and negative answers about the story. Correct the past form answers. Use the following explanations when students begin having problems.

259

Irregular Past Verbs - Questions - Optional The past form is easy, but questions and negatives are a little hard. Write the following sequence of sentences on the board.

> I walked to school.

> Did you walked to school?

Circle the "ed" and draw an arrow to "Did." Then put a big X over the "ed" in "walked." "You walked" becomes "Did you walk," without "ed." Remind students that you only need to say the past one time. "Did" is first, so you take the "ed" out of "walked." The same rule is true for the negative. "Didn't" comes first so the "ed" comes out. Write on the board.

Did you walk to school?

> Yes, I did (walk to school).
> No, I didn't (walk to school).
> I didn't walk to school.

Write on the board.

I went to school.

Go back to the first example and say, "In 'I walked,' you SEE the present form, 'walk.' " (Underline "walk" in "walked.") Point to "went" and say, "But when you see 'went,' you have to REMEMBER that the present form of 'went' is 'go.' " To one side on the board write,

went = go + did

On the board below the word "went" in the sentence, write,

I went to school.
I (did + go) to school.

Say, "Flip the subject and verb just like you do with other helper verbs." Flip your fingers to show how "did" and the subjects "I" or "you" reverse in the question and reverse back in the answer.

Did you go to school?

> Yes, I did (go to school).
> No, I didn't (go to school).
> I didn't go to school.

Point to the question, short answers, and negative sentence above and tell the class to remember that when they use "did," they cannot use "went." They have to remember the regular form, "go."

Say, "Make a question from these sentences." Ask students to get out their list of irregular past verbs and use it to answer. They answer with "he" for every question.

He bought a sandwich.	DID HE BUY a sandwich?
He came to class yesterday.	DID HE COME to class yesterday?
He drank water at lunch.	DID HE DRINK water at lunch?
He ate an apple at lunch.	DID HE EAT an apple at lunch?
He did his homework yesterday.	DID HE DO his homework?

After students make the question, ask to hear the short answer in positive and negative.

Irregular Past Verbs - Negative - Optional Practice negative sentences in the past.

Remind students that the helper verbs of the present form are "do" and "does." The helper verb of the past form is "did." "Did" is the same as "ed." It gives the idea of past time. You only have to put "ed" one time. You don't have to say the past twice.

Put the example on the board.   He didn't walked.   WRONG

The past form is in this sentence two times, "didn't" and "ed." You only need it one time.

Cross out the "ed" in "walked."   He didn't walk.   RIGHT

Example   He went to school.
            He didn't went to school.   WRONG
            He didn't go to school.   RIGHT

Say, "Went" = "did + go." Point to the wrong sentence. Tell the students that it has the past time twice, one time with "didn't" and the other time with "went." That's wrong. They have to say the past with "didn't" and change the main verb back to "go." Point to the right sentence.

Point to the daily vocabulary list and say, "Give the negative form for these verbs." Students listen to each verb and consult the list if necessary to answer. Use "he" for every example.

He drove.	He didn't drive.
He forgot.	He didn't forget.
He had.	He didn't have.

Have students give the negative past form of the remaining verbs on the vocabulary list.

Return to the reading practice and continue to ask Yes/No and WH questions about it. Encourage students to give answers in complete sentences as well as short answers.

5. Irregular Past Verbs - Written practice If time, begin written practices. See **references, Day 65.** In all exercises, continue to practice questions and answers in the past.

LAST 1/2 HOUR

6. Possessive Pronouns - Introduce with jazz chant (See Day 22 and Sub Work 1 for procedure.) "This is Mine, That's Yours" and "Selfish" are two very good jazz chants to introduce and practice possessive pronouns.

Because possessive pronouns like "mine" and "yours" are confusing for students and difficult to explain, it's good to introduce them using a jazz chant so that students can acquire the rules by hearing the words in context. When they recite the chants, it is very easy to hear the S ending and the position of possessive pronouns at the very end of sentences.

7. Possessive Pronouns - Introduce with TPR

Hold up a pencil. Say, "This is my pencil. This pencil is mine."

Say, "Juan, hold up your pencil. That is your pencil. That pencil is yours."

Say, "Maria, hold up your pencil."

Tell the class, "That is Maria's pencil. That pencil is hers."

Say, "Juan, let's see your pencil again."

Tell the class, "Look at Juan's pencil. That pencil is his."

Make a sweeping gesture around the classroom. "This is our classroom. This room is ours."

Say, "Hold up your books, everybody." (Indicate all students.) "Those books are yours."

Hold up 3 pencils. "These pencils are mine."

Give 1 pencil each to 3 students. Point to the students. "Now the pencils are theirs."

Possessive Pronouns - Oral practice - TPR

Say, "Okay, now we're going to talk about shoes." (Choose 2 students with shoes of the same color to stand in one corner of the room. Place a boy or man in another corner and place a girl or woman in an area apart from the man. You are in front of the room.

Point to their shoes. (The class should point to the 2 students or to more than one person.)
Point to your shoes. (They should point to their own shoes.)
Point to her shoes. (They should point to the woman or girl's shoes.)
Point to my shoes.
Point to our shoes. (They should point to everybody's shoes in the room.)
Point to his shoes. (They should point to the man or boy's shoes.)

Point to mine.
Point to his.
Point to theirs.
Point to ours. (They should point to everybody's shoes in the room.)
Point to hers.
Point to yours. (They should be pointing to their own shoes.)

The teacher should point to each person or couple to help students answer. Say, "Tell me the color of everybody's shoes."

Mine are _____.
Juan, yours are _____.
Hers are _____.
Theirs are _____.
His are _____.

Choose students who have backpacks or purses of the same color, and put them into several different groups. For example, three students with black purses are in one group. Two students with blue backpacks are in another group. Use your own bag and get into a group with bags of the same color. If you can't get enough similar bags, use shirts or colored pens or markers instead. Add a single male and a single female.

Say, "Let's talk about bags." Point to each person or group in turn. Students should answer with the correct color.

His is _____.
Hers is _____.
Mine is _____. (Step aside from your group and point only to yourself.)
Ours are _____. (Go back to stand in a group with bags of the same color.)
Yours are _____. (Point to a group with a different color.)
Theirs are _____. (Point to a group across the room with a different color.)

Day 65

Vocabulary

hold - held
know- knew (Don't drop the K.)
leave - left (Compare to live, which is regular.)
lose - lost
make - made
meet - met
put - put
read - read (Stress the different pronunciation of the past form.)
ride - rode (a bike, a motorcycle, a horse)

Agenda

1. Opening routine
2. Irregular past verbs #2 - review with pictures, acting, flashcards
        Collect homework, quiz
Irregular past verbs #3 - repeat 2-3X, practice with pictures, acting, flashcard review
        HOMEWORK - copy 20X with forms together
3. Irregular past verbs - reading and questions - popcorn reading with pages from Day 64
        Oral practice with True/False questions
        OR
        Pop quiz with True/False questions, check orally
4. Irregular past verbs - written practice
5. Pronunciation - aw sound #1 - al and all (list attached)

IF TIME

6. Possessive pronouns - review quickly, compare to possessive adjectives on big chart
        Jazz chant - oral practice - chant from Day 64
        HOMEWORK - copy chant 1-3 times for 1-3 points of credit
        Written practice - 1 page
7. LAST 20 MINUTES - 1/2 HOUR - BINGO - Use "VIDEO" for title

Stuff

1. List of irregular past verbs
2. Pictures if available and flashcards for vocabulary words for today's quiz
3. Pictures if available and flashcards for vocabulary words for tomorrow's quiz
4. Copies or projectable file of pronunciation list of AW sound #1 (with AL) (attached)
5. Copies, chart on large Post-it paper, or projectable file of chart in #6, below
6. Copies of jazz chant
7. Bingo game and rewards

Lesson Plan

1. Opening Routine

2. Irregular Past Verbs #2 - Review Use pictures, acting, and flashcards to practice. Collect homework and give the quiz.

Irregular Past Verbs #3 - Introduce Repeat new verbs several times. Practice with pictures, TPR, acting, and flashcard review. HOMEWORK is to copy new verbs 20X with forms together for quiz.

3. Irregular Past Verbs - Reading - Review with popcorn reading Reread a story from Day 64 one time. Use "popcorn reading." Each student reads one sentence each. Make sure students stop when they come to a period. Then they choose the person to read the next sentence. Popcorn reading is a popular technique with younger students. Adults may not like it. If you don't use it, still have students read only one sentence and stop at the first period.

Irregular Past Verbs - Reading - Review - True/False questions Review with True/False questions. You can do the True/False part orally or in writing. When you go over the answers, correct the false ones orally.

For example, if the reading says, "Linda Smith flew to Mexico City."

The True/False question is, "Linda Smith flew to New York." FALSE

Or the reading says, "He went to France last year."

The True/False question is, "He went to China last year." FALSE

When going over answers, for the false answers, students must give the correct information.

She didn't fly to New York. She flew to Mexico City.
He didn't go to China. He went to France.

Alternative Activity - Review with pop quiz Do a quick "pop quiz" on the reading in #3 above with True/False questions. See Day 8 for pop quiz suggestions.

4. Irregular Past Verbs - Written practice Practice with **Practical English, pp. 211-219, 247; Writing Practical English, pp. 149-152, 174; Side by Side, pp. 149-155, 160-161; New American Streamline Departures, pp. 44, 45, 51, 52.**

5. Pronunciation - Aw Sound with al and all Practice the "aw" sound when spelled with "al" and "all." Use the attached list.

IF TIME

265

6. Possessive Pronouns - Compare to possessive adjectives - Chart Present the following pronouns on a pre-written chart. Quickly review the first 2 columns with subjects and possessive adjectives. (See Day 13 and Day 64 for practice with possessive adjectives.)

I	my	mine
you	your	yours
he	his	his
she	her	hers
it	its	its (This form is never used. You will cross it out when you review the list.)

we	our	ours
you	your	yours
they	their	theirs

Pointing to the third column, give several sentences using possessions from the class for each form.

I like my purse.	This purse is mine.
You need to give me your paper.	Is this paper yours?
He needs his pencil.	Is this pencil his?
She wants to eat her lunch.	That lunch bag is hers.

("Its" as a possessive pronoun is rarely used. When you come to "its" in the third column, circle it and heavily cross it out. Tell students that they will never see this. However, they can use "its" as a possessive adjective. Point to the form in the second column.

   I have a phone, but its battery is dead.

Remind students that "its" does not have an apostrophe. (Point to the second column and to the example.) Repeat that they cannot use "its" the way they use "mine" or "yours." Continue.

We need to go to our car.	Which Toyota is ours?
We want to pick up our children.	
Which is their classroom?	Which classroom is theirs?

Possessive Pronouns - Jazz chant - Practice Practice the jazz chant from Day 64. (See Day 22 for ideas on how to practice.) HOMEWORK is to copy the chant 1-3 times for 1-3 points of credit.

Possessive Pronouns - Written practice Do 1 page. **Practical English, pp. 107-108; Writing Practical English, p. 75; New American Streamline Departures, p. 18.**

7. 20 MINUTES to 1/2 HOUR - BINGO Use "VIDEO" instead of "BINGO."

AW Sound with AL and ALL

AL (middle)

salt
also

always
already

(You don't want
3 consonants together
in the middle of a word
so no double L here.)

WRONG
"allways"
"allready"

ALL (end)
(1 syllable = stressed)

all
tall

call
fall

wall
hall
mall
ball

BUT NOT
(2nd syllable = unstressed)
= L similar to "le"

pedal
medal
metal
legal - illegal

1. All the tall boys are standing by the wall in the mall.

2. Don't throw the ball in the hall!

BUT

3. Don't put the pedal to the metal. (Don't speed.) It's illegal!

Day 66

Vocabulary

see - saw
shine - shone
sing - sang
sit - sat (vs. seat) Compare "sit down" with "have a seat."
speak - spoke
stand - stood
understand - understood (1 word)
swim - swam ("Went swimming" is more common.)
take - took

Agenda

1. Opening routine
2. Irregular past verbs #3 - review for quiz with pictures, acting, flashcards
        Collect homework, quiz
Irregular past verbs #4 - repeat, practice with pictures, acting, lots of examples, flashcards
        HOMEWORK - copy 20X with forms together
3. Irregular past verbs - written practice - continue and new practice
4. Possessive pronouns - begin, continue, or finish written practice from Day 65
        Jazz chant - 1 more time in group (See Day 64.)
        Collect homework (copied jazz chant)
5. Punctuation - short written practice
6. Guided composition - a trip to different city or country

Stuff

1. List of irregular verbs
2. Pictures if available and flashcards for today's vocabulary quiz
3. Pictures if available and flashcards for tomorrow's vocabulary quiz
4. Copies or projectable file of jazz chant
5. Copies of your own short, simple paragraph that students can write on. Leave out all capitals, periods, and question marks.
6. Transparency of attached guided composition to help check work

Lesson Plan

1. Opening Routine

2. Irregular Past Verbs #3 - Review Use pictures, acting, TPR, and flashcards. Collect homework and give the quiz.

Irregular Past Verbs #4 - Introduce Repeat the forms together a few times. Practice with pictures, acting, and flashcard review. HOMEWORK is to copy the forms 20X for a quiz.

3. Irregular Past Verbs - More written practice See **references, Day 65. Also Side by Side, pp. 162-163 (a long reading with exercises); GrammarWork, pp. 131 and 129-130 (WH questions with "did").**

4. Possessive Pronouns - Written practice Continue and finish pages from Day 65.

Possessive Pronouns - Jazz chant Recite the chant from Day 64 one or two more times. Collect the homework of the copied chant.

5. Punctuation - Short written practice Write your own short paragraph and type it with no periods, capital letters, or question marks. Pass out copies. Students add periods, question marks, and capitals on the sheets. Don't include commas. Tell them to make the capital letters and periods very large and dark. Review their answers orally and project a corrected version if possible. Unless there were very few errors, students should copy the paragraph one time correctly.

6. Guided Composition - A trip to a different city or country Review the basic paragraph format on the board. Dictate the sentences with capitals, punctuation, indent, and title. Students write the dictated sentences and fill in the blanks with their own information. Walk around and correct their work as you dictate. When finished, project the sample with blanks and fill in the answers together, or orally review the paragraph with students contributing their answers. You can also project a completed paragraph which is an example of good work. Collect the papers to check for understanding and formatting.

Guided Composition with Irregular Past - sample

(Dictate title with capitals. Tell class to center it.) A Good Trip

(Dictate indent = 5 letters or 1 thumb) Last summer, my family went to _____. It

was great! We ate _____ and _____. We also had_____. We drank a lot

of _____ and we liked that very much! We visited _____

and _____. We saw_____ and _____. We

didn't see any_____. We bought _____for souvenirs, and

we brought them back for my family members and my _____. I hope we can

go to _____again soon, because we had a really good time!

Day 67

Vocabulary

teach - taught
Compare to
think - thought

tell - told - He told me.
Compare to
say - said - He said to me.

wear - wore (not use)
win - won (not earn)
write - wrote (compare with ride-rode)

Agenda

1. Opening routine
2. Irregular past verbs #4 - review for quiz - pictures, acting, flashcards
    Collect homework, quiz
Irregular past verbs #5 - introduce - repeat, practice with pictures, TPR, and many examples
        Explain problems of meaning and pronunciation of words on list
        Individual students pronounce past forms in mixed order
        Taught/thought - #1#2 to practice
        Review negative form - students repeat affirmative and negative forms of past 2X
        Review with flashcards
        HOMEWORK - copy 20X with forms together for quiz
3. Irregular past verbs - optional - oral practice - negatives - make complete past sentences
4. Irregular past verbs - further written practice - 1-2 pages
5. Words with aw sound #2 - aw, au and aught/ought - pronunciation and spelling (list attached)
IF TIME
6. Possessive pronouns - second jazz chant "Selfish" - begin (See Day 68.)

Stuff

1. List of irregular verbs
2. Pictures if available and flashcards for vocabulary words for today's quiz
3. Pictures if available and flashcards for vocabulary words for tomorrow's quiz
4. Projectable file or copies of new jazz chant - "Selfish"
5. Projectable file or copies of pronunciation list - words with aw sound #2

Lesson Plan

1. Opening Routine - Past form review Ask questions about where students went, what they ate, what they drank, and what they saw. The goal is a conversation in the past form.

2. Irregular Past Verbs #4 - Review Use pictures, acting, and flashcards to review. Collect homework and give the quiz.

Irregular Past Verbs #5 - Introduce Repeat new homework verbs several times. Practice with pictures, TPR, and a lot of examples. Explain problems with pronunciation and meaning. Ask individual students to pronounce the past forms in mixed order.

Pronunciation - Taught vs. thought Use the #1#2 game to practice. (See Day 3.)

Irregular Past Verbs - Negatives - More review Class repeats negatives 2X going down the homework list. For example: wore - didn't wear, wore - didn't wear

HOMEWORK is to copy the vocabulary 20X for a quiz. Review with flashcards.

Using "wear" Some students have problems using the verb "wear." For practice, **GrammarWork, pp. 63 and 60; New American Streamline Departures, p. 24.**

3. Irregular Past Verbs - Oral practice - Negatives - Optional Coach students to help them answer in complete sentences. This may be too difficult for some classes.

TEACHER	STUDENT
He didn't come to school yesterday. When did he come to school?	He came Tuesday.
Did she go to the store? (or other location) Where did she go?	No. She didn't go to the store. She went home.
Did you speak to his mother? Who did you speak to? When did you speak to him?	No. I didn't speak to her. I spoke to his father. I spoke to him yesterday.
Did you take the white car? Which car did you take? Where did you go?	No. I didn't take the white one. I took the black car. I went to school and the store.
Did you teach in Italy? Where did you teach?	No. I didn't teach there. I taught in Spain.
Did you understand the lesson?	I didn't understand it very well. I only understood a little.

If this is difficult, don't continue it. Don't explain "who" and "whom" here.

4. Irregular Past Verbs - More reading, dialog and written practice Continue. See references, **Day 64, Day 65, and Day 66.**

5. Aw Sound #2 with aw, au, and aught/ought - Spelling and pronunciation Review and practice with the attached list.

6. Possessive Pronouns - Second jazz chant Begin the jazz chant "Selfish." (See Day 68. For how to do a jazz chant, see Day 22 and Sub Work 1.)

AW Sound #2

AU	**AW**
laundry	saw
author	draw
audio	awful
fault	jaw
cautious	law
haul	paw
	raw

automobile
automatic
autobiography

(prefix "auto" = you do something yourself)

AUGHT   **OUGHT**

caught (catch)   bought (buy)
taught (teach)   brought (bring)
                                             fought (fight)
                                             thought (think)

(Only 2 verbs with
"aught" instead of "ought")

BUT NOT!!!   **BUT NOT!!!**

laugh   rough
                                             tough

Day 68

Vocabulary

No vocabulary today. The quiz list could be a retest of common errors from the irregular past verb quizzes. You could also look ahead and start covering vocabulary from the final exam.

Agenda

1. Opening routine
2. Irregular past verbs #5 - review - pictures, acting, flashcards. Collect homework, quiz
3. Irregular past verbs - finish written practice - 1-2 pages
4. Pronunciation - oh/out sounds #1 - start today, finish Day 69 (sheet attached)
5. Possessive pronouns -
    Jazz chant "Selfish" - begin and practice
    Possessive pronouns - more written practice
6. Review possessive pronouns with forms on chart (from Day 65)

OPTIONAL EXPLANATIONS

7. Possessive pronouns - review rules - Okay/Not okay - optional
8. Whose - optional
9. Confusing forms - review - optional
10. Possessive pronoun as a subject - optional

Stuff

1. Pictures if available and flashcards for vocabulary words for today's quiz
2. Projectable file or written copies of jazz chant "Selfish"
3. Projectable file, copies, or chart of possessive pronouns - optional (See Day 65.)
4. Projectable file and written copies of the pronunciation list "Oh and Out Sounds"
5. Flashcards for the words on the attached pronunciation list. Have one pack of flashcards for each sub-list.

Lesson Plan

1. Opening Routine

2. Irregular Past Verbs #5 - Review Use pictures, acting, and flashcards. Collect homework and do the quiz.

3. Irregular Past Verbs - Reading, dialog and written practice - Finish Continue and finish. See **references Day 64, Day 65, Day 66, and Day 67.**

Irregular Past Verbs - More reading Use **Side by Side, pp. 154-155.**

274

4. Pronunciation - Oh and out sounds #1 Continue this practice over 2 days. These words are easy to confuse and just have to be memorized. Students will know many from previous work. Others are fun to include because they sound funny.

Begin by reading all 4 lists. Then point out that there are two different sounds on the lists. One is written with OA and pronounced like the word "Oh!" The other is spelled with OU and pronounced like the word "out." BUT as they can see on List #3 and List #4, both sounds can also be written with OW.

First, read List #1 and contrast it with List #2. You are contrasting the two different spellings for the two different sounds.

Then read List #1 and List #3 together. You are showing the students that the "oa" sound is often written with OW.

Now read List #3 and compare it with List #4. You are showing the students that the "ou" sound can also be written with OW. Also, OW is not always pronounced the same way.

After going over all 4 lists, have the students practice Lists #1 and #2 from flashcards. Don't allow them to pronounce two separate vowels in "boat" and "coat," as in "co-at" and "bo-at." Practice List #1 by itself and then pronounce List #2. Then show words from both lists and see if the students can pronounce them.

On Day 69 or later, you can do the same with List #3 and List #4 together.

These spellings cause a lot of reading problems, but beginning students can try to memorize the words as sight words. Don't use the words for vocabulary words or make students responsible for them on a test. Give the students paper copies of the list so they can study them at home.

Create flashcards for all the words on the attached pronunciation list. Have a pack of flashcards for each list. After practicing each list separately with its own flashcards, you will mix up all the flashcards and have a pronunciation bee to see how well the class remembers the words on the lists. (See Day 70.)

5. Possessive Pronouns - Jazz chant "Selfish" - Introduce and practice (See Day 22 and Sub Work 1 for how to use a jazz chant.) If students have any questions about "whose," add the optional lesson in #8 below.

Possessive Pronouns - Written practice Compare forms. **Practical English, p. 243 (top); Writing Practical English, p. 170 (top).**

6. Possessive Pronouns - Review Display the comparison chart from Day 65. Review the concepts of a subject, a possessive word before a thing, and a possessive word at the end of a sentence. If you wish, you can label the columns "Subject," "Possessive Adjective," and "Possessive Pronoun." (See Day 64 and Day 65 for introduction and practice.)

I	my	mine
you	your	yours
he	his	his
she	her	hers
it	its	XXX (never used)
	(Note: No apostrophe!!!)	
we	our	ours
you	your	yours
they	their	theirs

Don't expect students to use the grammatical terms. The important idea for them to remember is that the three forms do different jobs and we find them at different places in the sentence. The subject words are usually first. They tell us who is doing the action.

"My" and "your" are called "possessive adjectives." Adjectives talk about a thing (a noun), and they come before the thing. Possessive adjectives tell who is the owner of the thing.

> a big car (adjective)
> a blue car
> my car (possessive adjective)
> his car

You cannot leave a possessive adjective alone, without the thing it describes. You cannot say, "That car is my." My what? You have to say, "That car is my car." If you don't want to repeat the word "car" twice, you have to say, "That car is mine." "Mine" substitutes for both "my" and "car." That's why it is called a "possessive pronoun."

Possessive pronouns often come at the end of a sentence. They are alone. They do not need a thing after them, because a pronoun is used in place of a thing. Write examples.

> Which car is your car?
> That car is my car.

OR

> That car is it.   "It" is in place of "my car." "It" is a pronoun. You can use "it" instead of a thing.

OR

> That car is mine.   "Mine" adds the idea of "my" to "it."
> Mine = my + it

Again, "mine" is in place of "my car." If we both understand that we are talking about our cars, you don't need to repeat "my car," "your car," "his car," etc. You can just say, "mine," "yours," or "his."

7. Possessive Pronouns - Rules - Okay or not okay - Optional Remember the rule that adjectives don't have singular or plural.

That is my car.
Those are my cars. (Draw circles enclosing the singular and plural forms of each word. You
            will have circles around that/those, is/are, and car/cars. The only word in
            sentence 2 which does not become plural is "my.")

That is my new car.
Those are my new cars. (Again draw circles around the singular and plural forms of each
            word. Show that the word "new" does not become plural either.)

Give more examples.

It is her car.	OKAY
They are hers cars.	NOT OKAY
They are her cars.	OKAY

Take the class back to the list with 3 columns. Point to the list and say, "If you look at the list, all of the words except "mine" have S on the end, but they are not plural. They are like adjectives. They stay the same if you are talking about one thing or many things."

That car is mine.
Those cars are mine. (Draw circles around that/those, is/are, and car/cars. The only word in
            sentence 2 which does not become plural is "mine." You have a plural
            S on "cars," but not on "mine.")

That car is hers.
Those cars are hers. (Draw the circles. There is an S on "hers," but it is on "hers" in both
            sentences.)

That car is theirs. Two people own one car.
Those cars are theirs. Two people own two cars. (The S is on "theirs" in both sentences.)

Say "okay" or "not okay."

It's mine.	OKAY
They're mine.	OKAY
They're mines.	NOT OKAY "Mine" never has an S.

They're hers.   OKAY
They're hers cars.   NOT OKAY

Put a big X over the S on "hers." When "hers" goes before a thing, there is never an S on it.

The car is her's.   NOT OKAY

Put a big X over the apostrophe. Point to the chart. Say, "There is no apostrophe on this list."

8. Possessive Pronouns - Whose - Introduce - Optional   You may want to introduce "whose" to better understand the jazz chant "Selfish." If you do teach it, don't test on it much at this level. Write on the board.

Who's =   Who is your teacher?
                 Who's your teacher?   My teacher is Mrs. Lockwood.
                 's = "is"   (Circle 's and "is" in the 2 sentences above.)

Whose =   Who has
                 Who owns

        Whose pencil is this?   =   Who has this pencil? Who owns this pencil?
        Answer =   It's the teacher's. It's your pencil. It's my pencil.

Write on board together.

        Who's your teacher?
        Whose pencil is this?

What is the verb here? "Is" in the first sentence in the form of apostrophe S. "Is" in the second sentence. (Circle both of them.)

"Whose" does not have "is" or 's on it. It's one word. It is not a verb. It has the word "is" in the sentence with it. "Whose" is a question word, like "who," "what," and "where." Point to various objects in the room. Stress the verbs in your questions.

        Whose bag IS that?   It's hers. (Point to the owner.)
        Whose shoes ARE those?   They're his. (Point to the owner.)
        Whose room IS this?   It's ours. (Indicate yourself and the class.)
        Whose books ARE those?   They're yours. (Point to one student.)
        Whose books ARE those?   (Point to all students.) They're yours.
        Whose bags ARE those?   (Wave at students far away.) They're theirs.

278

9. Confusing Forms - who's/whose/they're/their/there - Optional Write on board.

Who's this?   Who is this person?
Whose (car) is this?   Who has this car?

They're   They are
their - theirs   two people have a thing
there - over there   (Wave to indicate a point across the room.)

Write the forms on the board and review them quickly to remind students of the differences between them. These words will be continuing problems for your students.

10. Possessive Pronoun as a Subject - Optional

Say, "Sometimes you use the possessive pronoun as a subject. Then you put the possessive pronoun first in the sentence." Write the examples on the board.

Where are our cars?   My car is here and your car is over there.
                               Mine is here and yours is over there.

My kids are in high school.   Mine are out of school now. (We both understand that we are talking about kids.)

Oh and Out Sounds
(Continue over 2 days.)

LIST #1 Oh!
(NOT "oh-ah." It's one sound.)

OA

boat
coat
road
coast
toad
goat
loan
moan and groan
roar
oatmeal
Goal!
Whoa!

LIST #2 Out!
(Gesture toward the door.)

OU

out
couch
house
sound
cloudy
count
bank account
about
loud
noun
pound (the weight, impound your car)
around

LIST #3 OW
(Pronounce like "Oh!" The W is silent!)

bow (hair bow, rainbow)
know (vs. now)
low
grow
blow
crow
tow truck
elbow
snow
show
slow

LIST #4 OW (Pronounce like "Ow! That hurt!" Act it out.)

bow (action)
now (time)
bow wow (dog talk)
meow (cat talk)
brown
cow
downtown
frown
crowd
crown
clown
vowels
wedding vows
howl
allow
Wow!
Pow!

Day 69

Vocabulary

No set vocabulary

Agenda

1. Opening routine
2. Pronunciation - oh vs. out - continue (See lists attached to Day 68.)
3. Modal helper verbs - can/can't - review
4. Modal helper verbs - will - introduce will for future time, compare to can
   Oral practice
5. Will - written practice - 2 pages
6. Will - oral practice - each student uses will to make 1 sentence about the future
   Won't - pronunciation
IF TIME
7. Will - short form - introduce
8. Will - oral practice - questions
LAST 15 MINUTES
9. Will - jazz chant "Meet Me in the Morning" - begin

Stuff

1. Flashcards with the pronunciation words separated into 4 groups
2. Big full year calendar with large numbers
3. Projectable file or copies of jazz chant "Meet Me in the Morning"
4. Index cards - 5x7 inches

Lesson Plan

1. Opening Routine

2. Pronunciation - Oh and out sounds with two letters - Review and continue See lists attached to Day 68. Remind the class of the pronunciation bee with these words on Day 70.

Read Lists #1 and #2 one time each. Review the two different sounds on Lists #1 and #2. List #1 is written with OA, pronounced like the word "Oh!" That is a long O sound. Words on List #2 are written with OU and pronounced like the word "out."

Look at Lists #3 and #4. Read the words. The lists show that both sounds ("oh" and "out") can also be written with OW. Reread and compare List #1 and List #3, with the vowel sound "oh." Then reread and compare List #2 and List #4, with the "out" sound words.

Read and repeat Lists #3 and #4 several times. Define the meanings of the words. Review with flashcards of the two lists spelled with OW. Tell students that tomorrow they will have a pronunciation bee where they must read the word correctly or sit down.

3. Modal Helper Verbs - Review can/can't Write charts on board.

He can swim.
Can he swim?
      Yes, he can.
      No, he can not. No, he can't.
He can't swim.

I can swim.
You can swim.
He/she/it can swim.
We can swim.
They can swim.

Review "can" with 1 or 2 other verbs. Stress "can't" to show that it has stronger emphasis.

4. Modal Helper Verbs - Will - Introduce All modal verbs follow the same rules. "Can" is a modal helper verb and so is "will." "Can" adds the idea of ability."Will" adds the idea of future time. Go back to the chart of "can" and write the chart for "will" next to it.

He will study.
Will he study?
      Yes, he will.
      No, he will not. No, he won't.
He won't study.

I will study.
You will study.
He/she will study
We will study.
They will study.

Compare forms on the chart. "Will" is always the same. The main verb "study" is always the same. Like can, "will" reverses order to make the question. It goes back to regular order to make the answer, short answers, and negative. (Show flipping fingers or crossed arrows when you use the words "reverses order.")

The negative of "will" is "will not." The short form is "won't." Ask several students to say "willn't." They will see that it's difficult to say, so the sound has changed to "won't." See below for more practice on short forms of "will."

Write on the board.

Can = able or possible
Will = future

Will - Oral practice Go to your classroom calendar and point to future dates. Ask a few students some sample questions.

What will you do next week?

I will go to the movies.
I will go downtown.
I will go to a party.

What will you do in December?

I will go to visit my grandma.
I will buy presents for my family.
I will take a vacation.

5. Will - Written practice Start work with "will." **Side by Side, Book 2, pp. 30-31 (basic) and 32 (reading and listening); Composition Practice, Book 1, pp. 75-83.**

6. Will - Oral practice - Pronunciation of won't Ask students, "What will you do in the next 10 years?" Alone or in small groups or pairs, they write on 5x7 index cards 5 complete sentences of things they will do in that period of time. If class ends in the middle of this practice, collect the cards to use in future practices.

I will buy an expensive car.
I will have 3 children.
I will have a cat.

Ask volunteers to report 1 each to the class. As the students report, write a few of the answers on the board. When 5-7 students have reported, go back and write the answers as negative answers underneath each sentence.

I will buy an expensive car.
I won't buy an expensive car.

I will have 3 children.
I won't have 15 children.

I will have a cat.
I won't have a dog.

Ask students to give you a few negative answers. Remind them to pronounce the "oh" sound in "won't." Don't let them pronounce it as "wunt."

Won't - Review spelling Review the contractions spelling rule. Apostrophe (') means a letter or letters are taken out. Then the two words are pushed together. Write on the board.

will not = will n't   (Put X over the O and replace it with an apostrophe.)
willn't   (Push the 2 words together. That's too difficult to say.)
won't   (Cross it out and change it to "won't.")

IF TIME

7. Will - Oral practice - Short form - Introduce Write the short forms on board. Repeat in pairs 2-3 times.

> I will - I'll
> you will - you'll
> he will - he'll
> she will - she'll
> it will - it'll
> we will - we'll
> they will - they'll

Ask 5-7 of the students to repeat their answers using the short forms.

8. Will - Oral practice - Questions Ask students some questions with short answers.

Juan, will you pass this class?   Yes, I will.
                                               No, I won't.
                                               Maybe I will, maybe I won't.

Mrs. Garcia, will you leave class early tonight?   No, I won't.
Will you go home on the bus?   No, I won't.
How will you get home?   I will drive my car.

Maria, will you get married next year?   Yes, I will.
Will you get married in June?   No, I won't.

Mr. Garcia, will you buy a car this year?   Yes, I will.

Ask students a few questions which need a complete answer. Don't continue the practice too long.

Will you buy a new car or a used car?
What kind of car will you buy?
What color car will you get?

LAST 15 MINUTES

9. Will - Jazz chant "Meet Me in the Morning." This jazz chant is short. Do it in the last 15 minutes of class. Read and repeat it several times as a review.

NOTE: Many grammar texts leave "will" to the second semester. It is easier, but not as much used as "going to" for future time. See Day 73, Day 74, Day 76, and Day 77.

Day 70

Vocabulary

You can choose 10 common restaurant menu items taken from the restaurant activity below.

Agenda

1. Opening routine - announcements with "will"
2. Will - jazz chant "Meet Me in the Morning" - repeat
    Written practice - continue from Day 69
    Oral practice - continue from Day 69

IF TIME

3. Restaurant vocabulary - begin - read and practice with menu and food words (See **references, Day 71**.)
    Practice with pictures
    HOMEWORK - optional - choose 10 menu items, repeat, copy 10X for quiz

LAST 40 MINUTES

4. Pronunciation - oh and out sounds - read from lists 1X
    Pronunciation bee - 1 time through flashcards
5. REMAINING TIME, if more than 15 minutes - BINGO - use "ZEROS"

Stuff

1. Pictures of common restaurant menu items
2. Flashcards with the pronunciation words with "oh" and "out" sounds
3. Copies of the "oh" and "out" pronunciation list
4. Big full-year calendar with large numbers
5. Copies, projectable file or copy on board of jazz chant
6. Bingo game and rewards

Lesson Plan

1. Opening Routine Use "will" to make classroom announcements. Also talk about what the class will do today, including pronunciation bee and Bingo.

2. Will - Jazz chant - Begin or continue See Day 69. If continuing, repeat the chant only once or twice.

Will - Written practice Continue. See **references, Day 69.**

Will - Oral practice See Day 69. Continue or start. If continuing the reporting activity, practice the short forms first. Then have 5 or 6 more students report to the class 1 thing they will do in the next 10 years using the short form of "will." Then they repeat the same sentence, but as a negative sentence.

Finish by hearing 1 "will" sentence from students who have not yet reported.

IF TIME

3. Restaurant Vocabulary Begin reading and practice with a restaurant menu and food vocabulary. OPTIONAL HOMEWORK - Choose 10 common menu items and practice them with pictures. Copy the words 10X for a quiz tomorrow. See **references, Day 71.**

LAST 40 MINUTES

4. Pronunciation - "Oh" and "out" sounds with two letters - Pronunciation bee Do this on an easier day, like Friday or the last class of the week, together with Bingo. Repeat the sample words several times with copies of the list. Then do a pronunciation bee using flashcards from all 4 lists. Students compete as 2 teams or in one long line as individuals. Mix up the flashcards and show one to the next student in line. Students must pronounce the word correctly. If they don't, they have to sit down. Reward the last student standing, the last student standing in each team, or all students left when the other team is out. If results are poor, review the words again with the flashcards. This will be fun, but difficult, so when you have done one pronunciation bee, move to Bingo.

5. REMAINING TIME - BINGO Instead of "BINGO," use "ZEROS." Tell students this is their last Bingo game of the course. From now on, they will have an irregular past verb bee for rewards instead of Bingo.

Day 71

Vocabulary

restaurant, kitchen
waiter, waitress, server
hostess
cook
busser

FOR QUIZ
knife
fork
spoon
napkin
plate
saucer
bowl
cup
mug
glass

Agenda

1. Opening routine - announcements with will
2. Will - written practice - finish
    Short form pronunciation - practice when checking
3. Will - short form - pronunciation - review
    Pronunciation - #1#2 game
    Oral practice - answer new questions
4. Restaurant vocabulary - optional - review with pictures, quiz - food words if assigned
Restaurant vocabulary #1 - introduce with text, pictures, TPR with realia, acting, repeat
    Oral practice with questions (attached)
    Review with flashcards
    HOMEWORK - copy 20X, quiz
5. Restaurant dialog or reading - read
6. Restaurant dialog - order food role play

Stuff

1. A textbook page with a simple menu
2. Textbook page or picture of a restaurant showing a table setting
3. Several menus from local restaurants or copies of a very simple menu from local place
4. Pictures and flashcards of today's vocabulary
5. "Realia" (actual objects, in this case real or plastic plates and eating utensils) to practice today's vocabulary

Lesson Plan

1. Opening Routine Make announcements and talk about today's schedule with "will."

2. Will - Written practice Finish written work. See **references, Day 69.** Check using short form of "will." Remind students to pronounce the "oh" sound in "won't."

3. Will - Pronunciation - Review Review the pronunciation of short forms of will. Write on board.

I'll
you'll
he'll
she'll
it'll
we'll
they'll

Have students repeat the short forms a few times. The L sound is going to be difficult for them.

Remind students that you cannot use a short form in a short answer which is affirmative.

Will you do the homework tonight?   Yes, I'll.   INCORRECT
                                     Yes, I will.   CORRECT

Point out separate problems for each form.

I will	I'll	Pronounced like "isle" or "aisle," but often "Ah'll." Sometimes students will write "Ah'll" because that is what they hear.
You will	You'll	
He will	He'll	After writing "he'll" and "she'll," show that the pronunciation of "he" and "she" doesn't change. "Hell" and "He'll" are pronounced differently.
She will	She'll	Same problem. "She'll" and "shell" are pronounced differently.
We will	We'll	Same problem. "We'll" and "well" are pronounced differently.
They will	They'll	

Take the apostrophes out of "he'll," "she'll," and "we'll," and pronounce the new words to show the students that you now have 3 completely different words, "hell," "shell," and "well."

Pronunciation - 'll Practice the difference between "he/he'll" and "they/they'll" with the #1#2 technique. (See Day 3.)

288

Will - Pronunciation - Oral practice Practice correct pronunciation when answering the following questions. Write the answer blanks on the board or help students to answer.

Where will you eat lunch?　　　　　　　　I'll eat at _____.
　　　　　　　　　　　　　　　　　　　　We'll eat _____.
What will you have for lunch?　　　　　　I'll have a _____ and _____.

Where will you eat dinner tonight?　　　　I'll eat at _____.
　　　　　　　　　　　　　　　　　　　　We'll eat _____.

Who cooks at your house?
Will she cook your favorite food?　　　　　Yes, she will.
　　　　　　　　　　　　　　　　　　　　No, she won't.
What will you have for dinner?　　　　　　I'll probably have_____.

Will you go out to eat soon?　　　　　　　Yes, I will.
Where will you go?　　　　　　　　　　　　I'll go to _____
Why will you go there?　　　　　　　　　　I'll go there because _____
　　　　　　　　　　　　　　　　　　　　　　　　　　　it's cheap.
　　　　　　　　　　　　　　　　　　　　　　　　　　　I like Chinese food.
　　　　　　　　　　　　　　　　　　　　　　　　　　　it's close to my house.

4. Restaurant vocabulary - optional Review yesterday's food words with pictures if assigned. Collect homework and give the quiz.

Restaurant Vocabulary #1 - Introduce Review or introduce the new restaurant vocabulary list with texts or pictures, acting, and TPR routines using realia. (See Day 2 for a sample TPR routine with objects.) Repeat the list several times. Practice the words by answering the attached questions. Review with flashcards. HOMEWORK is to copy the words 20X for a quiz.

5. Restaurant Dialog or Reading with vocabulary Read about a trip to the restaurant. **Practical English, pp. 167-168; New American Streamline Departures, p. 54; Composition Practice, Book 1, pp. 30-35, 36-37; Side by Side, Book 2, p. 25.**

6. Restaurant - Dialog - Order food Use the following sentences to order food.

　　　　I'll have the _____.
　　　　I'll have a _____.
　　　　He'll have the _____.
　　　　We'll have some _____.

Role play with copies of real menus, or use **New American Streamline Departures, p. 11; Side by Side, Book 2, pp. 23 (role play) and 27 (order fast food); Lifeskills, p. 63 (fast-food menu); Skill Sharpeners, p. 46 (menu).**

Restaurant Words - Oral Practice

1. What do you use for soup?   spoon, bowl, cup

2. Who helps you?   waiter, waitress, server, busser

3. Who helps the waiter?   busser

4. Who makes the food?   cook, chef

5. How do you cut the meat/food?   knife

6. How do you clean your mouth?   napkin

7. What goes under your cup?   saucer

8. Which is bigger (more big), plate or saucer?   plate

9. Which one is small, appetizer or entree?   appetizer

10. What do you drink?   beverages

11. What is sweet?   dessert

12. Which steak is pink?   rare

13. Which steak is brown?   well done

14. How do you like your hamburger?   rare, medium, well-done

15. How much is the tip?   15-20%

After talking about the answers, you can ask students about where they eat out, what they like to order, if they take the food out, etc.

Day 72

Vocabulary

appetizer
entree
beverage
dessert (vs. desert)
tip
rare
medium
well done

Agenda

1. Opening routine
2. Restaurant vocabulary #1 - review with text, pictures, menus, TPR, acting, flashcards
    Collect homework, do quiz
Restaurant vocabulary #2 - introduce new vocabulary using text or pictures, TPR, acting
    repeat list 2-3 times
    Practice the words with questions including those attached to Day 71
    Review with flashcards
    HOMEWORK - copy 20X, quiz tomorrow
3. Pronunciation - oi and oy - attached list
4. Restaurant reading - finish reading and dialogs from Day 71
5. Restaurant dialog - introduce - I would like, I'd like = I want
    Oral practice - short - from a menu, student asks for 1 drink and 1 food item
    Oral practice - groups of 4 - practice sample dialog (attached), then write similar
    dialog, deliver to class as a group
6. Restaurant - would like - reading and oral practice - continue
IF TIME
7. Will - reading

Stuff

1. Pictures and flashcards of today's vocabulary
2. A textbook page with a simple menu, or copy of a very simple fast food menu
3. Picture of a restaurant with a table setting
4. Copies of attached restaurant dialog
5. Copies or projectable file of attached list of OI and OY sounds, or have it on the board

Lesson Plan

1. Opening Routine Make announcements with "will."

2. Restaurant Vocabulary #1 - Review Use a text, pictures, TPR, and acting. Repeat the list and review the words with flashcards. Collect homework and do the quiz.

Restaurant Vocabulary #2 - Introduce Practice the new vocabulary using a text or pictures. Ask students to place a few foods into each category of appetizer, entree, beverage, and dessert. Repeat the list 2-3 times. Practice the words with questions. Repeat the questions attached to Day 71. Review with flashcards. HOMEWORK is to copy the vocabulary 20X for a quiz tomorrow.

3. Pronunciation - OI and OY sounds See attached sheet.

4. Restaurant Reading Finish or start reading about a restaurant visit. See Day 71.

5. Restaurant Dialog - Order food Finish or start a dialog. See Day 71.

Restaurant Dialog - Would like - Review Use "I would like, I'd like" to mean "I want."

I like	I like hamburgers.	Hamburgers are good. (every day)
I would like	I would like a hamburger.	means "I want to order a hamburger." (More polite)
I'd like	I'd like a hamburger.	short form of "I would like"
I want	I want a hamburger.	same as "I would like" but not as polite to the waiter

Restaurant Dialog - Would like - Oral practice With pictures or a short menu, each student asks for 1 food item and 1 drink. Teacher models first with several students. See **references, Day 71.**

Teacher: Are you ready to order?

Student: Yes.   I'd like a _____ and some_____.
                          I'll have a _____.
                          Can I get a _____?

Restaurant Dialog - Would like - Practice and write Students practice the attached dialog at least 3 times in groups of 4. Then the group writes a short dialog between 2 people and a server and delivers it to the class as a group. They use the attached dialog as a guide. Students can write directly on the dialog copies to help them write the orders.

6. Restaurant Dialog - Would like - Use **New American Streamline Departures, p. 11.** For more with "would like," **New American Streamline Departures, pp. 15, 39.**

IF TIME

7. Will - Reading More reading. **Side by Side, Book 2, p. 32.**

Restaurant Dialog

SERVER: Hi, my name is _____ . I'll be your server tonight.

GROUP: Hi.

SERVER: What would you like?

CUSTOMER #1:   I'll have a _____ with _____ and a _____ .

SERVER: Would you like fries with that?

CUSTOMER #1:   Can I have a salad instead of fries?

SERVER: Yes, of course.

CUSTOMER #1:   Okay, I'll have the salad.

SERVER: And you? (HE LOOKS AT CUSTOMER #2.)

CUSTOMER #2:   I'd like the _____ and the _____ .

SERVER: What would you like to drink?

CUSTOMER #2:   I'd like _____ .

SERVER: Would you like any fries?

CUSTOMER #2:   No, thanks. I don't like fries.

SERVER: Okay. And you? (HE LOOKS AT CUSTOMER #3.)

CUSTOMER #3:   I'll just take some coffee, please.

SERVER: Are you sure?

CUSTOMER #3:   Yes, thanks. I'll ask if I want anything else.

SERVER: No problem. I'll be back with the drinks in a minute.

OY and OI

"Y" AT END OF WORD OR END OF SYLLABLE	"I" IN MIDDLE OF WORD WITH CONSONANT AFTER IT
boy	boil
toy	toilet
joy	soil
enjoy	
royal	coin
loyal	point

Day 73

Vocabulary

No specific vocabulary. An option is to create a list from food items used in today's readings. Among words often misspelled: coffee, ice cream, apple pie, juice, spaghetti, cheese.

Agenda

1. Opening routine
2. Restaurant vocabulary #2 - review with text, pictures, TPR, realia, acting
   Repeat list 3X, review with flashcards
   Collect homework, do quiz
3. Count/noncount nouns - written practice - easier pages
   Rule for count/noncount nouns - food and drinks - introduce briefly
4. Count/noncount nouns - introduce rule in more detail
   Oral practice
   HOMEWORK - optional - copy list of food items 15X for quiz tomorrow
5. Future with going to - review present continuous form
   Introduce future with going to
   Written practice - 2 pages
6. Future with going to and will - compare
   Pronunciation
   Written practice, do same 2 pages with going to and will

Stuff

1. Pictures and flashcards of today's vocabulary quiz
2. Pictures and flashcards of vocabulary list for tomorrow, if any
3. Pictures of food divided into groups by count singular, count plural and noncount. Examples: water, milk, beer, bread, cheese, butter, cake, cookies, muffins, nuts, grapes, apples, a sandwich, a hamburger, a taco
4. Post-it paper sheets with separate lists of food to fill in the blanks in number 4 below
5. Large calendar with all months and holiday pictures if possible

Lesson Plan

1. Opening Routine

2. Restaurant Vocabulary - Review
Use texts, pictures, and menus to review. Repeat the list several times. Review with flashcards. Collect homework and do the quiz.

3. Count/noncount Nouns - Written practice
It's easier to introduce count/noncount nouns with written pages. Do easy pages. **GrammarWork, pp. 50, 52, 54, 56; Skill Sharpeners, p. 44 (foods); Side by Side, Book 2, pp. 11 (vocabulary), 12-13, 17.**

4. Count/noncount Nouns - Introduce rule After doing the written practices, the students will be confused. Explain the rule for count/noncount nouns, including food and drinks, with examples. Don't do too much oral practice.

Noncount **(Never add S)**	**Count** **(Can add S)**
money	dollars, cents, bills, coins, quarters
hair on your head	a hair in your food
coffee (liquid)	a coffee (one cup)
water	a water (a bottle of water)
beer	a beer (one can, one bottle)
milk	a milk (a small carton of milk, like in a school cafeteria)
paper	a sheet of paper, a piece of paper, papers (documents)
rice	a grain of rice
corn	an ear of corn

Give the class sample sentences.

I need money. I only have two dollars in my pocket.
Do you have (any) quarters? No, I don't have any money at all.

Would you like a cup of coffee? OR
Would you like some coffee?
No, thanks. I like coffee, but I don't want any coffee right now.

Let's go have a beer.
Sorry, I don't drink beer.

There is a milk on the lunch tray, but I'm allergic to milk. ("A milk" is one small carton.)

Could I borrow some paper?
How many pieces do you need?
Two or three sheets.

Count/noncount Nouns - More food - Oral practice Show a picture of customers in an eating place. Write the sentences with blanks on the board. Have each list of food on separate pieces of poster paper and let students choose from the list.

What are they going to eat? They're going to eat some _____.
pasta, cereal, pie, bread, chocolate, candy, ice cream
OR
tortillas, Cheerios, hamburgers, hot dogs, candy bars, French fries, potato chips

What is he going to drink? He's going to drink some _____.
soda, Coke, beer, wine, tea, mineral water, milk, orange juice

What is she going to buy? She's going to buy some _____.
tomatoes, apples, oranges, cookies, nuts

What are we going to have for dinner? We're going to have (some) _____.
chicken, steak, spaghetti, spinach, salad, coleslaw, apple pie

What are you going to have for lunch? I'm going to have a _____.
sandwich, burrito, Caesar salad, hot dog, bagel with cream cheese

At the end of this exercise, show each list and ask students to label the list "count singular," "count plural," or "noncount."

HOMEWORK - OPTIONAL - Choose 10 items which students did not know or had trouble pronouncing. Have them copy the words 15X for a vocabulary quiz.

5. Future with Going To - Review present continuous Write the forms on the board.

> I am working.
> She is working.
> We are working.
> You are working.
> They are working.

Remind students that a verb in present continuous means that the action is happening right now. (Point to the floor and the clock, dramatically.) BUT!!! It can also mean future time.

Future with Going To - Introduce Write on board.

He is going to the cafeteria.	(right now) (The main verb is "go.")
I am going to see a movie Saturday.	(future time) (The main verb is "see.")

I am going to graduate in June.
You are not going anywhere. This is not June. The main verb is "graduate."

I am going to make a cake tomorrow.
You are not going anywhere to bake. It's not tomorrow. It's today. The main verb is "make."

Here you are talking about your plans to do something in the future. Future words like "Saturday," "June," and "tomorrow" tell when the action will happen. "Going to" is much more common than "will" to talk about future time.

Present continuous without "going to" can also be used to talk about future time, especially with travel plans. However, don't teach that rule in this class. It's too confusing.

Future with Going To - Written practice Check the answers and save the papers for use in number 6 below. **Practical English, pp. 223-226; Side by Side, Book 1, pp. 128, 130-131.**

6. Future with Going To and Will - Compare going to and will

I'm going to eat at 12.	I'll eat at 12.
You're going to eat at 12.	You'll eat at 12.
He's going to leave at 12.	He'll leave at 12.
She's going to leave at 12.	She'll leave at 12.
The bell is going to ring at 12.	It'll ring at 12.
We're going to eat at 12.	We'll eat at 12.
They're going to eat at 12.	They'll eat at 12.

Remind students that the simple form of the verb comes after the word "to," and you always have the simple form of the verb after a modal helper like "will."

Future with Going To and Will - Pronunciation Read these lists with their typical pronunciation.

Ahmunna eat at 12.	Ah'll eat at 12.
Yer gonna eat at 12.	Yull eat at 12.
He's gonna eat at 12.	Heel eat at 12.
She's gonna eat at 12.	Sheel eat at 12.
Wur gonna eat at 12.	Weel eat at 12.
Thur gonna eat at 12.	Thell eat at 12.

Explain to students that it's okay to pronounce the sentences this way. They will see "gonna" in cartoons or hear people say it, but they cannot write "gonna" in school. It is not correct.

Future with Going To and Will - Written practice After checking answers on the written work in number 5 above, write some of the answers again with "will." As shown above, **Practical English, pp. 223-226; Side by Side, Book 1, pp. 128, 130-131.**

Before writing, repeat that students need to replace 3 words, "to be" + going + to, with one word, "will." Write on the board.

I **am going to** see him later. = 3 words
I **will** see him later. = 1 word

Dramatically underline once or twice "am going to" and "will." Count the words to remind them again that 3 words become one. Point out that "see" does not change in either sentence. As they write, walk around and make sure students do not write "will to."

Vocabulary

Study list of irregular past verbs for verb bee tomorrow.

Agenda

1. Opening routine
2. Vocabulary - food - optional quiz - if assigned, review vocabulary (food items) with flashcards, collect homework, give quiz
Vocabulary - verb bee - repeat all irregular past forms 1X from flashcards
   HOMEWORK - study entire list for verb bee tomorrow - teacher will say present form, student will say past
3. Going to/will - review will, short forms 'll and won't
   Begin or finish oral and written practices from Day 73
4. Future with going to - review rule - okay or not okay
   Dialogs and reading practice
   Reading and oral practice with calendar - optional
5. Pronunciation - Y as consonant and short vowel
6. Count/noncount nouns - more difficult written practice - optional
   Review rule for count/noncount nouns with food and drinks
   More difficult written practice - 1 or 2 pages

Stuff

1. List of all irregular past verbs
2. Flashcards of all irregular past verbs
3. Large calendar with all months, illustrated with holiday pictures if available

Lesson Plan

1. Opening Routine

2. Vocabulary - Food - Optional quiz If assigned, review the food items with pictures and flashcards, collect the homework, and give the quiz.

Vocabulary - Verbs - Practice Class repeats all the irregular past verbs one time quickly with flashcards. HOMEWORK is to study the entire list for a verb bee tomorrow. Students will stand in one long line or play in two lines as teams. The teacher will say the present form. The student up will respond with the correct past form. If the teacher doesn't understand the student's pronunciation, the student has to sit down.

3. Going to and Will - Written and oral practice Quickly review "will" and "won't." Begin or finish the written practice with "going to" and "will" from Day 73.

4. Future with Going To - Okay or not okay Students read sentences from the board and say, "Okay" or "Not okay." When they say, "Not okay," ask, "What's wrong with it?" Help them explain the errors. Or they can volunteer to make the corrections on the board.

I going see a movie.	NOT OKAY	You need to add "am" and "to."
I'm going see a movie.	NOT OKAY	You need to add "to."
I'm going to see a movie.	OKAY	
I'm going to seeing a movie.	NOT OKAY	After "to" you can use only the regular form of the verb "see."
I will to see a movie.	NOT OKAY	"Will" is a modal like "can." It doesn't need "to."
I will see a movie.	OKAY	

Future with Going To - Review rule Compare forms.

will +   simple form of verb
am/are/is going to +   simple form of verb

Remind students that you always have the simple form of any verb after the word "to" and also after modals like "can" and "will."

Future with Going To - Problems with "go" - Optional When you teach "going to" + verbs, avoid using "go" as a main verb. Sentences such as "I'm going to go to school now," will confuse the class. If necessary, write on the board

I am going to school.
I am going to go to school.

Ask, "When?" Next to the first sentence, write RIGHT NOW. Next to the second sentence, write FUTURE TIME. Explain that "going to" is like a helper verb which talks about future time. That's why you can have two "go" in the second sentence. The first "going to" is similar to a helper verb. The second "go" is the main verb.

NOTE: Again, don't try to explain at this level why the two examples above could mean the same thing. It will confuse the class. In the first semester, teach the simplest rule and keep the different verb forms separate.

Future with Going To - Dialog and reading practice When doing dialogs and written practices, use sentence stress which shows how "will" and "going to" are swallowed and the emphasis goes to the main verb. Remind students of pronunciation habits. (See Day 73.)

People pronounce I'll as Ah'll
People say I'm going to as Amanah
People pronounce go to as gotah

New American Streamline Departures, p. 27 (dialog); Side by Side, Book 1, p. 132.

Future with Going To - Reading and oral practice - Optional A longer reading with calendar months and future plans is in **Side by Side, Book 1, pp. 136-137.** If you do this reading, use a large classroom calendar with seasonal illustrations and add the oral practice below.

Future with Going To - Oral practice with calendar For each month, tell one thing that you are going to celebrate or do. Use holidays, your school schedule, vacation plans, etc.

In December I'm going to celebrate _____

> my birthday
> my son's birthday
> my anniversary
> Christmas
> New Year's Eve
> other?????

In June, I'm going to _____

> take my summer vacation
> visit Las Vegas
> drive to San Francisco
> watch my daughter graduate
> buy a _____

5. Pronunciation - Y as consonant and vowel Put examples on the board.

AS CONSONANT (beginning of word or syllable)

SHORT "I" SOUND (rarely)

year
yellow
yes
yesterday

gym (CVC)
physical (CCVC)

canyon

Double L is the same as single L.

6. Count/noncount Nouns - More difficult oral and written practice - Optional Write examples on the board before doing writing the more difficult practices.

1 thing = is	There <u>is a</u> cup on the table.
some things = are	There <u>are 2</u> cup<u>s</u> on the table.
	There <u>are some</u> cup<u>s</u> on the table.
	(2 or more, not a lot. You can count them and add "S" to "cups.")
some (a quantity) = is	There <u>is some</u> coffee (no S) in the cup.
	(This is a quantity that you did not count, so you can't add S. Because you did not count more than one, use "is.")

Count/noncount Nouns - More difficult written practice - Optional - See **Practical English, pp. 103, 106, 104; Writing Practical English, pp. 170-171, 169; GrammarWork, pp. 51, 53, 55; Side by Side, Book 2, p. 17; Skill Sharpeners, p. 52; New American Streamline Departures, p. 10.**

Day 75

Vocabulary

The homework for today was to review all irregular past verbs for a verb bee. One option for a vocabulary quiz tomorrow is to start previewing and pretesting the vocabulary on the final.

Agenda

1. Opening routine
2. Pronunciation - Y as end vowel (list attached)
3. Can/may/could - ask for permission - introduce
       Oral practices - in pairs, then as class
       Written practice
       Dialogs
4. Guided composition - introduce yourself (attached sample)
5. LAST 25 MINUTES - irregular past verbs - verb bee

Stuff

1. Copies or projectable file of Y pronunciation list attached
2. Transparency or projectable file of guided composition attached
3. Flashcards of irregular past verbs
4. Reward candy

Lesson Plan

1. Opening Routine

2. Pronunciation - Y as end vowel
Compare pronunciation. See attached page.

3. Can/may/could - Ask for permission - Introduce
Give examples of "can," "may," and "could" to ask for permission.

Can I have a piece of paper?	Everyday conversation
Can I go to the office now, please?	"Please" makes it more polite.
Could I see your paper, please?	Put "can" into past ("could") to make it even more polite.
May I go to the bathroom, please?	"May" is the most formal and polite.

If you have a class of teenagers, you might want to warn them that "may" is very formal and might be too polite to use with other teenagers.

Can/may/could - Ask for permission - Negative short answer - Oral practice   With modal helper verbs asking permission, it's better to give an excuse instead of a negative short answer. Write examples on the board and review them. Students practice the dialogs in pairs.

Can I have a piece of paper?

Sure.
Of course.
I'm sorry. I don't have another piece.

Could I see your paper, please?

Yes, of course.
I'm not finished with it.
Can I show it to you later?

May I go to the bathroom?

Yes, you may.
Yes, you can.
No, not right now.
Please wait until the bell rings.

Can/may/could - Oral practice with questions   Students request to do the following things. The teacher answers. (Students and teacher choose from the lists on the board.)

May I
smoke in the room?
sharpen my pencil?
sit in the front of the class?
borrow a pencil?
use the stapler?
open the window?
turn up the TV?
turn on the air conditioning?
borrow an eraser?

No, it's illegal.
Okay, but quickly.
If you see an empty seat.
If you give it back after class.
Sure.
If it's okay with the other students.
If the students don't mind.
It's okay with me.
Sure. Here's one.

Can/may/could - Ask for permission - Written practice - Skill Sharpeners, p. 15.

Can/may/could - Ask for permission - Dialogs - New American Streamline Departures, pp. 23, 19, 7.

The teacher acts out each dialog at least once. The class should repeat the dialogs several times as a class and then practice in pairs or groups. Students should copy the dialog at least once as HOMEWORK.

Some topics, such as polite requests, are easier to teach with a "Notional-Functional" approach. This means that you practice set phrases in specific situations. As stated above, many people do not deny polite requests with short answers because it can sound sarcastic or angry. Instead of trying to explain why such answers are uncomfortable, it is easier just to practice typical requests with answers that students are likely to hear.

4. Guided Composition - Introduce yourself See the attached sample.

LAST 25 MINUTES

5. Verb Bee Line students up for a bee game. (See Day 11 for ideas on dividing teams and giving out rewards.)

Using past form flashcards in mixed order, the teacher reads the present form. Students respond with the past form. The teacher must understand the answer. If students can't answer, they sit down. Anyone caught giving answers or looking at verb lists must sit down. If there is one consistent winner, you may have to reward him or her to sit out the contest or to act as the reader, so that others have a chance to win. You will probably have time to go through the cards 2-3 times.

There are commercially available past verb Bingo games. They may include some verbs which are too advanced for beginning students.

Y as End Vowel

LONG I SOUND
(1 syllable = stress)

my
Why?

cry
fry
fly
sky

rye (bread or whiskey)
dye (hair or clothes)

crying
flying
frying

trying
lying

LONG E SOUND
(2 syllables. Last syllable is unstressed.)
(I at the end of a word is unusual.)

family
happy
lucky

easy
activity
hobby

jelly
sticky

study
story
scary
creepy

Many of these words become adverbs.

easy   easily
lucky   luckily
happy   happily

The end Y changes to I and adds LY. The new I is short.

(Put an X over each Y on "easy," "lucky," and "happy." Change each Y to I and add LY. Pronounce the new syllables as you add them. Write the new adverbs again to make the change very clear. Go down the list and pronounce each adjective together with its adverb two or three times.)

Guided Composition - My Life

Walk around the room as you dictate and make sure that the students are observing margins. If not, fold their papers back on the pink lines to force them to stop and start at the margins.

Dictate the title, "My Life." Walk around the room to make sure everyone is centering the title. Make sure they are capitalizing only the first letters of the title. Watch out for students putting periods or quotation marks on the title.

Before you begin dictating the paragraph, write on the board "indent = 5 letters." Write five letters at the left margin of a piece of notebook paper to show students the right size for the indent. You can also put your thumb in the indent space to show students how to use their thumbs to measure the width of the indent.

(Dictate the indent) My name _____. (Dictate all commas and periods.) I am

_____ . I am from _____. I live in _____

with my _____, my _____, and my _____.

Every day, I go to ____(worksite)_____. I **like/don't like** my **job/school**. On the

weekends, I _____. I spend a lot of time with my _____.

In the future, I want to _____. I would like to _____(dream job) _____.

That will make me very happy!

The teacher dictates the composition, leaving time for students to fill in the blanks with their information. Dictate the indent, the commas, and the periods. You can also dictate capital letters. Make sure students choose only one answer from like/don't like and job/school. Students will need help to do the activity. You can coach them by suggesting various endings for each sentence.

Count 1 point for the title, 1 for the indent, 1 for each margin, and 1 for mostly correct periods and capitals. Don't count spelling.

To preview the assignment or to review the work, you can project a transparency or file and fill it in as a class.

Day 76

Vocabulary

No set vocabulary.

Agenda

1. Opening routine
2. Pronunciation of long and short OO and could, should, would - introduce (attached list)
3. Future with going to - reading practice
        Written practice
4. Past Verbs - reading - optional - read a longer story with irregular verbs
        Activities with regular and irregular verbs
        Oral practice with Yes/No and WH questions
        Pop quiz with True/False questions - no grade - check in class

Stuff

1. Photocopied copies of a long reading that students can mark up
2. Yellow markers to mark verbs in story
3. Copies or projectable file of attached list of OO words

Lesson Plan

1. Opening Routine Give information about the final exam using "going to."

2. Pronunciation of Long and Short OO, and could, should, would Introduce and practice with the attached sheet. 15 minutes maximum. Practice again on Day 77.

3. Future with Going To - Reading Use **New American Streamline Departures, p. 28 (wedding); Skill Sharpeners, p. 89.**

Future with Going To - More written practice Use **Practical English, pp. 232-233D, 248-249P; Writing Practical English, pp. 157-162; GrammarWork, pp. 69-74, 76.**

4. Past Verbs - Reading and oral practice - Optional Read a longer story with lots of irregular verbs. Student read one sentence each, making sure to stop at the period. Students in pairs or small groups mark all the verbs with pencils or yellow markers. Check their answers as a class. Choose a few verbs and ask the students how they know that the word is a verb. Make a T-chart of the first 10-15 regular vs. irregular verbs.

Ask Yes/No and WH questions about the reading. Then dictate a quick pop quiz on the reading with True/False answers. Check this in class and don't grade it. **New American Streamline Departures, p. 52; Side by Side, Book 1, pp. 154-155; Composition Practice, Book 1, pp. 87, 91.**

Food vs. Foot and Should, Would, Could

Long OO	Short OO	Compare to short U
food	foot	but
boot	book	buck
kooky	cookie	hut
kook	cook	mud
toot a horn	hook	puddle
boom	look	luck
fool		
room		rum
mood		
	good	
	shook (shake)	
	stood (stand)	
	cookbook (recipes)	
	hood	
	wood	
	would	
	could	
	should	

The sound in "would," "could," and "should" is short OO. Don't pronounce the L or the U.

I would like a Coke. = I'd like a Coke.	Please give me a Coke.
I could swim when I was 5 years old.	past form of can
You should study for your test.	It's a good idea.

1. Look at those boots!
2. I'm in a good mood.
3. Please take this book to the book room for me.
4. He stood up and shook her hand.
5. The food fell on his foot. He felt like a fool.

Day 77

Vocabulary

Don't assign vocabulary today because all future classes are review for the final exam. You could begin to assign vocabulary from the final exam. (See Day 78.)

Agenda

1. Opening routine
2. Pronunciation of long and short OO, could, should, would - finish
3. Future with going to - reading - finish
    Written practices - finish and continue
4. Count/noncount nouns - written practice - finish
5. Can/could/may/I'd like - oral practice (dialogs attached)

IF TIME

6. Irregular past verbs - reading - irregular verb review - finish (See Day 76.)

Stuff

1. Photocopies of reading and yellow markers used in Day 76
2. Menus or pictures of food and drinks
3. Photocopies of attached sheet of dialogs

Lesson Plan

1. Opening Routine Use "going to" to give information about the final exam.

2. Pronunciation of Long and Short OO, and could, should, would Finish pronunciation practice with the sheet attached to Day 76.

3. Future with Going To - Reading Finish readings. See **references, Day 76.**

Future with Going To - More written practice See **references, Day 76.** Also, for WH questions with going to, **GrammarWork, p. 75.**

4. Count/noncount Nouns - Written practice Finish. See **references, Day 73.**

5. Can/could/may/I'd like - Oral practice Students practice the attached dialogs several times in pairs or groups and then use them as models with food ideas from menus or pictures.

IF TIME

7. Irregular Past Verbs - Reading Finish the irregular verb review begun on Day 76.

Dialogs with Polite Requests

A

Would you like some soda?

Would you like Coke or Pepsi?

Yes, we do.
Sure.
Yes, of course.

B

Yes, please.
Yes, thank you.

Can I have some Coke?
Do you have any orange soda?

Could I get two bottles?
Could I get some water too?

What would you like for dessert?
Would you like some ice cream
on that?
Would you like milk or cream?
Do you want sugar also?

I'd like a piece of chocolate cake.

Yes, please. And some coffee, please.
Some cream, please.
No, thanks. I don't need any sugar.

Can I have a cookie, please?
Could I have a glass of water, please?

Yes, there are some in the closet.
Yes, but I'm sorry. There isn't any ice water.
We only have tap water.

Would you like a piece of chocolate?

No, thanks. I just had some.
No, thanks. I'm not hungry.
No, thanks. I'm on a strict diet.

Day 78

Vocabulary

For the vocabulary quiz tomorrow, choose 1/2 of the most difficult words on the final exam. Review them in class. The quiz should not be a dictation test for spelling. It should be multiple choice or True/False questions which test understanding of the words.

Agenda

1. Opening routine
2. Final exam preparation - review, practice test vocabulary for quiz
    HOMEWORK - study vocabulary for quiz
3. Final exam preparation - general review of sample test or test review material
    Do 1/2 of more difficult parts
    HOMEWORK - easier parts of practice test
4. Final exam preparation - explain essay topic
    HOMEWORK - think about or make notes for test paragraph, "My Family" or other assigned topic
    ADDITIONAL HOMEWORK - study for final - text and notes
    COLLECTION OF VOCABULARY LIST - If a course vocabulary list was assigned at the beginning of the course, teacher will collect before test for credit
IF TIME
5. Review game - Optional

Stuff

1. Copies of an official test review or a sample test duplicating all topics and types of problems on the final
2. Additional practice materials on test topics difficult for the class
3. Flashcards or questions on 5x7 index cards for bee on difficult material - vocabulary words, past form verbs, or a list of questions to be answered as a game

Lesson Plan

1. Opening Routine Give announcements about the final exam and end of semester information with "will" and "going to."

2. Final Exam Preparation - Review test vocabulary Review all of the vocabulary words on the final exam. Choose about 1/2 of the most difficult words and review them with pictures, flashcards, and questions. You could show flashcards of the words and ask the class for a basic meaning. For example, for a flashcard with the word "apple," students can say, "They're food," or "It's fruit," or "We can eat them." For verbs, they can imitate the action. For adjectives, they can point or describe something with that specific quality.

312

Explain that the vocabulary quiz tomorrow will not be a dictation test for spelling like previous vocabulary quizzes. It will be multiple choice or True/False questions which test students' understanding of the words.

To prepare students for other types of vocabulary on the test, such as helper verbs or location words (prepositions), you need to include them on a sample test. For example, if "don't" and "doesn't" are on the exam, the sample test should include them in at least one question and in more if students still have problems using them.

3. Final Exam Preparation - Review grammar Quickly review the whole sample test, pointing out the various sections. Do about /12 of the more difficult topics in class. If students have trouble with certain sections of the exam, focus on them and plan additional work in that area for the next class period.

Assign the easiest parts of the sample test for homework. Make clear to students that the homework is very similar to what they will see on their final and that you will give homework credit for this work.

The final should be a test only on material which students have already seen in class. If students are really weak in a certain area or if they haven't seen it before, they will probably not improve much in two days of final exam preparation. The purpose of the exam preparation is to review their knowledge, remind them of details, and clear up any confusion they might have on certain topics. It should also help them to be more confident when they take the test.

4. Final Exam Preparation - Assign paragraph topic Tell your class the topic for the final composition, which is an unguided paragraph. Tell them to think about and make notes on the topic. "My Family" is an example of a good paragraph topic. They will have about 1/2 hour to do one paragraph and will not be able to use notes.

IF TIME

5. Review Game - Optional Depending on what is on the final exam, students can do a bee game or other type of contest for rewards. They can pronounce or define words on the sample test from flashcards, give short answers to questions, or choose one correct sentence out of two.

Day 79

Vocabulary

Today's vocabulary list is the second half of the difficult words on the final exam. These words will be on the final exam tomorrow, so there will not be a quiz on them.

Agenda

1. Opening routine
2. Final exam preparation - quiz on vocabulary words from yesterday, check and collect
    Review and practice second 1/2 of test vocabulary for final exam
3. Final exam preparation - check homework of easier review materials
    Do remaining difficult parts of the sample test in class
    Practice difficult question formats from test
    Additional practice on grammar where students are weak
4. Final exam - additional component - Do an optional additional grammar test or other component which can be separated from the final exam, such as speaking, listening, or dictation sections.
HOMEWORK - study with their text, notes, and a final test review or sample test
    Prepare for the test paragraph, "My Family"
COLLECTION OF VOCABULARY LIST - If a main vocabulary list was assigned at the beginning of the course, it will be collected before the test for credit.

Stuff

1. Copies of official test review or sample test practicing all topics and types of problems on the final
2. Additional practice materials on weaker topics
3. Test on supplementary grammar materials - optional
4. Listening, speaking, or dictation components of final exam

Lesson Plan

1. Opening Routine Give end of course information with "will" and "going to."

2. Final Exam Preparation - Review test vocabulary Give a quiz on the first 1/2 of the difficult test words. Review the second 1/2 and tell students they will see those words on the test. There will not be a separate vocabulary quiz on them.

3. Final Exam Preparation - Review materials Check the simpler review materials done for homework. Do and check the remaining difficult parts of the sample test in class. Make sure to include all the types of questions and formats which appear on the test. Do additional practice on any weak sections. For example, if students are having problems with "do" and "does," have a worksheet on them.

4. Final Exam Preparation - Additional component If you want to add a grammar test to the final exam, like a multiple-choice test from a supplementary text or from supplementary grammar work, you should do it today or on another day separate from the mandated final.

If there is a listening or speaking section on the final exam, you should also do that on a separate day before the test, because if you need to test students individually, it will be hard to monitor the main test for copying at the same time. After the final exam, you may have lots of absences.

If there is a listening component to the test which involves dictation, you should always give it first or, preferably, on a day before the exam. This is especially important if you are afraid students will not have time to finish the final. It also gives you more time to make up the dictation for absent students.

It never hurts to do the final exam over several days, because there always seems to be at least one student who does not show up on the official test day but does turn up a day later.

HOMEWORK - Study for the final with the text, notes, and a corrected final test review. Remind students you will collect their course vocabulary lists before the test for credit. Remind them to think about and even make notes for the test paragraph, "My Family," although notes will not be allowed during the final. Give some sample ideas for the paragraph. For example,

> Give a little information about yourself.
> Who lives with you? Talk about them.
> Where does your family live?
> Give some information about your family home.
> What does your family do together?

Day 80

Vocabulary

Collect main vocabulary list from notebooks for credit.

Agenda

1. Opening routine - will and going to - end of semester announcements only
2. Final exam or last unit test
    Dictation - Do FIRST or on a previous day.
    Main section of test - 1 1/2 hours
    One-paragraph composition - last 1/2 hour - explain 1/2 hour before end of exam. They can finish after class if necessary.
    Reading passage with questions. Required or optional for extra credit if student finishes early.
    Listening or speaking part of test - Do as students finish the test or (better) on a previous day.
3. Past irregular verb bee with candy rewards - IF TIME (unlikely)

Stuff

1. Final exam or last unit test materials, pencils, erasers, Scantrons, lined paper for paragraphs
2. Past irregular verb flashcards and candy rewards
3. Puzzle or activity for students who finish the test extremely early

Lesson Plan

1. Opening Routine

2. Final Exam or Last Unit Test

If you don't have a mandated final exam or final unit test, you can use a multiple-choice test of 100 grammar items plus a one-paragraph composition. It should contain only items that students were tested on during the course. Avoid any surprises or tricky questions. If you use a standardized grammar test, write on the board the numbers of the questions that you did not cover and tell students to skip them. Or you can give them the answers.

If you do have a mandated test, but you feel that you need more information to decide who should move on to the next level, or if you have given a lot of supplementary grammar material, you can give the mandated final and a multiple-choice grammar test of your own as well. If you use two tests, they should be given on separate days for 1 1/2 hours to 2 hours each day.

One-paragraph Composition - "My Family" If writing is required in the curriculum, you can ask students to write one very basic paragraph, with mistakes, but understandable.

Interrupt the test and explain the paragraph assignment 1/2 hour before the end of the exam. Students can finish after class if necessary. Write the requirements (title, margins, etc.) on the board. Explain and write on the board how many points you will give for each part of the paragraph. You should give 1 point for the title, 1 total for both margins, 1 for the paragraph indent, and 1 total for using capital letters, periods, and understandable spelling. You should not insist on perfection. For example, every single capital letter does not have to be correct, but most of them should be.

Each piece of information or fact is worth 1 point. An introductory sentence and conclusion would receive many extra points. Ask the students to talk about their family at home. Give the following as examples, but don't write the prompt questions on the board or some students will write answers to the questions instead of writing a paragraph.

Who lives with you?
What are their names?
How old are they?
What do they wear?
What do they like to do?
Where does your family live?
What does your family do together?
Where do you go together?

Teaching assistants should not help students write the paragraph. The goal is to see how well the student writes independently. Their paragraphs will probably have 3-7 sentences and results will vary depending on the kind of student and class that you have. If the student doesn't do the assignment at all, that is useful to know and results in a zero grade in writing. You should roster the paragraph grade both together with other test results and separately, because a zero in writing will probably determine whether the student passes or repeats.

Reading Paragraph with Questions - Required or optional If you expect some of the better students to finish very early, add a short independent reading paragraph with questions for them to answer in complete sentences. You can give them extra credit or use the answers to further evaluate a student's ability to pass to the next level.

If you like, you can add this assignment as an additional test requirement. In that case, you should give the assignment on a separate day to allow all students a chance to do it. You should already have an idea of student reading comprehension from classwork. If your program promotes beginning students to an additional beginning level, your test does not have to be as demanding as when the next level is much higher.

Extra Material You may have very recent entrants to the class or other students who will not be able to do much of the exam and who will not be able to write the paragraph or read independently. You should have some kind of puzzle or activity for them to do when they can't go any further on the test. When you see that they have stopped working, collect their answer sheets and give them the alternate activity.

Dictation Component If there is a dictation or group listening component to the exam, you should always do it first. You could do it on a previous day, leaving you more time for the written exam. Don't have teaching assistants do the dictation for the whole class. They can do the make-up dictations if necessary.

Listening or Speaking Component If you want to add an individual listening or speaking section to the exam, you should try to have it on a separate day. Unless you have a teaching assistant, you will not be able to monitor the test for copying and questions while giving a listening or speaking test to individual students at the same time. Also it will distract others. You will probably have some idea of how well the student speaks and understands from his or her performance in class, but testing can be valuable if the students don't speak much in class.

IF TIME (unlikely)

3. Verb Bee There will probably not be enough time to play on test day, but it's fun to give out reward candy to all at the end of the test.

Unit Test Day minus 2

These activities are to prepare students for mandated unit tests or for periodic unit tests which are in a text or teacher-made. The final exam and final exam preparation suggestions are in Days 78-80. The "Unit Test Day" pages are similar, but they should be integrated into regular class periods as necessary, depending on the type of unit test you will give the students.

Vocabulary

Select 10-15 vocabulary words from the unit test for a quiz on the meaning tomorrow. This is not a spelling or dictation test.

Agenda

1. Opening routine
2. Vocabulary - Give previous day vocabulary quiz, if any.
3. Unit test - mandated test - vocabulary - half of the vocabulary from the unit test
    Choose 10-15 words - quiz tomorrow on meaning, not spelling
    HOMEWORK - study words
3. Unit test - test in text - vocabulary - optional - same as above, but optional
4. Unit test - all classes - Scantron - fill in computer answer forms
5. Unit test - mandated unit test - Use practice test with all test material and question formats.
    Do 1/2 of difficult questions in class and check
    HOMEWORK - easiest parts of practice test
5. Unit test - test in textbook - Show students where the test is
    HOMEWORK - review and study
    Optional - short practice test of most difficult material tomorrow
5. Unit test - Ungraded or nonacademic class - alert students to upcoming test
IF TIME
6. Unit test - review test grammar - optional - additional written or oral practice, correct
7. Lesson plans - complete unfinished work, no new topics

Stuff

1. Copies of practice test materials (for mandated tests)
2. Photocopied copies of test in book (for unit tests from texts)
3. Scantron answer sheets and sharpened pencils with good erasers
4. Sample "test" with 3-5 multiple-choice, very easy questions for Scantron training

Lesson Plan

1. Opening Routine

2. Vocabulary Collect homework and give a quiz on previous vocabulary, if any.

3. Unit Test - Vocabulary - Mandated test Go over about 1/2 of the difficult vocabulary from the unit test which will be in two days. Choose 10-15 words to copy for HOMEWORK. The quiz tomorrow will be on meanings (not dictation for spelling). This is required for the mandated test.

Unit Test - Vocabulary - Test in textbook - Optional Do the vocabulary as above, but it is optional.

4. Unit Test - Use a Scantron All students should learn to use a Scantron form or other type of computer-graded test answer sheet. If this is your students' first test with a Scantron form, some may not know how to use it. Teach students how to fill in their full name, date, and test information in the information area of the answer sheet. Mark up a sample Scantron to show them where they can write. Explain that on a bubble sheet, they can write only in the information box or in the answer bubbles.

Give a sample test with 3-5 questions. Show students using your own form how to match up the numbers of the questions and answers. Draw a little picture on the board to show them how to fill in the whole answer bubble firmly, but not too hard or they will not be able to erase errors. Don't allow anyone to use pens, markers, or unusual pencils on the form. Go around the room and check the answer sheets to make sure students are not filling in the bubbles with huge black blobs or tiny little faint marks.

While you are doing the sample questions, walk around the room to make sure that no student is using the same Scantron line for more than one answer. If students are mixing up the answer lines on the form, give them index cards to cover the answer lines that they have already completed.

Go over the test immediately. Ask students to explain why each wrong answer is wrong, and have them erase and change their wrong answers. Before they turn in the sample test, once again show students the areas that they can write in, the answer area and the information square. Ask them to check that they don't have any extra marks on the answer sheet, that they have answered all the questions, and that they have included their full name. Review each test form after they are collected to make sure that everyone has understood the procedure. This will save you a lot of time on test day.

5. Unit Test - Practice test If you are giving a mandated unit test, use a practice test which contains all the material and question types on the mandated test. Do about 1/2 of the most difficult sections in class and go over the answers. Make sure the students understand what they will have to do on the real test. Give the easiest parts of the practice test for HOMEWORK.

Unit Test - Test in textbook If you are using a unit test in a textbook, show the students where the test is located in the book and tell them to look at it for homework to see if they understand everything. Tell them exactly which pages to study. Show them the photocopies that you will use for the test, so they see that marking the correct answers in their text before the exam will not help them. (If you are using used books in a public school setting, many of

320

the answers will probably be checked off in the books already.) If the test vocabulary looks easy, or if you have used most of the text in class, you can skip the vocabulary practice and quiz. HOMEWORK is to study the text and any assigned vocabulary from the unit test. If you plan to have a short practice test tomorrow, you can warn the class to prepare for that.

Unit Test - Ungraded or nonacademic class A test is another way of reviewing and working with material. If you do not need to test students for grading purposes, you can still test them for your own information as well as to show them what they have learned. A test can show you what you need to reteach and help you decide whether to advance students to the next level. If a test is not mandated and passing to another level is not a concern, you don't have to spend as much time preparing them for tests.

Alert the class to the upcoming test. HOMEWORK - Ask the class to review their notes and textbook or workbook. Show them the sections that will be on the test.

IF TIME

6. Lesson Plans - Complete Return to daily lesson plans and continue uncompleted work. Don't introduce new topics.

7. Unit Test - Review grammar for test - Optional IF TIME, do additional practices on more problematic grammar topics. Correct the work in class. For example, for the first unit test, you could review the following with Correct or Incorrect? (See Day 10.)

singular/plural in this/these, that/those
is/are
noun plurals
adjective rules
present continuous is 4 parts - he + is + go + ing
a vs. an
in vs. on
separate words of location - next to, in front of

Unit Test Day minus 1

Vocabulary

Remaining vocabulary for tomorrow's unit test if necessary

Agenda

1. Opening routine
2. Unit test - vocabulary - mandated test or test in text - collect homework, do quiz, if assigned
Second 1/2 of vocabulary from test - review - quiz will be the test

3. Unit test - for mandated unit test - practice test - check homework (easiest parts of the practice test)

      Do last 1/2 of difficult questions in class, check answers

3. Unit test - test in textbook - optional - short pretest of most difficult questions, check

4. Unit test - mandated test - test separate components of mandated unit test

IF TIME

5. Lesson plans - finish uncompleted work

6. Unit test - review difficult grammar - additional practice, correct in class

HOMEWORK - All classes - study text and notes for unit test

Stuff

1. Copies of practice test materials (for mandated tests)
2. Photocopies of test in book (for unit tests in textbooks or supplementary texts)
3. Sample test questions similar to trickiest questions from test in textbook
4. Scantron forms and sharpened pencils

Lesson Plan

1. Opening Routine Make sure everyone understands there is a major exam tomorrow. Review the types of questions that will be on the test - multiple choice, a composition, etc. Advise students that their seats will be separated during test and that copying = 0. Briefly explain how the test relates to their grade and their ability to pass the class. You can draw a little graph on the board with a line showing the percentage needed to pass the exam.

2. Unit Test - Vocabulary Give a quiz on the previous day's vocabulary, if any was assigned. Collect the test and then go over the answers. Collect the homework.

Unit Test - Vocabulary Review remaining vocabulary for unit test tomorrow.

3. Unit Test - Practice test If you are giving a mandated unit test, quickly check the easiest portions of the practice test which were assigned for homework. Do the remaining 1/2 of difficult questions in class and go over answers. Make sure the students understand all the tasks which they will have to do in the exam.

Unit Test - Test in textbook - Optional If students seem weak on certain parts of the exam, you can give a short pretest of the most difficult questions. Go over all answers and do more practice on the difficult ones. If there is material on the test that you have not covered, don't try to teach the material in one day. Tell students that they will not be responsible for uncovered material on the exam.

HOMEWORK - Remind students that the unit test in the text is based on the text. Show them the previous unit in the book and write the page numbers they should study on the board.

4. Unit Test - Test separate parts of mandated unit test If your unit test is divided into separate components, such as a dictation, speaking, and listening, today give one or two parts which can be easily separated from the rest.

IF TIME

5. Unit Test - Review grammar Do additional practices for the grammar topics on the test if necessary. Correct in class.

6. Lesson Plans - Complete Return to the daily lesson plans and finish any uncompleted work. Don't start any new topics.

Unit Test Day

Agenda

1. Opening routine
2. Unit test - Give mandated test, unit test in textbook, or your teacher-created test.
3. IN REMAINING TIME - BINGO or other activity

Stuff

1. Mandated unit test forms. Check copies to make sure test booklets have not been marked.
2. If test is in the textbook, copies of an unmarked test page
3. Scantrons and sharpened pencils
4. Bingo game
5. Small candy reward for effort on test or Bingo prize
6. Puzzles or activity for students finishing early

Lesson Plan

1. Opening Routine Briefly remind students that copying gets zero credit. Tell them to choose the answer which they think is best if they don't know the answer at all.

2. Unit Test - Mandated test A periodic unit test is usually mandated by curriculum.

Unit Test - Test in a textbook or teacher-made test Some texts and supplementary books have unit tests. If you have no available test, put together a multiple-choice grammar test from exercises already done in the class. You can give the test before your grading period ends or every 4-5 weeks. If you are using a supplementary text as well as a mandated program, you can give both exams, but you should do it in separate weeks, or at least on separate days.

For a listening component, dictate questions and 2-4 answers labeled "a, b, c, d." Students mark the correct letter on their Scantron or write it on a separate piece of paper.

For a listening plus writing component, you can use a dictation taken from previous work, with the paragraph format and punctuation given as part of the dictation. You could also use sentences from homework dictated with periods and capital letters.

A reading component can be added. It should be a short paragraph with a series of questions to be answered in short answer, multiple-choice or True/False format. It could be directly copied from classwork or homework. This could also be extra credit work for people who finish early. It should not have a lot of new material. If the readings do not have questions, you can write them yourself. Readings which include several grammar points are **Lifeskills, pp. 26, 67, 98; Skill Sharpeners, pp. 17, 31, 39, 70, 79, 104; Practical English, pp. 48-50A, 109-110, 118-119, 137-138, 153-154, 174-177, 199-200; New American Streamline Departures, pp. 13, 25; Side by Side, Book 1, pp. 50-51; Composition Practice, Book 1, pp. 57-59.**

Writing component Most beginning students will not be able to write a short paragraph by themselves until the final exam about four months after their first day in class. Some will not write until the end of their second semester. You can have them do only parts of a composition. For example, they can complete sentences, re-order sentences from a book, or copy sentences into paragraph form.

Oral practice and paragraph component Student writing abilities within a class are usually very varied. Most students will need a lot of support. You can do the following activity in class, correct the paragraphs, and have the students rewrite the paragraphs once or twice for a grade on the final copy as part of the unit exam.

Talk about a picture where many people are doing things in a town, a party, or a school. Then have the students answer questions about the picture. For example, see **Practical English, pp. 122-123.** Then use the picture again. See **Writing Practical English, p. 87.** Ask the students a set of easier questions. They answer in complete sentences if possible. Then they write a guided composition. You dictate a general statement for the first sentence and they copy it. They then copy the answers they have written in the form of a paragraph after the general statement. When they are finished, ask if anyone can give you a "conclusion" about the picture, a sentence which has an opinion or an emotion in it. If they can't, you dictate one. Discuss a title which the whole class can use. Try to make sure that students are using paragraph format and punctuation as they write.

For sample questions, you could ask:

> Where are they?
> Give some information about the town.
> What time is it?
> How is the weather? (if shown in the picture)
> What do you see in the picture?

What are the people doing? (They're in school, they're working, etc.)
What is this person doing? (Point to 3 different people in the picture.)
How do they feel? (happy, angry, busy)
Do you want to visit this town? Why?

You can do this as a part of the unit test and grade the results generously based on the papers that you get. You can go backwards in your text and choose a picture or paragraph for the test which is easier than your students' present level. You can use a picture from a more difficult text but write questions which are easier for your students. You can work on a picture toward the end of the course with a lot of help and support as a sort of pretest and do it again for the final exam as a review and retest.

Unit Test - Ungraded or nonacademic class With this type of class, you may want to dictate the test questions and answers. Students can answer in multiple-choice form with 2-4 answers or in a True-False format, with "True" marked as "a" and "False" marked as "b."

Types of test questions for an ungraded class could include vocabulary, picture identification with pictures of everyday activities and work, listening exercises, and multiple-choice grammar questions with emphasis on questions and short answers. Reading problems could include schedules, instructions such as those on ATM and parking lot payment machines, real estate information, and advertising. If you are teaching a citizenship class, you can test on voter and jury information as well as the citizenship test for naturalization. A writing test could include writing complete answers to personal history questions and, later in the class, merging them into a personal history paragraph.

For sample listening exercises, see **Side by Side, Book 1, pp. 167-170; Side by Side, Book 2, pp. 140-144.** For vocabulary questions, commands on the citizenship interview, and civics information, Google "citizenship test."

3. IN REMAINING TIME - BINGO or other activity Play Bingo only if all students are finished. As long as students are still working, have extra test segments or an activity like a puzzle or a drawing activity for students who finish early. If only a few students remain and they have stopped working, collect their papers and play Bingo or do some fun activity.

You should not play Bingo for more than 30 minutes. If a lot of students finish very early give students some type of class-related art activity or project.

You can also go back and finish work begun in the previous unit. Don't introduce new topics after a long test.

Reward students for effort with small candy bars at the end of the class.

Unit Test Day plus 1

Vocabulary

At the end of class, introduce and practice vocabulary for the next day as usual.

Agenda

1. Opening routine
2. Unit test - all versions - review test - go over questions
    Testing tips - optional
    Writing paragraph or sentences - project an example of a good paper
    Chart of test results - pass out and explain
3. Unit test - Reteach material which many students got wrong, if it is not much
4. Vocabulary - introduce, practice vocabulary for next lesson
HOMEWORK - copy new vocabulary words for quiz
5. Lesson plans - return to regular lesson plans or begin new unit

Stuff

1. Scantron answer forms and test materials from unit test
2. Copies with chart of test results shown by number or by name. It should show student scores, the minimum passing grade, and the highest grade achieved in the class.
3. Projectable file, transparency, or copies of a good paragraph or written answers
4. Material for normal class

Lesson Plan

1. Opening Routine

2. Unit Test - Review Go over the test item by item and ask students for correct answers. Use the test checking to practice reading, speaking, and pronunciation just as you would in a regular class. Students are often most motivated after an exam, because they consider tests more important than regular classes.

Unit Test - How to answer a multiple-choice test - Optional Teach students how to answer multiple-choice questions. Choose 5 examples from the test in which the wrong answers are easy to find. Go over each example, reading the questions and answers, working as a class. Who, what, where, and when is the sentence talking about?

Read all 4 of the answers first. Look for 2 answers which are probably wrong and 2 which are more difficult. Draw a line through the "crazy answers" on the test materials, not on your answer sheets.

Look at the 2 remaining answers and compare them to the question. The following may be clues to a wrong answer. Explain only those which are found on your test.

- There is no capital on months or days of week.
- The answer sentence does not have a capital letter, period, or question mark.
- The helper verb in the answer does not match the helper verb in the question.
- A helper verb is missing in the answer.
- The question and the answer do not match in singular and plural. Look for "and" in the question or answer.
- The answer does not match the question in masculine or feminine.
- You need a certain answer because the question has a negative word in it.

- A word in the answer is very similar to the correct answer but it is wrong.
- The time of the verb in the answer does not match the time information in the question.
- The answer puts 2 past forms in the sentence.
- The answer doesn't have a/an or needs a/an.

Unit Test - Review paragraphs If a paragraph was included in the test, explain how you graded the paragraphs. Give copies or project an example of a good paragraph and point out what you are looking for in their work.

Unit Test - Review reading If reading questions were included, explain how you graded the answers. Reread the paragraph several times and answer questions orally as you would in any reading activity.

Unit Test - Review results on a chart Pass out a chart which shows individual results for each member of the class, as well as the minimum passing grade and highest grade. The chart can list students by number or by name depending on your school's policy. Again explain the test grading system and how the test will affect the course grade. Grades on the segments of the test should be added for a total score. They can also be broken out on a bar chart to show students their weak areas.

3. Unit Test - Reteach Some Scantron machines can be set to total the number missed for each answer on a Scantron test. You can also tally student errors on each question to find the answers most often missed. If there are not many errors on a specific topic, review the material briefly in this class. If there are a lot of problems in a certain area and the material will not be recycled soon in the regular course of the class, reteach it soon after the unit test and retest it in quiz form to see if there is improvement. Keep a list of the most common errors so that you can review problem vocabulary and grammar when you introduce new material, create oral practices, and give examples.

4. Vocabulary - Introduce Introduce, practice, and assign new vocabulary as usual.

5. Lesson Plans Return to your regular schedule. Begin new unit if necessary.

Sub Work 1

Vocabulary

No vocabulary homework

Agenda

1. Opening routine
2. Jazz chant or other simple dialog - read and repeat
    HOMEWORK - copy jazz chant, paragraph or dialog 1-3 times for 1-3 points
3. Pronunciation - letter names of consonants
    #1#2 technique
4. Alphabet - reading, dialog, or worksheet with letters and numbers
    Written practice
5. Reading practice - dictation or questions on any previously done paragraph
6. Alphabet grid game

Stuff

1. Paper copies of one jazz chant
2. Chart of alphabet or alphabet written on board in large capital letters
3. Copies of pre-made grid with 25 squares or textbook containing alphabet grid game

Lesson Plan

1. Opening Routine Substitute introduces himself and takes roll. If the sub is new, he can use opening routines to meet the class. (See Day 1.)

2. Jazz Chant Recommended jazz chants are "Snow's Not Hot" or "Where's Jack?" Other available jazz chants or easy dialogs can be used for these activities.

Pass out paper copies or write the chant on the board. The teacher reads it twice. Then the class reads each line after the teacher once. The class reads it together several times. Then divide the class into 2 groups. The 2 groups can read the chant as a dialog or compete to read it louder or better than the other side. Copy the chant once.

Explain the grammar in "Snow's Not Hot" and "Where's Jack?" Both of these jazz chants use short forms of "is," but instead of "isn't" they use "he's not, snow's not hot, she's not here." Show that the negative of "is" and "are" can be written 2 ways. Write on the board.

you are not here	he is not here
you aren't here	he isn't here
OR	OR
you're not here	he's not here

Both are correct and equally used. Practice the poems several more times.

Erase the examples and write the following list on the board. Have students convert the sentences like the example.

he isn't   he's not
she isn't
it isn't
you aren't
we aren't
they aren't

They can write answers on their papers or one student can write them on the board.

he isn't	he's not	you aren't	you're not
she isn't	she's not	we aren't	we're not
it isn't	it's not	they aren't	they're not

HOMEWORK is to copy the jazz chant or other dialog 1-3 times for 1-3 points.

3. Pronunciation - Consonants The teacher repeats the alphabet several times while pointing to the chart or board, breaking up the letters into the groups shown below. Then have students repeat several times while teacher points to the chart or board. The letters are divided the same way as in the alphabet song to prepare them to sing the alphabet song. Adults usually refuse to sing, but you can ask them to chant like the song. The teacher should walk around the class to hear more clearly.

AB CD EF G
HI JK
LMNOP
QRS TUV
W X Y Z
Now I've said my ABC
Tell me what you think of me!!

Go back to the chart and repeat the consonants which are difficult for them -- C, D, G, H, J, L, M, N, P, Q, R, T, V, W, X, and Z. Make faces while saying the letters very distinctly.

Compare the pairs which are difficult to distinguish.

B vs. P
B vs. V
C vs. Z
D vs. T
G vs. J
L vs. R
M vs. N

Repeat the pairs several times together. Don't practice the sounds of the consonants. Just read the names of the letters.

Pronunciation - Difficult consonants - #1#2 technique For 3 of the pairs above, write the pair on the board. For example,

#1 B
#2 P

Say the letters several times with their numbers, "Number 1 B, number 2 P," pointing to the letter which you are saying. Then you say one of the letters and the students raise one or two fingers to show which letter you said. Mix up the letters. After mixing up the letters several times, repeat the same letter 4 or 5 times to see if students actually hear the difference or if they are simply guessing. Don't do the game too long, since some students will not be able to hear any difference.

Continue throughout the course to practice consonant names which are difficult for your particular student group. Every now and then, take out the chart and repeat the alphabet once or twice. Review by asking students to spell words out or correct spelling mistakes from their homework that you write on the board.

4. Pronunciation - Alphabet - Reading practice Do a dialog, reading, or written practice. There is a telephone dialog with spelling practice on **Lifeskills, p. 16.** The page includes state postal abbreviations and practice with telephone numbers.

Pronunciation - Alphabet - Writing practice See **Side by Side, p. 5.**

5. Reading Practice - With a previously used paragraph Use a previously done reading or dialog. Read it again 1 or 2 times. There are several activities you can do, shown here in order of difficulty.

A. Dictate 5 selected sentences from the reading in the order they appear. Skip some sentences. Students search in their reading copy for each sentence and copy it.

B. Teacher asks questions about the reading. Students search for answers and copy them.

C. Dictate only 5 sentences from the reading in a list, mixing up the sequence of the sentences. Students do not copy the sentences. They write them as a dictation without looking at the reading. Allow the class 5 minutes to study before doing the dictation.

D. Teacher asks questions regarding the reading. Students write answers without looking at the reading.

Assure students beforehand that this is not a test. Go over the answers or let them look at the original copy and put a big X on their mistakes.

6. Alphabet Grid Game Use the grid from the **Hampton-Brown Reading Practice Book. (See "Texts" section.)** You can also create your own grid or have students make one on notebook paper. The grid looks like an empty Sudoku square with 25 squares, 5 boxes across and 5 boxes down. Dictate one letter at a time. Students write each letter, filling in the squares from left to right across the top of the box and then filling in the next row down. After you have dictated 25 letters, repeat all of the letters quickly one more time. Check by having students give you the answers and writing them on the board in the grid pattern.

Sub Work 2

Vocabulary

Monday
Tuesday
Wednesday
Thursday
Friday
Saturday
Sunday

Capital letters and correct spelling are required!

Agenda

NOTE: This agenda can be used at a low level by a substitute teacher. A higher level guided composition is included in case the sub day is later in the course.

1. Opening routine - What is today? What is the date/month/year?
2. Vocabulary - days of the week - review, pronounce 2-3X, flashcard review
    Compare Tuesday and Thursday, #1#2 technique
    HOMEWORK - copy 20X, quiz - includes capital letters, spelling
3. Days of the week - reading - days and activities - copy or write dialogs
4. Days of the week - oral practice
    Written practice - write activities on weekly calendar
    Written practice - puzzles
5. Days of the week - poem "Solomon Grundy" and quiz (attached) - optional - higher level
6. Days of the week - guided composition (attached) - optional - much higher level

Stuff

1. Calendar page for the month - large
2. Copies of smaller calendar page
3. Flashcards - days of the week
4. Puzzles from elementary school materials in the educational supply store - for example, a puzzle with names of the days scrambled
5. Copies or projectable file of poem and quiz (attached)
6. Blank white paper and colored pencils for the optional illustration of the composition

Lesson Plan

1. Opening Routine Add questions. What day is today? What is the date? What is the month? What is the year?

2. Vocabulary - Days of the week Show the days on the calendar. Repeat the list several times. Note the odd spelling of "Wednesday" and that all words start with a capital letter.

Compare "Tuesday" and "Thursday" using the #1#2 technique. (See Sub Work 1.)

Review all the days with flashcards. Go through the list on the board and put an accent mark on the first syllable. Do not stress the "day" syllable. HOMEWORK is to copy the days 20 times for a quiz tomorrow.

3. Days of the Week - Reading Read a paragraph or dialog about days and activities. Repeat the readings several times and copy them once in the correct format. Answer questions. **Side by Side, pp. 88-89 (easiest), 90-91 (harder), 92-93 (hardest).** For an additional listening exercise, see **Side by Side, p. 98.**

4. Days of the Week - Oral practice Write the following activities on the board. Students repeat and review them with pictures.

go to school
play soccer
shop at the supermarket
buy food
wash the clothes
go to the laundromat
clean the house
go to work
buy gas
wash my hair
go to the movies
visit my family
relax
go to a club
go out with my girlfriend

Write on the board. "On Monday, I _____." The students choose an activity from the list or use one of their own to fill in the blank.

Students use examples to write their weekly schedules on a calendar page. They report to the class about 1 day. **Lifeskills, p. 34; Skill Sharpeners, p. 13; Side by Side, pp. 90-91.**

Days of the Week - Puzzles or questions Practice with puzzles with scrambled names of days. Or do **Skill Sharpeners, p. 12; Lifeskills, p. 33.**

5. Days of the Week - Poem Read the "Solomon Grundy" poem several times. Define unknown words with pictures. Do "pop quiz" questions and go over answers. This is too difficult for students in the first weeks of the class.

6. My Favorite Day of the Week - Guided composition Use on a day later in the course or with a creative class. If class finishes very early, they can illustrate their composition.

Solomon Grundy

Solomon Grundy
Born on Monday
Baptized on Tuesday
Married on Wednesday
Got sick on Thursday
Worse on Friday
Died on Saturday
Buried on Sunday
That's the end of
Solomon Grundy.

(Dictate questions. One-word answers are okay.)

1. What is today?

2. Write 2 days that you come to school.

3. Write 2 days that you don't come to school.

4. What date were you born? (What is your birthday?) (Check ID cards to help them.)

5. What day of the week were you born? If you don't know, write "I don't know." (on board)

6. What day of the week was Solomon Grundy born?

7. What is your baptized name (if any)? If you were not baptized, write "none." (on board)

8. What happened to Solomon Grundy on Wednesday?

9. What happened to him on Thursday?

10. How long did Solomon Grundy live? How old was he when he died?

11. What is the title of the poem?

12. Who is the most important character? (person)

This poem is a traditional nursery rhyme.

Guided Composition - More Difficult - Optional

Usually with a guided composition, the teacher dictates the composition and pauses at the blanks so that he or she can prompt and help the students to fill in the information, even by writing vocabulary on the board. (If you project the composition or pass it out as a fill-in exercise, you run the risk that students will rush to fill in the information and then ask you for help while others fall behind.) Later in the course you can give this composition as a paragraph with blanks which students fill it in and then deliver to class as an oral report.

Dictate the title, "My Favorite Day of the Week." Say, "Make sure to center the title." Walk around to see if the students are centering the title. Dictate each capital letter.

Say, "Remember margins." Go around while dictating to check that everyone is observing margins on both sides.

Say, "Indent 5 letters or the size of your thumb." Hold up a piece of notebook paper and put your thumb where the indent should be, or write 5 small letters at the beginning of the line. Walk around to check that students are leaving an indent space.

Dictate the paragraph slowly, leaving time for students to write. Do not allow students to determine when you move on. Move on when almost everyone seems finished with the blank. Dictate capital letters and periods.

(Indent.) Everybody has a favorite day of the week. My favorite day is _____.

On that day, I usually _____. I also _____ and

_____. I enjoy these activities because _____.

That's why _____ is the best day of my week.

If the class finishes this very early, pass out blank white paper and colored pencils and ask them to illustrate their composition on one side and copy it on the other.

335

Sub Work 3

Vocabulary

January
February - stress R
March
April
May
June
July
August
September
October - O not U, not "Octuber"
November
December

Capital letters and correct spelling are required!

Agenda

1. Opening routine - point to date - What month is this?
2. Months - read the names from the big calendar
       Point to vocabulary list on board, read quickly several times
       Students repeat individually to correct pronunciation
       Note capitals and difficult spelling
       Read months in mixed order several times with flashcards
       HOMEWORK - copy list 10X for quiz tomorrow
3. Poem - "30 days has September" - recite 3X, copy, answer oral questions
4. Months - oral practice - birthdays
       Oral practice - seasons and holidays
       Reading or oral practice with pictures
       Written practice with months, including "before" and "after"
IF TIME
5. Months - puzzles

Stuff

1. Large calendar with all months, preferably with holiday or seasonal illustrations
2. Flashcards of months
3. Big Post-it chart paper for birthday list
4. Elementary school puzzles from educational supply store, for example, worksheets with months in scrambled order or with scrambled spelling
5. Teacher-made worksheets with months in scrambled order or spelling

Lesson Plan

1. Opening Routine What month is this? What month did we start school? What month will we finish school? What month will we go on vacation?

2. Months - Big calendar Read the months once in order from the big calendar. Read the months in order several times from the vocabulary list on the board. Individual students read the months in mixed order to correct pronunciation. Note that capitals are required. Point out R in February, no U in October, and the difficult pronunciation of "January," "June," and "July." Read the months in mixed order several times with flashcards. HOMEWORK is to copy the list 10X for a quiz.

3. Months - Poem - "30 Days Has September" Write the poem on the board. Students repeat it several times. Ask and answer the questions orally.

Thirty days has September,
April, June, and November.
All the rest have 31
Except for February alone.
That has 28 days clear
But 29 in each leap year.

1. How many months have 30 days? 4

2. What months have 30 days? September, April, June, November

3. How many days are in December? 31

4. How many days are in June? 30

5. How many days are in January? 31

6. How many days are **usually** in February? 28

7. How many months have 28 days? One

8. When does February have 29 days? Leap year OR every 4 years

9. What is a leap year? It's a year with 366 days, not 365.

10. How do we know if a year is a leap year? You can divide it by 4.

11. Is this year a leap year? (Divide the year by 4 and see if there is a remainder.)

12. What is special about a leap year? Girls can ask boys to marry them.

4. Months - Oral practice - Birthdays Ask each student, "What month is your birthday?" Write the model answer on the board.

My birthday is in _____.

Make a list of student names and birthday months on a big Post-it poster.

Months - Oral practice - Holidays Ask the class what holidays and special days they know. Write them on the big calendar or put them on smaller Post-it notes and stick them on the right pages. Include foreign holidays, but don't include too many that other students don't know. Try to talk about most of the months. For seasons and weather, see **Practical English, p. 194-195.**

In February, I give Valentines.
In December, we have Christmas.
In December, we go to Mexico.
In January, we celebrate New Year's Day.

Months - Reading Read **Side by Side, pp. 136-137** or just talk about the pictures.

Months - Written practice Use a page which practices "before" and "after" or write your own practice on the board. **Skill Sharpeners, p. 14.**

January is before/after February.
June is before/after July.
May is before/after March.

For written exercises on American holidays, see **Lifeskills, pp. 82-83.**

IF TIME

5. Months - Puzzles

Use commercial puzzles which involve scrambled or mixed-up months. Or use a teacher-made worksheet with mixed-up spelling and mixed-up order of the months and have students put them in order.

Sub Work 4

Vocabulary

one - first
two - second
three - third
four - fourth
five - fifth   Note spelling.
sixth
seventh
eighth
nine - ninth Note spelling.
tenth

Agenda

1. Opening routine
2. Ordinal numbers - introduce, practice with 10 students in a line
      Talk about the first ten page numbers in book
      Repeat vocabulary 2-3X
      Note spelling problems
      Pronunciation - practice with #1#2
      Written practice
      Oral practice - school schedule and important dates, like birthdays, Christmas
      Review rules for writing date
      Review with flashcards - HOMEWORK - copy vocabulary 20X, quiz
3. Months - review with ordinal numbers - oral practice

Stuff

1. Large calendar
2. Flashcards with regular numbers on one side, ordinal numbers on other

Lesson Plan

1. Opening Routine

2. Ordinal Numbers - Introduce Put 10 students in a line. Pointing at each student, say, "You're the first/second/third person. You're the fourth person." Stress the "th" sound. Then ask questions. "Who's the tenth person?" "Who's behind the sixth person?"

Open the textbook and show the first 10 pages. Say, "This is the first page. This is the tenth page," etc. Give the class orders to go to a few pages and hold up their books to show the page.

Read the vocabulary list several times. Point out difficult spelling.

Ordinal Numbers - Pronunciation - Pairs with "th" Read the vocabulary list in pairs several times. Practice 3 pairs with the #1#2 technique. Ask, "Which am I saying?" (See Sub Work 1 for explanation of the #1#2 technique.) Students raise 1 or 2 fingers to indicate which word they hear you say.

> #1 five or #2 fifth?
> #1 eight or #2 eighth?
> #1 nine or #2 ninth?

Ordinal Numbers - Written practice Use **Practical English, p. 196; Lifeskills, p. 34 OR Skill Sharpeners, p. 13.**

Ordinal Numbers - Oral practice Talk about the school schedule and important dates like birthdays and Christmas. For more questions, **Practical English, p. 195.**

> We are on vacation November 24th and 25th.
> My birthday is December 24th.
> Christmas is December 25th.
> What day is your first child's birthday?
> Who is your second child? What day is his birthday?

Writing dates Quickly review rules for writing dates. Pointing to the complete date written on your board, show students that October 10, 2016 does not have "th" after the "10." We read it "October tenth" but we do not write the "th." That is the correct form for a business letter. On a personal letter, you can write "October 10th" without a year, or any way you like.

Review with flashcards. Show the regular number and students give the ordinal number and vice versa. HOMEWORK is to copy the vocabulary 20X for a quiz.

3. Months - Review with ordinal numbers - Oral practice Help students to answer.

What month is January?	It's the first month.
What month is February?	It's the second month.
Which month is March?	It's the third month.

What is the fourth month?	It's April.
Which month comes first, July or June?	June comes first.
What is the eighth month?	It's August.

Which is the ninth month, September or October?	It's September.
What month comes after the ninth month?	October
What month comes before the twelfth month?	November
What is the twelfth month?	December
What is New Year's Eve?	It's the last day of the last month.
What is New Year's Day?	It's the first day of the first month.

Verb List Continuous

Verb	Continuous form	Add ing, drop final e	Double final consonant? Does it follow CVC rule?
arrive		arriving	
attend	attending		No - 2 consonants
begin	beginning		Yes - accent 2nd syllable
build	building		No - 2 consonants
carry	carrying		No - keep Y
change		changing	
clap	clapping		Yes
clean	cleaning		No - 2 vowels
close		closing	
come		coming	
cry	crying		No - keep Y
dance		dancing	
draw	drawing		No - don't double W
drink	drinking		No - 2 consonants
eat	eating		No - 2 vowels
erase		erasing	
fill	filling		No - 2 consonants
fix	fixing		No - don't double X
give		giving	
go	going		No - don't double vowels
have		having	
hear	hearing		No - 2 vowels
laugh	laughing		No - 2 consonants
leave		leaving	
lie	lying		No - IE changes to Y
light	lighting		No - 3 consonants
listen	listening		No - accent 1st syllable
live		living	
look at	looking at		No - 2 vowels
look for	looking for		No - 2 vowels
make		making	
open	opening		No - accent 1st syllable
paint	painting		No - 2 consonants
pick	picking		No - 2 consonants
point	pointing		No - 2 consonants
practice		practicing	
put	putting		Yes

read	reading		No - 2 vowels
ride		riding	
run	running		Yes
shut	shutting		Yes
sing	singing		No - 2 consonants
sit	sitting		Yes
sleep	sleeping		No - 2 vowels
smile		smiling	
speak	speaking		No - 2 vowels
stop	stopping		Yes
stand	standing		No - 2 consonants
study	studying		No - keep Y
take		taking	
talk	talking		No - 2 consonants
throw	throwing		No - don't double W
tie	tying		No - IE changes to Y
try	trying		No - keep Y
wait	waiting		No - 2 vowels
walk	walking		No - 2 consonants
wash	washing		No - 2 consonants
wear	wearing		No - 2 vowels
whisper	whispering		No - accent 1st syllable
work	working		No - 2 consonants
write		writing	

Texts for Beginning - Low Intermediate

Introduction

If you want to buy only one additional textbook to accompany this manual, the following would be good choices. See more detailed information below.

- For secondary students and adults who need reading and writing, **Practical English 1**.

- For students who have studied English before and need to review or to improve speaking skills, such as EFL students, **New American Streamline Departures.**

- For adults in a non-academic situation who need mostly speaking skills, **Side by Side, Book 1, and part of Book 2.**

  A Conversation Book 1 would also be valuable, as would **Skill Sharpeners 1** or **Lifeskills 1.**

- For a reading class of students who also have a grammar class, the **True Stories** series.

Some of the books recommended in this manual are older, but most are still available new from the publisher or through Amazon. Sometimes the first edition of a text is more entertaining or simpler to use than later editions. A good course text not only practices grammar, however buried the grammar practice may be, but gives the class something to talk about. A character using a dial telephone in an older book can stimulate an interesting discussion on phones then and now.

The focus of these books is survival English. They may have been replaced as classroom texts by others deemed more modern, but their replacements are not necessarily as useful for very low students.

A new teacher will find all of these texts worth buying. Some also have cassettes and teacher's editions available. Other course texts can be found in community college and university bookstores or in general bookstores like Barnes and Noble. Outside the U.S., course texts available in ordinary bookstores usually teach British English.

Grammar Program

1. Practical English l, Second Edition, with a workbook, Writing Practical English 1, Second Edition, by Tim Harris and Allan Rowe. The series also has a level 2 and a level 3.

These books were last updated in the 1980s, but they are so valuable that they continue to be popular. They are especially appropriate for adult students or teenagers with a lower literacy level who need practice in reading, writing, and punctuation. An inexperienced teacher will learn to teach a sequenced, organized course of low level ESL grammar by using these books. They are available used as well as new on Amazon, Alibris, AbeBooks, etc. The text has lots of pictures, and on many pages of the workbook there are illustrations with each question.

Practical English 1 has periodic unit tests which can be merged or adapted to create a grammar final or a pretest. It covers a 6-month beginning class. Some material from **Practical English 2** can also be used.

Google "Tim Harris and Allan Rowe" at amazon.com

2. Side by Side, Book 1, Third Edition and Side by Side, Book 2, Third Edition, by Steven Molinsky and Bill Bliss

These are books for low-level students which use dialogs practiced in pairs. The dialogs are very common everyday English. The books have lots of pictures. If your class does not do well with the paired conversation technique, the books can still be used with the teacher acting as one partner. Students can also write the dialogs. The exercises and pictures are especially helpful for certain topics like present continuous verbs and home vocabulary. There are excellent listening exercises and a good 2-video set is available.

When buying this series, be careful, because the texts and workbooks can be bought divided into 1a, 1b, 2a, and 2b, and online sources may be confusing for that reason. Your beginning class would use Book l and part of Book 2.

The third edition of this series contains excellent reading practice material which was previously in the older **Line by Line** readers, as well as additional discussion topics. It also has charts which help you align your course to the various standards which may be required by your program.

Search Molinsky + "Side by Side" at amazon.com or go to pearsonelt.com.

3. New American Streamline Departures (whole book, Units 1-80) by Bernard Hartley and Peter Viney

This text was originally written to teach British English under the title **Streamline English Departures,** but the British version has never been updated and its availability will have to be researched. The book was revised for the American market under the title **American**

Streamline Departures. That edition can be bought, but it might be difficult to get enough new copies for a class set. The series was then updated under the title **New American Streamline Departures**.

This series is very entertaining, with funny stories and cartoons. The text has one grammar topic per page with a dialog, story, or schedule, plus a few grammar practice exercises. The book is a good review for students who may have studied a lot of English, but who don't speak much. If you want to use this as the sole text for students with less background in English, you will need to add more grammar practice. There is a teacher's edition available.

Grammar summaries at the back of the book show exactly what grammar is practiced in each unit. You can use this book as a fun review of topics which you have already taught using a simpler book such as **Practical English**. The first few pages are very basic, but the level rises quickly, so you use it at the very start of a beginning class and then start using it again after a few weeks.

When buying online, be careful that you don't buy the workbook instead of the text. Also, the workbooks and texts can be bought divided into units 1-40 and 41-80. I would buy the whole book and then decide if you want to get a divided book for classroom use. The last quarter of the **Departures** book goes into an intermediate level.

Google "New American Streamline" (no s) + OUP (Oxford University Press). At the OUP site, you have to click on the country where you want to get the book. You can also go to viney.uk.com/streamline or try amazon.com or amazon.co.uk.

Supplementary Grammar

4. GrammarWork 1 (2, 3, and 4 also available), Second Edition, by Pamela Breyer

This book provides easy grammar practice in a logical sequence with one grammar point per page. The format provides repetitive writing practice for less literate students. The exercises may seem simple, but they are demanding enough for most beginning ESL students.

The book is self-explanatory, with an example of the grammar in each assignment at the top of every page. It can be used as additional work for students who finish other assignments early. An answer key at the back has perforated pages, making it easy to remove.

Google GrammarWork + Breyer.

5. Regents English Workbook 1, Beginning, New Edition, by Robert J. Dixon

Books in the Regents series are not texts, but worksheets on points which students get wrong. They have one grammar point per page, with blanks for answers and no illustrations. They are self-explanatory, with an answer key at the back. They are good for substitute work and extra work for students who finish assignments early, as well as for homework or test review.

Google "Regents English Workbook" + Dixon

Reference Grammar

6. Basic English Grammar by Betty Schrampfer Azar

Some of the exercises in this book are good, but it is not an introductory text. It has valuable charts which break down and explain the grammar. There is no chartbook for **Basic English Grammar (red)**. You have to buy the whole text to get the charts.

Chartbook: A Reference Grammar - Fundamentals of English Grammar by Betty Schrampfer Azar

This is a convenient book with only the charts from the textbook by Azar called **Fundamentals of English Grammar (black)**. The textbook is for an intermediate level class but the charts cover some lower-level grammar.

Chartbook: A Reference Grammar - Understanding and Using English Grammar (blue) by Betty Schrampfer Azar

This is the chartbook which goes with the advanced grammar text of the same name. The grammar level starts at high intermediate.

These chartbooks are a quick and valuable resource for teachers who feel unclear on a grammar point or find a topic difficult to explain.

Google "Azar grammar chartbook"

Literacy

7. Access: Fundamentals of Literacy and Communication, by Molinsky and Bliss

This book by the authors of **Side by Side** has very simple dialogs which are usable for a beginning class, as well as alphabet-level writing practice and word discrimination work for students with a very low literacy level. It has exercises with clocks and money and good listening exercises.

Google Access + Molinsky

Survival Skills

8. Lifeskills 1, 2, and 3, Second Edition, by Judy DeFilippo
Skill Sharpeners 1, 2, 3, and 4, Third Edition by DeFilippo and Skidmore

Skill Sharpeners and **Lifeskills** are almost the same book, but **Lifeskills** is easier than **Skill Sharpeners**. Both are good for teaching names, time, money, family trees, housing, and food. Both have grammar practice with plenty of pictures, signs, graphs, and schedules. Both include an objective and a short lesson plan on each page, making them useful for substitute days. Both series have several levels, but you will only use Book 1 for beginners.

Lifeskills 1, Second Edition has some pages good for citizenship classes.

Skill Sharpeners 1, Third Edition includes some short reading selections with questions. It also has an end-of-book test with a vocabulary review, a grammar test, and reading questions.

Google title plus DeFilippo

9. A Conversation Book 1, Third Edition, by Tina Carver and Sandra Fotinos

This book has many excellent illustrations of everyday situations, with lots of specific items shown for vocabulary development. There are activities for partners and groups. Although the goal of the book is English through conversation for adults, the pictures can be used for grammar practice as well.

Google "A Conversation Book" + Fotinos for a range of editions with different offerings.

Speaking

10. Jazz Chants, by Carolyn Graham
Jazz Chants for Children, by Carolyn Graham

Jazz Chants are page-length poems for oral recitation and repetitive chanting, with the chants for children being shorter and happier. They are fun and very popular with students. Jazz Chants are very valuable for reinforcing and sometimes introducing grammar concepts.

Google "Jazz Chants" + "Carolyn Graham." Also "Jazz Chants for Children"

Phonics

11. The Basics Reading and Language Practice Book Set, High Point program published by Hampton-Brown

The Reading Practice Book which comes in this set is the reading practice book of the High Point program. It can be bought separately from the rest of the program. It has photo illustrated exercises matching pictures to letters and sounds. It has grid games for letters and words, which I have adapted in the lesson plans above. There are also phonics-based stories geared toward young teenagers.

You may not be able to get the Reading Practice Book separately from the Language Practice Book. Make sure you are not ordering other reading products which go with the series.

Google "High Point" + "The Basics Reading and Language Practice Book Set." You may have to search quite a few sources to find one which has the book available.

Reading

12. Very Easy True Stories, A Picture-Based First Reader, by Sandra Heyer
All New Very Easy True Stories
Easy True Stories, A Picture-Based Beginning Reader
All New Easy True Stories

This is a series of truly awesome readers starting at level 0, where there is a picture accompanying every sentence. The stories, adapted from real news articles, are really interesting, even for the teacher. Exercises help students focus on words and sentences, learn vocabulary, and practice pronunciation. There are answer keys at the back. These books can be used in a general grammar class for review, reading practice, or discussion.

The titles are a little confusing. There are now two different books at the easiest level ("Very Easy") and two different books at the next easiest level ("Easy"). The Very Easy books have 14 units each and the Easy books have 20 each. The series then continues to almost an advanced ESL level, so the series can be extremely useful in a multi-level ESL reading class.

Fiction written or adapted for low-level readers is hard to find and almost always terrible. That's why these non-fiction books are so valuable. They are entertaining, stimulate discussion, and, although they are easy, they are not edited down to the point that they are meaningless or hard to explain. The stories are appropriate for teenagers or adults.

Google Heyer + "True Stories"

Composition

13. Composition Practice, Book 1, Third Edition, by Linda Lonon Blanton

This is a basic composition book which has a series of pictures and a reading for each unit. It then encourages the student to write his own paragraph using the reading as a model. Graphics illustrate the organization of a paragraph and a composition. Most of the composition assignments are too difficult for a very low-level class, but the readings and exercises are easier. Each unit has an easy assignment involving Internet research.

Google Blanton + "Composition Practice"

Essential Equipment

- Large elementary school clock - cardboard with moveable hands
- Calendars - month, year, daily agenda page
- Bingo games - numbers, past form verbs
- Educational equipment store - charts of alphabet, numbers, colors
- Educational equipment store - elementary worksheets - alphabet, numbers, colors, days, months

- World map, U.S. map, state map

- Most common office supplies - pencils, pens, erasers, stapler, notebooks, paper
- Squares of the most basic colors, including gold and silver, mounted on cardboard
- Large plastic cups in basic colors
- Pencils in basic colors in different lengths, also crayons, colored markers

- Picture collection organized by topic - qualities (like tall, short, big, little), famous people, jobs, weather, activities, clothes, family members, vehicles, food, sports, etc

- "Realia" if convenient - clothing, coins and bills, fake fruit and flowers, real or plastic plates and eating utensils, food boxes and cans

- Menus from local restaurants - short
- Advertising fliers from local supermarkets and other stores
- Transportation schedules
- Travel brochures

Troubleshooting

The whole class is failing.

If your whole class is failing, the material is too difficult for them. The mandated curriculum may be poorly written or it may not be appropriate for students like yours. For example, ESL students may be given material more appropriate for special education classes or elementary students. If you have not taught beginners before, you may need to look at other beginning ESL texts to see if the material you're giving them is simply too high level. It's also possible that you're not breaking the material down into easy enough pieces or giving them sufficient practice.

A few students are failing.

A student who fails while others in the class are passing could be in a level too high for him. Of course, in a Beginning ESL class, there is no lower level, but the student may be illiterate. People who did not have a lot of schooling in their own language, especially if they cannot read or write, may have more trouble learning a second language, especially if reading and writing are a large part of the course. You can usually see this lack of school experience in their written work. It could have very uneven lettering, be missing a lot of letters, and generally show lack of format. The words could rise or fall off the lines of the paper. The student may avoid writing at all.

A less literate secondary student will usually have to repeat the class. A literacy class which also teaches ESL may be available at a public library or adult school.

Struggling students could also be learning disabled. It's possible that they have trouble tracking words or lines in a book or on the board. Second language students who are also special education students may learn oral English easily but have difficulty in reading and writing.

The difference between low literacy students and special education students is that the low literacy students may learn more slowly but show progress over time, whereas special education students may have more difficulty as they go from a beginning class to a higher level class where reading and writing become more demanding.

The student could have hearing problems or need glasses. Many ESL students do need glasses. In public schools, students entering after the elementary level are not always tested for both distance and reading vision. A student may have glasses but refuse to wear them.

Ask the student if he needs glasses, or ask him to read the board from the back of the room. You could try rotating class seating once a week to see if this is a problem. Ask the problem student to try on a pair of reading glasses, which can be bought at a drugstore or even at the dollar store. Public health programs for children may be able to provide glasses.

A failing student may have come into the class too late to catch up. Communicate to late entries that you are happy to have them but that they may have to repeat at the end of the semester. As long as you present this as a positive opportunity, most students are willing to repeat. You should check for placement errors in the files of students entering late.

It's possible that a low-performing student could simply be a poor language learner who will do better with time if he repeats a semester.

Most students in the class are failing, but several students are having no problems.

There are two types of beginning ESL students, True Beginners and False Beginners. True Beginners know very little English when they start. They may sit in your class for six months or even a year before they begin to speak. This is completely normal.

So-called "False Beginners" are students who have already learned some English somewhere. They may have been in an American school previously, or have relatives who speak a lot of English, or have studied in their home country. It might be difficult to tell how much English False Beginners know, but you can see that they know more than the rest of your class. They usually end up in a beginning class because they did poorly on a placement test. Sometimes they have been required to repeat the class several times in a previous program.

You need to investigate their records to see if there has been some mistake. If they have gone to school in the United States or are very fluent, you should move them to a higher ESL class or even a "Sheltered English" class. They will not be happy in a class of True Beginners. Students who are too high for your group are not making progress and may even become discipline problems. If there is no suitable class for them, you will have to give them higher level work or assign them an aide until they can pass to a more challenging class.

Unfortunately, False Beginners make students who are correctly placed look less competent. You have to meet the needs of the greatest number of students in the class, rather than gearing the level of the class to a few of the highest level students. It's better to move one or two students up than to have a whole class fail.

Avoiding placement problems

In order to avoid placement mistakes, have the class fill out an information card. (See Day 1 in the lesson plans.) You should also give your own placement test. If the student comes in later in the semester, do the same.

Your program counselor should have information on when students first entered the U.S. and their prior education, along with placement test scores. If the counselor can give you a sheet with this data for the whole class, it makes a good reference. Even if this information doesn't help students to succeed, it will help you understand their situation, and you will be alerted to possible misplacements.

Connected Ideas

Am/is/are

name, address, etc
nationality, country of origin
jobs
classroom teachers at school
famous people
objects in a classroom
objects in a house
colors
favorite possessions

Have/has

clothing
favorite possessions
furniture and fixtures in rooms and houses
family members and children

Adjectives

clothing
describing friends and family
colors
possessions
gifts or things you would like to buy
opinions - great, wonderful, interesting, fabulous, beautiful

There is/there are

objects in a classroom
furniture in a room
rooms in a house
places in a community
numbers
some and any
much and many

Ordinal numbers (first, second, etc.)

days, weeks and months of year
dates and holidays
age order of family members
to-do list

Weather and seasons

names of cities, countries and regions
senses and feelings
present simple and adverbs of frequency
seasonal clothing

Present continuous verbs

daily routine verbs
job requirements, tasks
activities in a room or in a place
hobbies and sports

Present simple verbs

all of the categories under present continuous
thoughts and emotions - wants, needs, likes, loves, hates, thinks, believes
habits and vices - smokes, drinks, eats - with too much, a lot of
adverbs of frequency - always, sometimes, never, etc.
schedules and daily routines
clothes, "wears"
food habits and preferences
have/has

Can/could/will/have to

offers of help
invitations and excuses
chores, housework, requirements
sports, skills, talents
adverbs

Will/won't

future time words
dates with days of the week, months of the year
promises
refusal to do something

Should/shouldn't

school rules
healthy habits and vices
tips for success

Rationale

Goals of the Beginning ESL Class

Learning another language is stressful for most people. The most stressful part is the phase when students go from understanding nothing to being able to get by. Your beginning students will be in that painful process the entire time they're with you.

In six months your students need to:

> Understand classroom directions.
> Understand and use basic survival vocabulary.
> Be able to understand and express simple personal and business information.
> Become alert to grammar indicators so they can improve in future ESL classes.
> Read enough to understand survival information like signs and brochures.
> If in an academic track, start to read and write in formal formats.

Your goal is to develop the student's ear for spoken English while you make the use of language as easy and natural as possible. You want them to try hard to produce any sentence at all, but you are also trying to reduce the number of errors that they hear.

Errors are corrected so that students don't form habits of speaking with the very common mistakes that all learners make. You correct pronunciation as much as possible and teach basic rules of phonics to improve their reading skills and accents. Basic writing and spelling rules are practiced from the very beginning to reduce problems in future classes.

You would not expect to play the piano perfectly after six months of lessons, and beginning students will not do anything perfectly after six months or a year of ESL. Unless they are unusually gifted language learners, they will need more time to become fluent, probably two to three years.

The "Goldilocks" Goal

Students want to feel that their class is not too easy or too hard, but just right. That's why you include listening, speaking, phonics, reading, writing, vocabulary and some idioms (which are popular, but not easy to teach). Teaching your curriculum in all of these aspects provides a variety of activities and uses the best skills of each student. Some students depend on the written word. Others learn everything by ear. Your goal is to teach the whole class without boring the higher level students or frustrating the lower level students.

The Downside and Upside of Teaching Beginners

Many ESL teachers prefer not to teach complete beginners. It strains the voice, and it takes a lot of energy. It's labor intensive, with lots of materials to organize and store. On the other hand, a beginning class will be more similar in level than other classes, and you will see marked progress by the end of a semester. Very few students get stuck at the lowest level, which is why beginners can be more rewarding than any other group. You will also find that your students recognize and appreciate your know-how.

ESL beginners do not get as bored as other students; they're too stressed out. Most beginners try very hard. They want to learn. They want to see results, and they know they need a coach. They are hanging in there, trying to get the sense of what you're saying while trying not to feel silly. They will be happy as long as they can comprehend a reasonable amount of what you're doing in class.

Nobody's Perfect

Beginning language students don't master one concept and then move on to the next, as much as you might want them to. On one hand, you are teaching specific material, like vocabulary words or grammar rules, so student effort counts. On the other hand, you are conducting the class in English, so the student is also learning words and grammar just by sitting in class.

All of your students are learning, though you don't see evidence of it at first. Even after they acquire a word or a concept, students continue to give wrong answers for many reasons. The word slip out of their brain when they need it. They get one word or rule confused with another one. They're not sure what you asked. They're not sure what rule to use in a new situation. Sometimes they'll write something wrong in one sentence and correctly in the very next sentence. They make typical errors over and over. That doesn't mean that they don't understand what you've taught them. They are just unable to integrate the new words and habits into their speaking at that moment. Different students need more time.

That's why you cannot wait to go on to new material, or test and retest until everyone has mastered the material to a certain level. Move the bulk of the students along at a reasonable pace and if a student has fallen too far behind by the final, he should repeat the class. He'll be better able to keep up after his introduction to the course.

As students progress in your class, they will make more mistakes, because they have more forms to confuse. For example, after a student learns to use "he will go" and "he can go," he may say "he will can go." That's good. The student is thinking creatively and trying to use his knowledge to express himself. The most you can hope for is to grade on the material that you have taught in class and listen proudly as your pupils make mistakes at higher and higher levels.

Something for Everyone

For some reason, people like to argue over their approach to teaching ESL. No grammar! No translating! No reading! Repeat the same sentence over and over! Correction! No correction! I believe the best approach is an eclectic one. Your main concern should be whether the class is learning the curriculum. Can they go to the next level and succeed? If not, what can you do to help them improve?

Some students will like one approach more than others. Students previously taught under one system may need a different system to compensate for their deficiencies. If you use a lot of different approaches to teach and reteach the same material, you can satisfy everyone. Before a student can get too frustrated with one activity, you're on to one they like better. All techniques have some merit, even those old-fashioned exercise books with long lists of grammar drills on each page. You should use all approaches. If you do, you can provide the review and repetition that beginners need without boring yourself and your class.

Adapt a Curriculum

If you are required to teach a mandatory curriculum, you must follow it. However, just because materials are required does not make your students understand them any better. If your text is too difficult, you will have to build up to it. If the text is too easy or too skimpy, you will need to supplement it. Even the best text has some sections which are less effective. You must decide what to teach in depth and what to glide over.

It's difficult to use a curriculum which you have not chosen yourself, because you have to work from your own understanding of the subject. Some texts are obviously written for students in an environment very different from yours. Even if you hate the curriculum provided for you, work with it. Parts of it may work for your particular students and compensate for areas in which you are weak. Keep an open-minded attitude and keep looking for materials to help you teach it the easiest way for you.

A good text should make the material clear and have pictures with a lot of content, not just color balloons and graphics, which are decorative but distracting. If it takes too much effort or too long a time to explain something in the text, it's too difficult for the class at their current level. A beginning level class is not the place to try to extend the students' vocabulary with exotic or unusual words. If a text contains such words, you can define them for the moment and move on.

If you know teachers with experience in teaching your group, don't be ashamed to ask them for advice and materials. Usually they will be happy to give you suggestions and copies of their worksheets. Teachers are helpful people and they don't want their own incoming students to be poorly trained. This could save you a lot of work. It can be difficult to work with another teacher's materials, but even if you don't like or use them, you will better understand the students in your program.

Levels

Try to avoid mixed level classes in the same room. Even when your students have been pretested and leveled correctly, they will have different abilities, and you will always have adjustments to make. Having very different levels in the class makes your job very, very difficult. Administrators sometimes try to help in this situation by giving you teaching assistants, but you will have to train and organize your teaching aides well. Make sure they understand why you don't want them to simply translate everything for the group.

Correction

There is nothing wrong with correcting a student if you do it in a nice way. If students have not been corrected consistently, they can get frustrated if suddenly challenged at higher levels. Although most students at the beginning level don't have this attitude, correcting them from the beginning shows them that it's important to be correct, and that correction is not a bad thing, but an opportunity to learn. You cannot assume that their future teachers will fix basic errors.

If you correct all of the students in a very neutral way, they will not feel bad about it, especially if you make correction fun or competitive. Correction is a form of attention. "I am listening to you, and I want to help you improve." You should never feel frustrated when students make mistakes, because mistakes help you assess their level of competence.

Later in the course, you will need to use specific correction less. You merely write a quick review on the board or give a hint as to the rule and see if somebody in the class can provide the right answer without your help. You can just lift your eyebrows significantly, repeat the error in a shocked tone, or write what the student just said on the board. If he doesn't self-correct, you can try weeping copiously and banging your head against the wall or gasping for breath and acting as if you're having a heart attack. Usually somebody will yell out the right answer. The idea is to make it cool and fun to give the right answer.

Adult students want feedback. They don't want to make speaking errors any more than they want to make any other social mistake. Your adult students' co-workers are probably reluctant to correct them when they are speaking, feeling that it is rude or time-consuming. However, people sometimes complain that certain co-workers are hard to understand and should go to English class. This may even affect their colleague's career.

In the recent past, correction went out of fashion. It was thought to be too discouraging to the students. Teachers were taught that after students make errors, they should "model" the sentence, which means to repeat the sentence correctly and expect the students to learn the right form by hearing it. This "Natural Approach" is valid, especially when the student can hear the correction easily, when correcting double negatives, for example. However, not everybody picks up this type of correction. The student may be listening only for the content of your answer and ignore its form. It's possible that he may not hear the correction very well or will remember it better if he sees it written down. Some people need direct instruction.

The value of teaching grammar is that it enables students to learn lots of things about English that are difficult to hear as well as hard to understand. That's why you practice over and over with "does," "doesn't," "did," and "didn't." The "n't" is a small and subtle sound which some people don't even notice. English also places significant meaning to "s" on the end of words, which is ignored in some languages. You can highlight certain difficult facets of English in beginning ESL courses by stressing them in your own pronunciation and then correcting student errors.

Details, Details

There are a lot of details that you don't need to get into in Beginning ESL. Grammar terminology is one area to minimize. Many rules have exceptions. Teach only the exceptions that students really need. There are many ways to ask a question. You should teach only one way. There are at least four ways to express future time, but with beginners, you teach only one or two. Teach the most common usage and explain exceptions and alternatives later, if they ever come up.

Beginning students don't usually bring up exceptions to the rules or grammar that is too high for the class. Occasionally they ask about something that you plan to cover in the near future. Say that you will explain the point soon or that you can explain it after class. You can't spend a lot of class time on a topic which doesn't involve everyone.

Pictures

A picture saves you a thousand words. Never tire yourself out explaining anything when you can show a picture. It saves explanation time and allows the student to experience meaning directly without a lot of interference from words they may not understand.

You need a collection of textbooks and worksheets with lots of pictures. You need pictures from newspapers and magazines filed in folders by topic like Weather, Workers, and Places. Commercial flashcards for elementary school with pictures of animals, birds, and musical instruments can be useful. If you have no other alternative, you will have to draw the picture yourself.

Examples

The best explanation is a picture. The second best explanation is an example. Keep giving examples until the class begs you to stop.

Easy Grammar to Teach Vocabulary; Easy Vocabulary to Teach Grammar

Some texts expect students to use and be tested on new grammar and new vocabulary together in the course of one unit. I think this is asking too much. It's easier to learn new things in small pieces and on a foundation of familiar things, so teach a new grammar point using common vocabulary and very easy ideas, comparing the new form to familiar forms. Teach the vocabulary in the easiest way possible. Students can learn new grammar and new vocabulary separately and use both together just as they do in their first language.

You shouldn't require students to learn long lists of words in a beginning level class, even if the words are related. Throughout the course, students should be using basic words which will be reinforced outside of school. If the students want to learn specific words to match their interests, provide them with pages from a picture dictionary to study at home. You could also do some extra vocabulary in class with groups studying different lists.

Boredom

No matter how enthusiastic your students are, you should have a new activity every 15-30 minutes. Reviews should be about 10 minutes. Introduction and speaking practice of new material can be about 20 minutes. If the class is writing, end it after about 30 minutes. Most people's attention span is 45 minutes, but you can't expect students to listen or write that long. Leave the easiest, most repetitive written practice for homework. If you have a few minutes at the end of class, fill them with an open-ended activity like a flashcard review.

When writing, someone usually finishes early and needs something else to do. You never want students, especially teenagers, to sit around waiting for their next assignment. Even adults can become discipline problems that way. Save yourself stress by always having more material on hand than you think you need. It's better to have longer exercises or worksheets with several stages instead of completely different extra material, because if you give faster students something completely different to do, you then have to personally explain the new assignment to each person as they finish.

With experience, you will be able to estimate a time limit for every reading or writing activity. Some students do not like to stop working if they are not finished. However, you can't hold the whole class hostage to the level of your lowest students. If the whole class protests when you call time, extend it a few minutes, but when most students are done, start going over the answers. Tell the slower students they can finish the work for homework or during a break.

Reading and Writing in the Beginning Classroom

Some very intelligent friends have begged me to say that the first one to three months of learning a language should be devoted only to speaking. It's true that if literate adults are shown written words, they will use them as a crutch rather than focusing on the spoken sounds. They will be influenced by the written word to pronounce the new word as they would in their native language.

If you are teaching adults in a non-academic situation, you can give them only as much reading and writing as they need to do. However, if left to themselves, some will resort to phonetic spelling, writing words exactly the way they would look in their native language. You do not want your students imagining the spelling of words that may be much more complicated in English than they expect. For that reason, even at a low level, it helps to teach basic phonics rules as well as the spelling of the most common words.

Reading and writing practice should not be a substitute for speaking and listening. It's good to introduce the grammar and vocabulary orally, with pictures. Students should see the words they are pronouncing at the same time or soon after. Any written work should be read out loud and answered orally before the students start writing, then checked orally when they are done. Reading material can be read out loud or with a tape and then repeated or dictated. Even tests should be reviewed out loud after they are graded.

Reading, writing, and phonics work are less stressful than listening and speaking. They also provide you with alternate activities to keep the class interested. Sometimes you may want to have the students read the new material first to introduce it. Often teenagers pay closer attention when they're shown something they don't understand. This creates a "teachable moment," an education term for a point at which your students feel more motivated than usual to learn what you are teaching.

Correction of Punctuation and Writing

It's easy to think that details like capitals, periods, and spaces between words do not need to be corrected at a very low level because they can be dealt with later. In reality, if students have been in classes which did not correct these almost imperceptible details, it is very difficult to change their ingrained bad habits later, when they are speaking fluently in a higher level class.

Periods and capital letters mark the limits of a complete sentence. Understanding this concept is essential to success in regular English classes. Furthermore, tiny, pesky little things like apostrophes and commas are disregarded by a lot of students, so they are guaranteed to appear on state standardized exams. That's why your secondary ESL students need to be sensitized to them as early as possible.

Rule for your class: If it's a complete sentence, but it doesn't have a capital letter and a period or question mark, YOU SHOULD FEEL SICK! And to my old Spanish teacher, who corrected all the accent marks that I had somehow thought were optional, I apologize!

Homework and Good Copying

When homework is extremely easy, more students are willing to do it. Copying is very easy, and because it's a form of repetition, it's a good technique for basic language learning. Rewriting sentences reinforces spelling, and a page of written work will show you if the student has a problem distinguishing letters and tracking sentences. This is work which is too boring to do in class except to give students a rest.

Some students will not or cannot do homework. This is why you can't depend on homework assignments to provide enough practice, and you cannot base your class on work done for homework the night before. If you keep a class roster just for homework credits, large blank spaces will make it easy to spot and easy to show which students are not doing any. You do have to give some kind of credit for assignments done outside of class, because people have given up free time to do them.

You can include homework points in overall grade totals or reward homework with effort and cooperation grades, but do not fail anyone just for lack of homework. There are always a few students who manage to pass without doing any.

You should not spend too much time correcting homework. Homework is for practice and for your information. You can underline a few errors, but most students will not correct the errors, or even look at them. You can see if students understand the material just by skimming the pages. If a paper is all wrong, you will notice the problems, and you can explain the material again. However, if someone has obviously copied the homework, give the student zero points, because you can't evaluate anyone based on someone else's work.

In any written work, students should copy the questions and write the answers in complete sentences. It's always harder to form questions than to write affirmative sentences, so copying questions may actually be more valuable than finding the answers. One-word answers are not useful, because they're too easy to copy and don't show you anything about the student's abilities. If students are answering questions about a short paragraph, have them copy the paragraph in correct paragraph format first.

If you train students in class to write answers in complete sentences with punctuation, you can assign text pages for written homework. Some textbooks on the recommended list are very good for homework because they have very clear models for the answers. Even at the end of the course, require students to copy the models, because some students will not even look at the examples if they don't have to copy them. After you explain an assignment, have students do the first few questions in class while you walk around the room making sure that everybody understands what to do.

If you do give homework, especially at the secondary level, it's a good idea to assign something every day to establish a habit. At the very least, your class can copy their daily vocabulary words 10-15 times. If you have a text without much written work, you can choose some sentences out of the classwork for students to copy 3-5 times each at home. Tell them that they need to repeat the sentence out loud each time they copy it. No one can complain that this homework is too difficult, and parents can understand it as well.

Bad Copying

There are always some students who resort to copying on tests and homework. At the end of a quiz, take the quiz papers immediately, before students can copy from neighbors or look up the answers. Original written paragraphs should never be done at home.

Secondary students are often quite brazen in insisting that copied work is their own, but copying is easy to spot. The work may have entire sentences missing or weird spelling because the copier has misread his friend's handwriting. You have to explain to teenagers that no two brains work exactly alike. Show them the two papers side by side with the identical answers highlighted.

If you spot a teenager copying his neighbor's work, you can grab the paper and dramatically pretend to tear it up while yelling, "Rip! Rip!" The class will be fascinated by this. Give the guilty person one more chance. Most of the time, you won't have to really tear up a paper. Watch how your students react when you merely threaten to rip up their work. Most younger students consider this funny. I would not try it with adults.

Handwriting

When you write on a board, you must print because many ESL students cannot read cursive writing. Their own printing is sometimes very hard to understand. Some students need a lot of practice just in the physical act of writing, which is another reason to have them copy. If they complain that their hand hurts, then they really need this practice. Check their grip to make sure they're not holding the pen in some strange, uncomfortable way.

Secondary students must write legibly with pens because some standardized tests still require compositions in the students' own writing. However, even though it is valuable to be able to read and use cursive writing, you simply do not have time in an ESL class to teach it. Most people would much rather read printing than poor handwriting. If a student can only print, don't force him to do more. If a student insists on writing in all capital letters, ask him to make the necessary capital letters bigger than the rest.

Movies and Simplified Readers

Movies and cartoons are a good way to practice listening. Students think they are getting a reward when they are actually working harder. If you want to use a movie or cartoon in class, show only short 10-15 minute segments at one time. Give the class questions about the segment they will see. Repeat the segment more than once, and then ask the students to report what they have seen and heard. Ask for very basic information. Repeat the segment again before going on.

Movies in class can be a problem. Administrators sometimes assume that if you are showing a movie, you're a lazy teacher filling time. In some programs, they are banned completely. The second problem is that most movies, even cartoons made for children, are too difficult for absolute beginners. If you find a movie which is useful for your class, invest in buying it. You can use it forever, and it may not remain as easily available as you expect. Don't count on borrowing movies from colleagues. You're the one they will resent when the movie disappears.

Some programs and textbook companies offer simplified readers and story collections. These can be educational and fun if they are written well, but many are not well-written. Out of a series of titles, one or two might be great while the rest are terrible. If you open a book storage cabinet and find multiple unused copies of one reader and a few battered copies of another, you are looking at the difference between a book that students like and one that bores or confuses them. Never order class sets of readers without reading the whole sample copy first. If you find the book clear and amusing, your students may like it also.

If a book that you have bought for a class set turns out to be popular and easy to use, buy extra copies immediately so that you aren't stuck when the book goes out of print or is reprinted in a heavily revised format that makes your older copies unusable. Even for class sets, it's good to assign books by number to each student personally to reduce graffiti and unwanted artwork which renders expensive books useless. Teach students how to cover books using newspaper without glue or tape. The difficulty of buying replacement copies in a public school setting can be a shock, so it is a good idea to control your own books if you can.

Testing and Grading

If you are teaching in an adult education or volunteer setting, you may not be required to give tests, but it's a good idea to do so anyway. Adults like to know where they stand and see how much they have accomplished. You need some idea of when you should move students to a higher level class, and testing itself is a class activity.

Class Tests and Quizzes

Tests and quizzes should be easier than the classwork. You should test only on concepts that you have practiced a lot. You should not grade on a curve or use tricky questions as a challenge to more competent students. They can be given an additional test segment, such as a reading or writing assignment, instead of making the class test harder to reflect their achievement.

At the beginning, students are learning English passively, by listening. Asking for complete responses before students are ready to give them is a waste of time. Passive knowledge can be tested by asking questions which students answer with "yes" or "no," with very few words, by pointing to an object, or by choosing from a list. Ask them to tell you if your sentences are correct or incorrect or to complete sentences which you start. Ask them questions with answers that are easy to find.

Multiple choice tests were out of fashion for a long time, but they are a good way to measure student knowledge quickly and with little stress. If the test is well written, it will include common errors among the wrong answers. Toward the end of the course, show students how to use the questions to help get the answers.

You should not expect independent thoughts at a beginning level. It's very hard to be creative as a beginner in another language. Most ESL students are not "test wise." If they see a word they don't already know, they may get confused. They will ask you to define a word even though it is part of the test.

Students can mark their own or other students' tests if you don't need the results for a grade, although they will not usually find all the errors. You can give the class a test as an activity or a practice and then give the real test. You don't have to grade or record every test. Some teachers allow students to erase one or two of their lowest test scores from their grade.

When students repeat a test as a do-over within a short period of time, they don't usually do any better.

Grading

If you give one vocabulary quiz a day, with one point per correctly spelled word, you will have a daily quiz grade plus one additional point for homework completed. This will encourage the students to do the homework to prepare for the quiz. Short grammar quizzes are good for student review and teacher feedback. You can give longer tests when class grades are due.

At the end of the course, you can ask for a short paragraph about the family or a friend. See Day 80 for suggestions on how to grade this paragraph. Some programs want you to grade paragraphs based on a rubric, for example, from 1 to 4, but a rubric is difficult to explain to a beginning student. If there is no "0" category in the rubric, this will also be a big problem, because a student who fails to do the assignment at all will receive the same rating as a student who tries, but performs poorly.

The best way to teach paragraph writing is by reading and discussing model paragraphs, copying paragraphs, guided compositions, and rewriting. Students usually reach a point after one or two rewrites where their paragraphs don't improve any further.

Final Grades

In general, if your school's placement system is good and your grading system is valid, most students should pass and succeed in the next level. However, out of a class of 30, you can expect several who will need to repeat at the end of a semester. If you pity students who are marginally passing, for example, achieving under 60% compared to others with 80%, they may fail the next level if you move them up anyway. Promoting them too fast is not doing them a favor. They will just be more confused in the higher class.

Marginal students require difficult decisions. Most students should repeat a class only once. You should investigate the quality of the students in the next level to help you decide if your marginal student can succeed there. In fact, no matter what level you teach, it helps to be familiar with the materials and, if possible, the students in the levels before and after your own.

The way that you grade your students at the end of the semester is actually Pass/Fail, but P/F is too general to use throughout the course. It doesn't show the students exactly how well they are doing.

The easiest grading system is to simply add test scores, composition points, and homework together and divide each student's total by the highest total in the class. That way you are measuring both effort and good results, and you don't have to manipulate lots of different percentages. You can consider speaking and listening skills separately based on student performance throughout the class or on a separate test at the end.

The problem with establishing a grade system based on 100% is that a native speaker of English has created the tests. It's easy for a native speaker to get 100%! Your test might not be as easy as you think, and there are always some questions which confuse students in ways you don't expect. I used the highest student score as the top score as 100% and calculated grade percentages based on that. However, I still often had to adjust for students whose top score was too high.

Here's a sample scenario. "Daniel" is very bright and has studied English before. His work totals 120 points at the end of the grading period, including test scores and homework points. Everybody else in the class scores much lower, with two students scoring 95 and a group scoring in the 80s. The two students scoring 95 started at a low level of English at the beginning of the class, and both paid attention and did homework. This tells me that I taught the class 95 points worth of English. The students with 95 get 100% and an A. Daniel gets 126% and an A, plus we consider him a candidate to skip a level at the end of the semester.

In other words, the 100% achievement is based on what most of the class actually learned, and what you evidently taught, not what you hoped they could learn. You are giving some credit for effort and diligence, but you're not basing the whole grade on those.

A student may get a higher grade just because they do all of the work while others don't bother. That does not always mean they should be jumped into a higher class. Students should only skip a level if their skills are much higher than the other students in their current class. Their current teacher is the only person who can judge this. You will have problems if parents, counselors, and athletic concerns become part of the process. On the other hand, you should not hold back students who could clearly succeed in a higher class just to follow a general sequence detailed in your curriculum.

Reducing Stress

Some techniques are good for passive learning and are relaxing and easy. Use choral repetition of short word lists, sentences, dialogs and jazz chants. Chanting is especially good for teenagers. Everyone gets a chance to talk, and even to yell (politely). Memorizing the chant or poem for a grade is stressful, but it gives a feeling of accomplishment and allows the student to claim the attention of the class.

Copying is to writing what repeating out loud is to speaking. It allows the students to go over and over spelling and grammar forms without a lot of thought, so it's a low-stress activity. Everybody can do it and everybody can benefit from it. If your class seems tired or stressed out, give them something to copy. Maybe you've been working them too hard.

If the students have been working, you can occasionally reward them with word searches, puzzles, or Bingo to review the material in a relaxing way. Projects and artwork also provide some stress relief while reinforcing material which has already been taught. However, games, projects, and artwork at the beginning level reflect the student's knowledge more than they add to it. They are not a substitute for a class, and they are time-consuming.

The Notional - Functional Approach

Certain expressions are necessary for social life but difficult to teach at a low level. You can teach your group exactly what they need to say in a certain situation, without explaining the grammar. Teach the expressions as a group of sentences. For example, greetings are always the same, and you learn them together. You learn to say, "How are you?" Nobody is going to practice, "You are how. You aren't how. Are you how?" People never say any of those things. So you learn the greeting, "Hi, John. How are you? Fine, thank you," as one typical expression.

This approach, which is called "Notional-Functional," is the basis of some texts. It may not be the fastest way to learn everything at a basic level, but it's the easiest way to learn some necessary phrases, and it's fun to sit and practice social dialogs with as much drama as possible.

Computers

Computer programs such as "Rosetta Stone" are a very valuable introduction to English for beginning to low intermediate students. They can also be a fun way to practice or review, but don't count on such a program to replace a teacher or a course. Students need a real person to interact with, and they need to interact at other people's pace, not just their own. Students can only concentrate on a computer language program for about 45 minutes. You might expect hyperactive students to learn more using a computer, but that does not always happen. Some students, unless closely supervised, simply play with the program or spend their time experimenting with the computer.

Talking and Phones in Class

Before starting your class, you should read your school's policy on using phones in class. You should determine how you are going to deal with this issue and decide how strict you want to be before it comes up in the room.

Even in a program higher than secondary school, like community college or adult education, some students may use phones or carry on personal conversations while you or other students are talking. This is not okay. You always have to speak not only clearly, but a little bit louder to help your students understand you, and a conversational buzz in the room can be very distracting. Also, you want students to be in "English mode" as much as possible in class.

You may want to communicate to the whole class at the beginning of the course that if they want to converse or use a phone, they are free to leave the room and come back when they're finished. Then when you notice students on the phone, you just discreetly point to the door and smile. They probably won't take this personally if you have informed the whole class before a specific incident occurs. This is important enough to act it out at the beginning of the course, or communicate it through written rules or a translator if you have access to one.

The best discipline tool is keeping students focused and occupied at all times. If they begin checking their phones or the talking gets out of hand, you might need to replace your next activity with a dictation, a pop quiz, or an oral activity like a jazz chant. If adults are talking too much, it might mean that the class is too teacher-centric and that you should do more small group activities.

Absences and Lateness

First and foremost, the teacher should never be late. Even if an entire class of adult students comes late, the teacher should not. Adults hate that.

Don't try to finish up material after the designated ending time of the class. When that time rolls around, especially if it is late at night, students are done. They're no longer paying attention, so it's pointless to go on.

The best solution for lateness is to give all quizzes and tests at the beginning of the class. You may want to have a policy that you will not give make-ups for dictated tests, only written tests. Otherwise, you will spend a lot of your time personally giving make-up quizzes, and there will be no consequences for regular absences and tardiness. If students get upset at this policy, you can allow the whole class a certain number of missed quizzes so only extreme cases will suffer.

Only you can decide how to deal with persistent lateness. As amusing as a excuse-mongering, chronically late entrant may be to you and to the other students, he is wasting everyone's time. If you have such a student, you can teach the class how to come in late. Sneak in quietly, signal "sorry" to the teacher, and don't bother to give a lot of excuses. You can act this out for the class. They'll get the idea.

You may want to give adults one or two extra absences beyond the number allowed, and tell them that in exchange for this, you want them to save their absences for true emergencies. If adults perceive you as sympathetic to their problems, they will try hard in return.

If you have a box of files with copies of classwork and homework handouts organized by date, it will save you time when absentees return and ask for them. You can also give their copies to a friend. Don't interrupt your class to deal with a person who is late.

Your Success Rate

In an adult program, your employers will look at your retention rate to gauge your success. They will want to know how many students drop out of your class and how many sign up for the next semester. The school administration may ask your students how they like the class.

Native English speakers, including your supervisor, will be bored to tears if they have to sit in your class for any length of time. If the people who evaluate you are not themselves ESL or foreign language teachers, make sure that they have a copy of the materials and the text. Explain the level of the class and what you are trying to do.

Immigrant secondary students need a good ESL class when they first enter school in the U.S. or academic success will be impossible for them. You don't want to let them become lost and failing in their first experience with English. If their ESL classes are effective, there is no reason why beginning ESL students cannot be successful later in an all-English curriculum and eventually graduate from high school.

Standardized Testing

For legal reasons, in many schools, beginning ESL students take standardized tests written for the general student population. The reasoning is "We need to measure their achievement." Until students have obtained a certain level of English, they will not be able to demonstrate any achievement, because the tests are not written at a level of English low enough for them. Unless your beginning students can be exempted from taking the exams, this is a problem without a solution at this time.

Sink or Swim

When you teach ESL, people often inform you that their grandparents came from this or that country and became successful in the U.S. without any ESL classes at all. Therefore they think that "sink or swim" is the best way to learn another language. Actually, "sink or swim" has several problems as a language learning technique. It's true that anyone constantly exposed to another language can pick up quite a lot. However, sometimes people make progress for a while and then get stuck at a level where they're hard to understand because of limited grammar or a strong accent.

Most people don't really know how much school their immigrant grandparents attended here in the U.S. The census returns for 1930 and 1940 ask if the person had attended school or college in the past year. (Ability to speak English was noted in the naturalization column.) High school was considered an important part of the assimilation process. The impression is that quite a few people were going to available ESL classes, just as they do today.

In any case, you want your students to learn as quickly and easily as possible. Just because Grandma and Grandpa attended the school of hard knocks, it doesn't mean everybody has to. That's why you don't allow your students to sink or swim. They'll be doing enough of that when they leave your class.

CPSIA information can be obtained at www.ICGtesting.com
Printed in the USA
LVOW09s2120121016

508496LV00017B/227/P